ENTREPRENEURSHIP FOR THE EIGHTIES

Gordon B. Baty

General Manager
Imaging Products
Burroughs Corporation

Reston Publishing Company, Inc.
A Prentice-Hall Company
Reston, Virginia

LIBRARY OF CONGRESS CATALOGING IN PUBLICATION DATA

Baty, Gordon B.
    Entrepreneurship for the eighties.

    Previous ed. published in 1974 as: Entrepreneurship.
    Bibliography.
    Includes index.
    1. New business enterprises--Management.
2. Entrepreneur. I. Title.
HD62.5.B38 1981   658.4'2   81-2864
ISBN 0-8359-1745-2   AACR2
ISBN 0-8359-1744-4 (pbk)

10 9 8 7 6 5 4 3 2 1

Printed in the United States of America

TO

ROBERT OAKLUND

engineer, entrepreneur,
and a very tough guy

1941–1974

Contents

PREFACE

"We are not here to sell a parcel of boilers and vats, but the potentiality of growing rich beyond the dreams of avarice."

> . . . Samuel Johnson
> presiding at the sale of Thue's
> Brewery, London

This book, like its predecessor, *Entrepreneurship—Playing to Win*, was written as a resource for the entrepreneur and would-be entrepreneur. As observed in the preface to the first version, entrepreneurship is one vocational calling for which there is really no apprenticeship. Working in other companies, even small ones, cannot prepare one for the challenges, the highs, the lows, the incessant demands, and the loneliness of running your own company. Since 1974, when *Entrepreneurship—Playing to Win* was written, however, a good deal of progress has been made on the periphery of the entrepreneurship area. Today there are over 200 colleges offering accredited courses in small business management, entrepreneurship, and related subjects; in 1974 there were only a handful. Moreover, today there is a robust academic literature in the field, whereas in 1974 it was very sparse indeed. I have cited some of the best, and they are highly recommended for further reading. Today, there are numerous seminars, retreats, multiweek training courses, and other ways to find out about being an entrepreneur; in 1974 there were very few. Today we are seeing recognition on the part of the public, local and state government, and even of Congress of the enormous role that small and new business plays in our economy in the creation of jobs, new products, new technologies, tax revenues, and exports. In February 1980 the Presidential Conference on Small Business gathered 2,500 delegates nationwide to draft recommendations to Congress for actions to strengthen the nation's economy by strengthening small business. Some of these recommendations have been enacted; others perhaps will be. Washington may be finally getting the message: Small businesses and the people who work for them are perhaps the largest "constituency" in the nation—one that is certainly beginning to feel its muscle.

At the same time, the incipient entrepreneur confronts a very different world now than in 1974. Numerous international crises, a floundering energy policy, near-collapse of major manufacturers, raging inflation, slumping productivity, and government economic policy flip-flops have all taken their toll in confidence in our institutions. The general inability of large companies and large government to get anything done causes us all to stop and wonder if we're on the right track. Salary increases that cannot keep up with inflation, pension plans guaranteed to leave retiring persons paupers in a very few years, reduced expectations for our children—these are the fuel for doubts among the most loyal big organization employees. One must ask, "Is this really the reward I can expect for investing a working lifetime of effort and loyalty? Is there a better way?" This, then is a book not only for the committed entrepreneur, but for the doubter, too—no longer certain that the present job or career path makes sense, yet not quite certain that he's ready to take the plunge into a new venture, either. It's my hope that this book will help the individual to resolve that dilemma.

This book is not intended to be a complete reference manual of what you need to know to start a company. Such a book would be so long and detailed that no busy entrepreneur would read it. For very specialized subjects (e.g., accounting, market research, negotiation) other excellent references exist. We have attempted at the end of most chapters to list a few of the more generally available of these, listed approximately in order of usefulness.

Our focus throughout is on the problems of the growth-oriented new enterprise, as opposed to the small business, although of course many of the same management considerations apply to both. We are interested in the problems of the person who is attempting to build a rapid-growth company by exploiting some new technological or marketing principle—a company with the potential for national or multinational marketing; the possibility of exponential growth; and the probability of making its founders millionaires in a surprisingly short time period.

This book is not offered as an academic, or even a balanced, study of entrepreneurship. It is written from a definite and pragmatic point of view which, badly stated is this: Neither innovative genius, nor hard work, nor even luck is in itself a guarantee of corporate success. Assuming that all of these are present in the new venture in at least trace quantities, the missing catalytic element often seems to be what we might call the "entrepreneurial state of mind." It might be characterized as a degree of tough-mindedness that stops somewhere short of truculence; a confidence in one's intuitive as well as one's rational faculties; a capacity to think tactically on one's feet, as well as to plan strategically in the business school sense; an attitude which stresses timely action based on frequently inadequate information, ahead of prolonged fact-finding; a mental set stressing integration of many facts into action plans, rather than endless differentiation and analysis. It is an attitude that says, in short: "I didn't just come to play the game—*I came to win.*"

If winning, then, is to be our goal, how shall we define it? Allow me the following provisional definition: *The entrepreneur shall have "won" when he succeeds in bringing his firm to a position where, in order to continue the growth of sales and earnings, a substantial infusion of new capital is required.* This definition by no means implies, of course, that all the perils are behind him. Indeed, many of the most challenging ones lie just ahead. Does he now go public? Sell out to a larger firm? Merge with a competitor? And how does *he* cash in? When and in what way will he manage to exchange some of his ever-diminishing share of the company for real, spendable money?

Clearly, our definition of "winning" merely assumes that the most basic, elementary business objectives have been met. The business has been born, has survived the perils of infancy, and has been set upon a trajectory of profitable, sustainable growth. From there on, the entrepreneur's problems are of the sort that many businessmen have, or would like to have.

We hope that this book will become a resource to be opened, reread—to stimulate your thinking, to get you talking to the right sorts of people, and reading some useful literature. We hope it will save you some time, some costly mistakes, some needless worry, and some irreplaceable entrepreneurial energy. We hope that it offers you, the incipient entrepreneur, some idea how to go about collecting your building blocks, and to the functioning entrepreneur, some glue to hold them all together.

G. Baty

ACKNOWLEDGMENTS

The people who have provided ideas and encouragement for this project over the years are too many to acknowledge individually. I am especially grateful to my friends in the academic, financial, and business communities, many of whose thoughts and attitudes have influenced my own. However, as is customary and proper, I must accept full responsibility for the results, including errors, omissions, and other peccadillos.

My thanks, too, to Carol McSweeney who prepared the manuscript and to Fred Easter of Reston Publishing Company, cheerleader extraordinary.

NOTE TO THE EDUCATOR

This book is quite properly placed in the category that one academic researcher has dubbed "normative folk wisdom," as opposed to "knowledge" (i.e., new research findings). It relies heavily on my own experiences in starting and building three companies, acting as investor and director in others, and eight years of attempting to teach my graduate students something about the process. Based on these experiences, it is my tentative conclusion that the student will be distinctly shortchanged if he is *not* exposed to a lot of folk wisdom in his attempt to learn about entrepreneurship—by working in small firms, by personal observation of live companies via consulting or project work, and by reading some "normative folk wisdom".

The very real-worldliness of entrepreneurial teaching is not always cogenial to the professional educator. He is by instinct an analyst; however, in this role he is attempting to train and to some degree motivate a synthesist, for that is what the entrepreneur really is. It is, of course, a mistake to think of the startup venture as a miniature version of the larger company. Intensive analysis of cases, of research findings, of markets and products, is without a doubt *necessary*—it just is not *sufficient*. An integral part of the student's experience should be exposure to some definite entrepreneurial points of view and some synthetical superstructures, to help him to form his own.

This book was not designed as a textbook. It may be reasonably asked, in fact, whether a course "text" in the normal sense is even appropriate for an entrepreneurship course. The book is intended for use along with other sources, some of the best of which are cited here. It is deliberately brief, intended for complete reading in one long evening. Finally, although not a scholarly offering, it is intended as an offering to the serious scholar, attempting to innovate educational methods to teach what seems to me to be the ultimate synthesis of business subjects.

Gordon Baty

FORMATION I

Chapter 1

WHY START A COMPANY?

"The reasonable man adapts himself to the world, the unreasonable man attempts to adapt the world to himself. Therefore all progress depends upon the unreasonable man."

. . . George Bernard Shaw

It should not be astonishing that entrepreneurs have been studied, as individuals and as groups, to a rather extensive degree. Psychologists are interested in finding out what motivates them. Investors are interested in finding some saliva test that will tell them in advance which entrepreneurs are going to make them rich. Business school professors have begun to be interested in the questions of whether and how entrepreneurial behavior pattern and skills can be taught. Legions of people in government (as well as their academic consultants) have begun seeking ways to engage entrepreneurs in programs of regional development, minority enterprise, leadership training, export promotion, and "technology transfer"—all in the name of the commonweal.

Needless to say, all of this activity has produced, not one, but several disparate literatures on entrepreneurial motivation and behavior. Books have been written, reports filed, symposia convened, theses and learned papers ground out. Some interesting specimens of this genus are listed at the end of this chapter, and are recommended reading. From a practical standpoint, however, it does the entrepreneur very little good to know that his statistical chances of

3

success are relatively poor if (a) he is a Gentile; (b) his father was not a businessman or self-employed professional; (c) he has a Ph.D.; and (d) he is not 32.2 years of age.

While it may be interesting to know this sort of average or modal information, much of it totally misses the point of entrepreneurship: the *diversity* (or if you will, statistical dispersion or variance) of the traits that have historically characterized successful entrepreneurs. If you don't seem to fit neatly into the traits profile of "successful entrepreneurs," you may take comfort from the fact that Edison, Ford, Land, and most of our other entrepreneurial geniuses probably wouldn't have, either.

The germinal question to ask at the outset is somewhat existential: Why should *I* start a company? The range of possibly valid answers to this question includes the following:

1. To make a lot more money than I could with some other application for my energies for a like time.

2. To get out of a professional rut—to see ideas through to completion, to gain professional recognition, to accept responsibility for the full consequences of my ideas.

3. To be my own boss, control my own destiny, set my own hours.

4. To prove to myself (my wife, my father, my ex-boss, etc.) that I can do it.

5. To advance technology, society, etc.

6. To develop and deploy talents I feel that I have outside my area of specialization.

7. To show up somebody with whom I intend to compete.

This list could be greatly extended.

None of these motives is without some subjective validity, and no doubt examples of companies founded on the basis of each could be shown. In real life, however, human motives are never unmixed. Your own answer will be a weighted sum of several of these, plus some additional twists resulting from your own unique outlook and experience. The question is, does the sum of *all* of these justify the cost, sacrifice, and risk of becoming an entrepreneur? The sum should be reckoned, but the yes-no answer should be held in abeyance, at least until you can more clearly evaluate some of the probable costs. Such evaluation is the subject of the next chapter.

From our list of possible motivations, it may appear that all are of equal merit, since all are of some subjective validity. Nothing could be further from the case. It appears that the most successful firms are started by men who are predominantly motivated by #1 in the list, and, to a lesser degree, by #2. To the extent that you are concerned with rebelling against your employer, proving yourself to your wife, advancing social causes, etc., you are least statistically allying yourself with less successful entrepreneurs.

The central objective of the business enterprise is to make money for its owners. To the extent that you are seeking to maximize a number of other effects, you will inevitably be diluting your energies from the central objective. When the business dies, *all* objectives are lost. And it will take most of your energy just to keep it alive.

"Why Start a Company?" is a question that can be answered on yet a different level. During the last decade, a variety of factors have turned many talented and capable people away from business enterprise as a means of self-fulfillment and social contribution. Charles Reich in *The Greening of America* epitomizes this mentality: We as a people have abandoned Consciousness I (the ruthless entrepreneurial spirit) in favor of Consciousness II (the gray organization man) but through enlightenment we should evolve soon to Consciousness III (the socially concerned man) to achieve the long-awaited Greening. How ironic it must seem to Reich that significant numbers of talented and educated young people appear to have come full circle, abandoning the beatitudes of Consciousness III for some sense of purpose and accomplishment of socially useful tasks through starting new enterprises—a return, it might seem, to Consciousness I!

Such enterprises are not necessarily trivial (from the economic standpoint) and are often begun by people whose talents range well beyond the making of leather belts or the fixing of bicycles. In the Boston area, some examples of such enterprises include computer dating and roommate matching services; newspaper and book publishing enterprises; health-care delivery systems; computerized legal reference systems; computerized medical diagnosis; specialized teaching systems designed for a myriad of clients with widely varying needs, ranging from retarded children to immigrants learning English; and consulting and hardware firms in pollution abatement.

The basic point is this: There is no inherent conflict between the possession of a social conscience and the possession of entrepreneurial drive. This "conflict" exists principally in the minds of journalists. Moreover, without talented and unique individuals who possess both qualities, little of significant value would be accomplished. Not only are most of our successful businesses started by such people, but also these same people start and operate our clinics, laboratories, dance companies, consumer action groups, museums, alternative schools, and most of the other new initiatives which contribute to what we consider our civilization.

This is in no way to say that there are no entrepreneurs motivated by cupidity and greed; nor is it to say that most or even many new enterprises are initiated with the intention, let alone the prospect, of accomplishing any significant social end. However, some successful new enterprises *are* organized to accomplish specific social goals, and there exists no inherent conflict between such goals and profit. Additionally, social ends are sometimes served even in the absence of conscious social goals. One hears, for example, that the purpose of our society has shifted from the creation of material goods to the creation of jobs. To the extent that even a mundane new enterprise creates jobs, incomes, payroll taxes, reduced welfare costs, and human dignity that might not otherwise develop, it is *inadvertently* playing a very desirable and constructive role in society. A similar case could be made for the creation of important products, desirable services, and much-needed exports.

There is another set of reasons why more talented and ambitious people should consider entering into a new business enterprise:

1. Going into business is not as difficult as is often supposed. Sacrifices, while you must be *prepared* to make them, are not always, in fact, *made*. Enormous talent is not necessary. As a matter of fact, it is sometimes a liability. Engineering, sales, and "business" people usually can be hired when needed. There is enough professional help available, on both a part- and a full-time basis.

2. At no time and in no place on earth have the conditions ever been more propitious for starting a new business. Hundreds of venture capitalists exist in the U.S., in a form all but unknown in other countries. Banks, accounting firms, investment bankers, and other institutions have acquired an understanding of new enterprise that is unmatched in any time or any place. The whole essence of capitalism and the Protestant Ethic (whether or not you take it neat) is at work, to the benefit of the new enterprise.

3. There are hundreds of companies who will design, manufacture, and package your product, to your specifications. There are inventors, consultants, lawyers, and vendors who will work with you, advise you, sell you their goods and services on very liberal terms—perhaps for stock. Maybe these people hope to develop a major new customer, or, more likely, just to share in the excitement of your venture.

4. In America innumerable ready-made channels of distribution exist for nearly any class of product. In an open, mixed economy of our type, there are commission representatives, distributors, wholesalers, house-brand buyers, and jobbers of every description—all waiting for the new product that will really "click" for them.

5. At no time and in no place have skilled people been so

readily accessible to the new enterprise. There are several reasons for this:

    a. At any given moment, many people are dissatisfied with bureaucracy, lack of recognition, and dead-end careers in large firms. They would seriously consider a stimulating, if less secure, position in a small new enterprise.

    b. Unlike many other industrial societies, ours does not stigmatize the job-changer. You can hire away the best salesman from your competitor without incurring the moral wrath of the entire community.

    c. People are more mobile than ever. It is common practice to recruit top people across town or across an entire continent—and top people *expect* to change employers when opportunity and growth dictate.

    d. Due to tax and emotional preferences, many professionals will work as hard for stock as they will for cash. A "piece of the action" is as much in the American tradition as winning the Rose Bowl.

    6. It is more difficult to fail than is often imagined. The business failure statistics collected by Dun and Bradstreet and mournfully recited by the press are compilations which include every type of venture from the doomed "ma and pa grocery" to moribund used car lots, gas stations, small jobbers, wholesalers, needle trades firms, and every other conceivable form of enterprise. When the lugubrious chant about 80 percent business failures starts, tune out. This is data, not information. A more interesting analysis was put forth by Professor Edward Roberts of MIT, who estimated that only about 20 percent of the large number of MIT spinoff firms ever fail completely. And, should disaster impend, the extraordinary bankruptcy laws of our land (discussed in a later chapter) provide still another mechanism to protect the struggling new enterprise.

    7. In Federal and local governments an odd political bias toward small business exists. The declared purpose, of course, is to permit small firms to compete on fair terms with large firms. The effect, however, is to produce a positive bias in some areas favoring small business. This bias shows itself in the small business set–asides in Federal government, in the existence of the Small Business Administration and the Small Business Investment Corporations, in the existence of a variety of regional development authorities, as well as in other ways. Our entire tax structure, with capital gains, "Subchapter S" corporations, tax-loss carry forwards and carrybacks, and "Section 1244" corporations also tends to create a desirable climate in which to raise capital for a new venture. It is debatable how effective these various measures have been in actuality in promoting the small business sector, but surely no one can doubt the *intent* be-

hind such legislation and appropriations. No government official wants to be considered against small business.

8. The personal and professional risks of a new enterprise are rather less than might be imagined. To be sure, you may be giving up a $25,000 job for a $10,000 job for a few quarters; you may miss some vacations and some professional meetings. Yet, assuming the worst, you lose your savings and go back to a $25,000 job having become a broader and more valuable person than you were when you left. None of this is to say that the process is risk-free; nothing worth doing ever is. It merely says that the downside risks are not only not unthinkable, but may be a lot less than you'd imagine.

9. Starting a business doesn't require as much experience as you might think. Naturally, business experience and contracts are usually an asset. However, the person who goes to work for a large company to get 10 or 15 years of solid experience before starting out on his own is just fooling himself. With a few notable exceptions, most big companies provide the poorest sort of background for the would-be entrepreneur. Most people find themselves working upward through a functional specialty, such as manufacturing, accounting, research, or sales, gaining experience that is negotiable only in that or a similar company. Moreover, experience teaches us our limitations all too well, and makes us pessimistic about the ability of new ideas to get anywhere. Some real-world experience is, of course, essential. More essential, however, is the enthusiastic damn-the-torpedoes spirit that one expects from youth (but which one is sometimes pleasantly surprised to find in the not-so-young). Enthusiasm, vigor, energy, and the skin of a rhinoceros are far more valuable assets than the "many years of experience" which are all too often the same year repeated many times.

10. Finally, we reach the consideration that is probably more significant than the rest together: Starting a new business is more fun than almost anything else. *Of course*, you're going to have to work long hours. But any professional worth his salt, no matter what his field, works long hours. Nights, weekends, holidays. Sixty- and seventy-hour weeks. *Of course*, there are going to be headaches—and maybe stomachaches, too. But how do you expect to avoid them in any other significant professional job? The big difference is this: Instead of immersing yourself in someone else's organization and struggling with *its* problems, in a new enterprise you create your *own* organization (with its own problems), and run it as you think it should be run. You stand or fall on the result. And that's about as much fun as most of us can handle.

Perhaps at this juncture, we can step back from the question, "Why Start a New Business?" and turn toward, "Why *not* start a new business?" The remaining chapters of this book are dedicated to those inclined to say, "Let's get on with it!"

References

1. McClelland, D. C.: *The Achieving Society*, D. Van Nostrand Co., N.Y., 1961.

This is the classic, a fascinating study of entrepreneurs and what makes them tick.

2. McClelland, D. C.: "Achievement Motivation Can be Developed," *Harvard Business Review*. November-December, 1965.

Discusses the philosophy, methods and limitations of efforts to develop entrepreneurial drive.

3. Mancuso, Joseph. *Fun and Guts: The Entrepreneur's Philosophy*, Addison-Wesley Co., Reading, Mass., 1973.

This is an amusing and generally accurate account of the stages an entrepreneur goes through in building a company.

4. Collins, O. V., and Moore, D. G.: *The Enterprising Man*, Michigan State University Business Studies, East Lansing, Mich., 1964.

This is a unique work in which 100 entrepreneurs from all different types of industries were studied with regard to personality traits. Entrepreneurs turn out to be a rather grubby, asocial, and generally unlikeable bunch. The book even includes a sort of psychoanalysis of the typical entrepreneurial type, examining his childhood deprivations, etc. Message: Nice guys don't win.

5. Roberts, E. B.: "How to Succeed in a New Technology Enterprise," *Technology Review*, December, 1970.

All you need is the right parents, the right age, the right religion, etc. Based on studies of about 300 MIT spin-off technology ventures.

6. Roberts, E. B.: "Entrepreneurship and Technology," *Research Management*, Vol. XI, No. 4, 1968.

Discusses the influence of various factors on technology transfer and, indirectly, on entrepreneurial success. Centers on the role of the entrepreneur himself.

7. Baumback, Clifford M., and Mancuso, J. R.: *Entrepreneurship and Venture Management*, Prentice-Hall, Englewood Cliffs, N.J., 1975.

This is a book of readings by some 35 contributors, giving research findings, normative advice, descriptions of the venture capital market, and other perspective-building materials, in an easy-to-digest form.

8. Myers, Gustavius: *History of the Great American Fortunes*, Modern Library, N.Y., 1907.

If you *really* want to know how the old rich got that way, read this first-rate bit of muckraking, written before Nader's grandfather was born.

9. Brooks, John: *The Go-Go Years*, Weybright and Talley, N.Y., 1973.

A ringside view of the wild bull market of the 1960s. Good entertainment, with a message.

10. Braden, Patricia L.: *Technological Entrepreneurship*, Michigan Business Reports, No. 62, University of Michigan, Ann Arbor, Mich., 1977.

Results of survey of 167 Michigan technology firms. Marketing turns out to be their major problem.

Chapter 2

RISKS AND REWARDS

"It is only by risking our persons from one hour to another that we live at all."

... William James

The decision to become an entrepreneur has two basic components: (a) Am I an entrepreneur? Do I have the abilities, the attitudes, the motivation? and (b) Are the potential rewards commensurate with the risks? Each of these questions has a number of components which should be explored before any decision is reached. The world is full of examples of successful and wealthy entrepreneurs. (Indeed, it is difficult to find examples of first-generation wealth made by people *not* in business for themselves.) In accounts of their experience, however, one seldom gets an accurate picture of the risks which confronted them or how they evaluated these risks at the outset. It is questionable as to whether these people even *recognized* many of the risks confronted when they started their businesses, or the role played by luck.

It all looks too easy. The unsuccessful entrepreneurs are seldom heard from. They are hard to find, since they don't usually identify themselves, and often give self-serving accounts of the failure mode (e.g., "Our product was too advanced for its time," and, "We did not have enough capital."). In these cases it is very hard to separate the effects of bad timing, bad management, and bad luck—even for the founder himself.

11

Financial Risks

Usually the financial risks involved in starting a new enterprise are numerically low, but of great importance to the entrepreneur. They involve his savings, his house equity perhaps, and some temporary reduction in salary. Maybe the spouse will have to go to work. Many people are unwilling to even consider a reduction in their standard of living or in their financial security, in order to start a new company. They are not entrepreneurs at heart.

However—and here is the crucial point—while you must be *prepared* to make financial sacrifices, there is a very good chance that you will never actually *have* to make them. It is much more important to *appear* willing to put your hand in the fire. To illustrate: Several years ago a businessman in Massachusetts decided to start a company in specialty food packaging. His personal assets consisted of equity in a house, the cash value of his insurance, and a few thousand dollars in savings. When the time came, at last, to leave his job with a food broker and set out on his own, he sat down with his boss and showed him the business plan. The boss, himself an entrepreneur, was impressed by the idea. He was, however, more impressed by the fact that the young man's business plan involved many months of deferred salary, as well as most of his savings and a second mortgage on his house. This guy had to be crazy, the boss thought, or else on to a sure bet. He decided it was the latter, and volunteered the necessary seed money in exchange for a minority equity position. As a result, both made a great deal of money, and a successful, growing company exists today. *Note*: Our entrepreneur never missed a paycheck, never refinanced his house, and never put over 25 percent of his savings into the venture!

So, when considering the financial risks, remember:

1. The *real* risks may be less than the *apparent* risks.

2. You can always get another job if the company folds.

3. You can rebuild your savings account.

4. Corporation law prevents you from being liable for more than you have in the company.

Career Risks

This is an important area, that is seldom discussed by business writers. Yet it may be even more significant than the financial risks encountered in a new enterprise. Simply stated, it is the risk that, having stepped outside your profession for a few years, reentry may be difficult. Certain professions, such as law, are structured to permit an interruption in one's career for a few years without excessive penalty. This is one reason why so many politicians and "public servants" are lawyers. Some other professional careers are not as easily turned off and on at will, however. A professor, leaving his post, may miss an opportunity to ever achieve tenure. A scientist starting a small company may discover that the demands on his time are so heavy that he loses touch with his colleagues, his funding sources, and the broader front of research progress in his field. A very senior executive may relinquish seniority, vested savings, stock options, or retirement benefits earned. A skilled machinist may relinquish seniority in his union, a nice thing to have when layoffs hit.

However, there is another side to the story. A take-charge person who has evidenced the courage to leave and start his own business, even if he in turn leaves *that* business, returns to his old employer as a broader, tougher person. At least some organizations seem to believe this—and if your old one doesn't, its competitor probably will. Moreover, those who start new companies are probably more inclined than others to find new and different uses for their training, and thus are among the least likely candidates to sit wondering if their old desk is still waiting empty at Titanic Industries.

Personal Risks

The level of personal risk is the most difficult of all to analyze. It is difficult because it involves one's own family members, social friends, and others whose reactions may be harder to predict than one's own. Unlike financial cost, which may be avoided under some circumstances, the commitment of almost all one's leisure time and energies is usually inescapable in starting a new company. Many marriages simply cannot survive the long absences of the breadwinner from hearth and home. Vacations have a way of getting postponed indefinitely. Meals get cold. Weekend outings vanish from the calendar. Social invitations go unaccepted and unrepeated. Reduced family cash flow may dictate fewer dinners out, less entertaining, and so on. These factors put a strain upon any household. Whether they might wrench *yours* is a question that deserves some sober reflection.

On the asset side, however, are the following considerations:

1. Your absence from the hearth may create the opportunity, necessity, or excuse for your wife's going back to work full- or part-time, or for your husband's doing some work around the house. This may be the best thing to happen, not only to your spouse but also to your marriage.

2. The necessity of constant absence from home diminishes with time. (Let your new sales manager make some of those trips to Cincinnati. Let your accountant prepare those draft budgets for

your review. Let your assistant deliver that paper at the Association meeting.) Eventually, you will be able to find more time to devote to your domestic life. Whether you exercise that ability is, of course, your choice. The company often provides a convenient excuse for staying *away* from home.

3. You must ask yourself what the future time demands of your present job are going to be, if you are to be successful. Many people, as they scale the professional ladder, find that their broadened responsibilities keep them away from home more, rather than less. The reasons are many: attending meetings with the West Coast subsidiary, troubleshooting the new plant in Kuwait, attending sales meetings, visiting the consulting client in Boise, delivering a paper to the Society in London, plus expanding one's social and civic responsibilities to fit the perceived desires of the firm—all at the expense of one's private life. The important thing is to compare your future life as an entrepreneur with your *future* life on your present trajectory.

In summary, of all the risks—those to your financial, career, and personal life—the last usually proves to be the most important, primarily because the costs are the least escapable, and secondly because its total impact is the hardest to predict. A demolished home life is a high price to pay for business success, and can ultimately undermine the company itself.

Here are some ways in which entrepreneurs have dealt with this problem:

1. Set aside a sacred day—Sunday is usually best—and make it an inviolable rule always to be home and never to schedule work or meetings. This is harder than it sounds.

2. Make sure your secretary reminds you of social engagements, your spouse's and your kids' birthdays, anniversaries, etc., so that something happens, even if you're not home.

3. Substitute the three-day weekend for vacations. Four or five short trips a year will go far in refreshing mind and spirit if time and finances don't permit a regular vacation.

4. Occasionally, conduct business over breakfast, and meet your husband or wife in town for lunch.

5. Put your spouse to work on specific company problems—for example, getting the mailing out, typing some memos, decorating the lobby, designing the brochure, and shopping for office equipment. As his or her time and/or interests permit, involve your spouse in a full- or part-time professional capacity, as a partner, employee, or consultant.

6. Keep your spouse informed. Even if he or she can't fully appreciate the breakthrough you're aiming toward in the laboratory,

or the big contract you're hoping to sew up, he or she *will* appreciate your sharing your hopes and problems, and your not shutting him or her out of your big adventure.

In addition to helping, they will gain insights into your problems, and a sense of sharing in the venture. But be sure that the company pays him or her whatever the going rate is for the work—even if he or she has to take IOU's! Don't hesitate to use him or her as a sounding board when you're thinking aloud about a problem.

You can imagine at least a dozen more ways in which to ease the strain upon your domestic life—and perhaps turn your venture into something of an adventure for your family, as well as for yourself.

Rewards

The rewards of successful entrepreneurship are legendary. There are few other ways in which wealth can be accumulated in this age, and fewer still that provide the sort of satisfactions that can be provided by the use of all of one's talents and energies in building a successful company of one's own. In a society such as ours which exalts commercial success above inherited status, cultural attainments, or even intellectual accomplishment, the successful entrepreneur is probably assured a disproportionately high return on his investment of energy, time, and worry, relative to other, equally talented, hard-working people.

An anonymous sage once observed, "Money isn't everything, but it's sure better than whatever's in second place." Among the second place contenders, excluding things that money can buy, we must list a sense of social contribution, professional satisfaction, esteem of peers, community status, and perhaps even a sense of power. Sometimes even not-too-successful companies provide these rewards to their founders in substantial degree.

Balancing Risks and Rewards

It may be that the accounting model can provide a useful way to structure your thinking about risks and rewards. Try making up a balance sheet along the following lines, to pull your thinking into focus in evaluating the "net worth" of your venture.

This sort of model is certain to seem excessively formal to some and hopelessly naive to others of a more scholarly bent. My own experience advising entrepreneurs has shown it to be useful, if only as a way of documenting some very crude *a priori* estimates, for later review.

How to Tell if You're An Entrepreneur: You're an entrepreneur if:

a. Your analysis of risk and reward shows that the probable gains outweigh the probable net costs by a substantial margin, and,

b. Your personal profile is not outrageously at odds with the known facts about successful entrepreneurs.

	Rewards (Assets)		
Reward/Risk	*Maximum Value*	*Probability*	*Expected Results*
a. Significant Wealth	9	50%	4.5
b. Professional Satisfactions—Sense of Achievement	8	80%	6.4
c. Community Status	4	20%	0.8
d. Power Being Boss	3	100%	3.0
e. Control Over Own Life	8	70%	5.6
TOTAL ASSETS			20.3
	Risks (Liabilities)		
a. Loss of Savings	10	20%	2.0
b. Reduction in Professional Status	7	30%	2.1
c. Diminished Leisure	6	80%	4.8
d. Increased Marital Stress	10	40%	4.0
e. Health Risk	5	20%	1.0
f. Psychological Cost of "Failure"	5	20%	1.0
TOTAL LIABILITIES			14.9
NET WORTH OF VENTURE =			5.4

Notes:
1. Your own asset and liability list may be quite different from those shown.
2. The maximum value attached can be any number, zero through ten.
3. The probability is your estimate of the likelihood of attaining the maximum value.
4. The expected result is then the product of maximum value times probability.

What Kind of Entrepreneur To Be?

There are innumerable patterns of entrepreneurship. Many people start out as one kind and end up as another. Vesper (1980) offers this list of entrepreneurial styles.

1. *Solo, self-employed individuals.* Ma and pa stores, dentists, doctors, consultants, accountants.

2. *Team builders.* One-man shows that build up teams of helpers (e.g., Ford, Coca-Cola, John Deere).

3. *Independent Inventors.* Bell, Edison, Kettering.

4. *Pattern Multipliers.* J. C. Penney, McDonalds, Col. Sanders, Stretch 'n Sew.

5. *Economy-of-Scale Exploiters.* For example, discount merchandisers.

6. *Capital Aggregators.* Banks, savings & loans, money-market funds, mutual funds.

7. *Acquirers.* Buy existing businesses, try to regenerate and improve.

8. *Buy-Sell Artists.* Turnaround, sell, liquidate; the realm of corporate raiders.

9. *Conglomerators.* Buy earnings with stock.

10. *Speculators.* Buy and sell land, war surplus, antiques, timber leases, without adding value.

11. *Apparent Value Manipulator.* Acquire assets at a discount, representing them for new use or market. Restructure balance sheet to improve current ratio.

Each of these entrepreneurial types implies differences in talents, commitment, circumstances, and interest of involvement for the individual. Any one of them may characterize you at some stage of your venture.

Conventional Wisdom. The risks and costs of failure are almost unthinkably high for a person starting a new company today.

Reality. Not only are the risks much less than is commonly assumed, but by planning, they can often be reduced, if not altogether eliminated. Your financial backers may be taking a lot more risk than you are.

References

1. McClelland, D. C.: "Entrepreneurs are Made—Not Born," *Forbes,* June 1, 1969.

   This is a painless capsule of McClelland's ideas on motivation in general. Message: Money does not motivate people.(!)

2. Hoad, W. M., and Rosko, P.: *Management Factors Contributing to Success or Failure of New Small Manufacturers,* University of Michigan, Bureau of Business Research, Ann Arbor, 1964.

   This study demonstrates the various risk elements of startup, with a sample of 100 companies.

3. Vesper, Karl: *New Venture Strategies,* Prentice-Hall, Englewood Cliffs, N.J., 1980.

   This unusual book explores the various ways in which people get into business, and discusses the usual ingredients needed for success. Plenty of ancecdotes and mini case histories. Excellent.

4. Liles, Patrick R.: *New Business Ventures and the Entrepreneur,* Irwin, Home-wood, Ill., 1975.

Basically a case text. This book nonetheless offers several excellent sections on venture risk, evaluation of going companies, raising venture capital, and the nuts and bolts of securities regulations.

5. Rubenstein, A. H.: *Problems of Financing and Managing New Research-Based Enterprises in New England,* Federal Reserve Bank of Boston, 1958.

This is an early but still relevant study of the risks and problems of technology entrepreneurs.

6. "How the High Fliers Take Off," *Business Week,* November 22, 1962.

Some wild case histories from the Zenith of the 1962 bull market.

Chapter 3

WHAT KIND OF COMPANY?

"The man with a new idea is a crank—until the idea succeeds."

. . . Samuel Langhorn Clemens

A cynic might divide all new venture into two groups: (1) those companies organized to profit from the sale of products, and (2) those organized to profit from the sale of stock. To draw this distinction is not to say that the two are necessarily mutually exclusive—they aren't. However, some companies with excellent earnings may not sell for much (i.e., for a low price-earnings ratio), while other companies with negligible earnings or even large losses may sell for a lot of money (i.e., infinite or negative price-earnings). The reasons are not hard to understand. A company with good earnings may sell cheaply because:

1. It is in a static or declining industry.

2. Impending events may cloud the future, such as patent expirations, growing competition, antitrust actions.

3. Its growth is limited by its local character (e.g., a dry cleaning plant), a saturated market, scarcity of raw material (e.g., fish processing), etc.

4. Its product or technology may be simply out of style in the investment community (e.g., computer software firms and nursing home chains, as of time of writing). Brokerage house customers may just have lost a bundle in similar companies.

19

Conversely, a company with a terrible earnings record may sell for a lot of money because:

1. It owns substantial net assets (i.e., high liquidation value).
2. It has a tax-loss status of value to the buyer.
3. It has a product or service that has tremendous potential.
4. It is in style.

The trick in deciding what kind of company you're going to start lies, of course, in finding a combination that will make money from product sales *and* from equity sales. Elementary, you say. But, as experience will verify, it is much harder to actually make money in a rapidly growing firm than is generally supposed. It is incredible how rising materials costs, expanding sales organizations, product redesign, product delays, and collection problems can devour that marvelous projected gross margin. The obvious hedge is this: Make every conceivable effort to be in one of the areas in which companies with less-than-zero earnings can be sold profitably, *or* be in a dead-end situation where the profits that can be milked are so great that you don't care if you have to throw your stock away in five years. Generally, one should avoid the middle of the intervening spectrum. As a matter of practical experience, it is probably true that the stylish company is the better choice for the first-time entrepreneur, while the turnaround or liquidation project is the province for more experienced venturers.

Most entrepreneurs like to think in terms of building a company which can eventually go public, thus allowing them to cash out via the founders' stock. Yet, many successful ventures are acquired by bigger companies, and some can be said to have been developed and groomed with that disposition in mind.

A third, if somewhat dated, philosophy is to build a solid company to own, operate, and pass on to one's children. There is nothing wrong with that. However, generally speaking, if you build a company which meets the tests of the capital markets in order to go public, the chances are that either of the other two routes will still be open to you, should you change your mind. The reverse is not always true.

Service vs. Manufacturing

It may be that there once was a bias, within the capital markets, toward companies whose product was hardware rather than services. It is apparent, however, that today an innovative idea in service or in service delivery can be quite capable of attracting both capital and investor interest. A roster of currently stylish company areas would include examples of both types of company. Service industries which have attracted investor interest in the last few years include computer timesharing, health-service delivery (e.g., nursing homes), medical monitoring, fast food merchandising, campground franchising, tax-preparation services, and parcel delivery services. In the gradual shift of our economy toward more service industries, entrepreneurs and investors alike should become increasingly sophisticated in judging the risks and returns of new service ventures. Both hardware and software offer opportunity for the entrepreneur with an innovative concept.

Fashions in Technologies and Markets

Although it is true that definite fashion trends may be found in capital markets, it is a bit unfair to use the word *fashion* when referring to the venture capitalist—unfair in that it connotes an irrational preoccupation with trivia (e.g., hemlines and lapel widths). In fact, most venture capitalists and "special-situation men" in brokerage houses are engaged in a rational, cold-blooded analysis of what they can *sell*.

Changing fashions come about in new ventures, not because someone wants to make the shares of stock which his customer purchased last year obsolete, but because new and exciting ideas and technologies are constantly being created. Innovative marketing ideas are emerging, and new market needs are developing. At the same time, as the glamour industries of yesterday mature and consolidate, competition reduces opportunities for large profits, and fewer new ventures come forth for capital from those industries. Moreover, some new technologies (e.g., cryogenics) and some new markets (e.g., the "Youth Market") are oversold, yield disappointing returns to their early investors, and are pushed aside in the venture capital market, in the next wave of changing fashions. For these and other reasons, discernible trends do exist in the market. It is up to the pragmatic entrepreneur to discern them.

The best way to discover the current trend is to find out what's being financed. A look at the annual reports of some of the major public venture capital firms will indicate what kinds of businesses have been added to and deleted from their portfolios. Conversations with management of some of the not-so-public ones can often yield similar information. One useful source for such data is the *OTC Review* (Box 115, Jenkintown, Pa.) which gives summary information on most new ventures presently in registration with the SEC, as well as rundowns on the product and stock performance of many over-the-counter companies. A still better source, if you can get your hands on it, is the monthly *SBIC/Venture Capital*, published by Venture Publishing Co., Wellesley, Mass. Reading such a publication over a period of time can also give one a very good sense of the investment patterns of different financial institutions and underwriters. One, for example, may specialize in computer companies, while another seems to follow medical firms, and so on. The reason for this pattern of specialization is fairly obvious: A firm simply gains experience in evaluating ideas and entrepreneurs of a particular sort, thereby reducing both cost and risk.

Once you have tentatively identified your general area of interest or have confirmed that your initial idea is sufficiently fashionable, you would do well to approach whatever underwriters are active in that area and have a long talk with them. You'll learn a great deal about who the present and future leaders are in your particular field, what's going on in the industry, and will get at least some idea of how much longer that industry will stay in the Top Ten. The editors of the industry magazines are another good source of this sort of information. It is their business to be alert to new trends and to evaluate the viability of new developments. They are generally interesting, interested people, and such an acquaintance can be extremely valuable to you, in terms of publicity and contacts, once your business is off the ground. Take an editor to lunch today. Or better yet, an editor *and* an broker. To paraphrase a tired cliché, "If you're going to sell steak, just be damned sure it's still *sizzling*."

Where to Look for Ideas

Despite the myth to the contrary, most new companies are *not* started on the basis of totally new or original ideas. Most are simply based on old ideas which have been updated: current ideas, repackaged for a new market; straightforward extensions of existing products; or products which are designed to fit into a niche between existing larger competitors. This is one of the reasons why ordinary people can start extraordinarily successful businesses. It is not necessary to be an innovative genius to come up with a suitable idea. Many of the most profitable and hence fundable, low-risk ventures are merely mundane looking extensions of existing products (e.g., a cheaper handheld calculator, a higher-performance servo motor, a fancier motor home). One of the best places to look for specific first-product ideas is right under your nose, in the development direction of product lines already being marketed in your target area.

What is required? What will sell? What will the market demand *next* year? This approach may pit you against established competition, but at least you don't have the enormous investment and lead-time required for the development of a new market. Investors look with favor upon this approach.

Here are some of the other idea sources which you might also look into, in rough order of descending effectiveness:

present job environment

successful entrepreneurs

trade shows

trade publications

editors

Commerce Business Daily

management consultants

idea brokers and patent brokers

venture capital firms

technology transfer agencies

regional development agencies

Official Gazette of the U.S. Patent Office

Once you have picked a general product, there are, of course, many ways in which to focus more closely upon alternative design approaches, existing and abandoned state of the art, probable research efforts by competitors, etc. Agencies such as the Library of Congress National Referral Center, the Smithsonian Institution's Science Information Exchange, and the National Technical Information Service of the United States Department of Commerce, are good places in which to find specific information, but aren't much good for browsing.

Once you get into it, you may find in your idea search that there are many people with ideas which seem better than yours— ideas just sitting there, waiting for the right person to match them up with the people and resources needed to exploit them. So don't lock yourself in a closet and try to think of the ideal product. It's probably sitting out there in the world, just waiting for you.

Criteria for First Products

It is important to remember that the product which is one firm's success may be another firm's disaster. Success and failure are determined by the nature of the organization and the people who will exploit the product. The criteria for a beginning company's first product are particularly stringent, due to its extreme limitations in terms of staff, experience, market contact, capital, and every other factor needed to make a new product sell.

Table 3–1 offers one general way of classifying your first product candidates. The examples in the boxes are illustrative.

Try placing your first product ideas into these pigeonholes. Then consider the following:

1. The closer you are to the northwest corner, the safer and easier-to-finance your product will be. This is often a winning combination for the first product, even though the potential payoff may be higher for future products.

Table 3–1
Classifying Products

	Existing Product	Modification of Existing Product	Totally New Product
Existing Market	"New" shaving cream	Disposable hospital bedding	Laser surgical instruments
Identifiable Market	Children's cosmetics	Home computers	Spanish language news—only TV station
Unknown Market	One-man submarines	Computerized home intrusion alarm	Internal combustion pogo stick

2. The further toward the southeast corner you get, the harder it will be to find financing and develop a profitable enterprise.

3. In general, a new company is better off in the northeast corner, where the market is, at least, *known*, than in the southwest where you may never make the first sale. This is true because new companies usually have less marketing competence than product development ability.

4. Since high rates of return nearly always involve higher risk, you ought to consider reserving riskier, higher-potential ideas for second or third products. By then you'll have a company going and (hopefully) some modest first-product success.

Here are some of the additional criteria to which the first-product candidates must be subjected:

1. *Is it proprietary?* This is the first question an investor will ask. It doesn't have to be patented (although patents are great window-dressing), but it should be sufficiently proprietary to permit a long headstart against competitors and a period of extraordinary profits early in the venture to off-set startup costs.

2. *Are the initial production costs realistic?* If your first product is plastic canoes, perhaps they are. If it is seagoing LPG tankers, perhaps they aren't.

3. *Are the initial marketing costs realistic?* A specialized scientific instrument may, measured in this way, be a better first product than a new razor.

4. *Does it have potential for very high gross margins?* This is almost a necessity for a fledgling company. By this measure, a "new" cosmetic product might be less of a risk than a new machine tool.

Note that gross margin is one thing which the financial community *really* understands.

5. *Is the time required to get to market and break even realistic?* If you have no idea how long it will take to get there, then you can't even estimate how much money you'll need. In most cases, the faster the better. You can always hold your new product in reserve, announcing it to the stockholders immediately *after* you announce your first profitable quarter.

6. *Is the potential market big enough?* By potential market, look ahead three to five years. By this gage, specialized instrumentation for student laboratories might be a better product than specialized instrumentation for metallurgical laboratories.

7. *Is your product the first member of a growing family?* If so, it's a better first product than a solo virtuoso. If it requires a lot of high-margin accessories or supplies, so much the better. Most of the best growth companies have products with this characteristic. Again, due to the enormous costs, delays, and uncertainties of market development, a stream of products aimed at the same market is a safer investment than trying to develop entirely new markets for your old product.

8. *Do you have some ready-made initial customers?* It is certainly impressive to financial backers when you can list your first ten customers by name.

9. *Are the development cost and calendar time realistic?* Preferably, they are zero. A ready-to-go product, with the development already paid for (by your old company, the Government, an offshore manufacturer, or *anybody* else) gives you a big leg up over other small companies that dissipate their initial stake in seemingly endless product development. Save your jazzy product-development efforts for your second, third, or fourth products.

10. *Are you in a growing industry?* This is not absolutely essential, if the profits and company growth are there, but there's less room for mistakes. A growing company in a growing market can survive a lot more management blunders and bad luck and still succeed.

11. *Can your product and the need for it be understood by the financial community?* If the product is super technical, financiers can always get a consultant in, to evaluate its merits. But if they can evaluate it themselves, you're golden. One of the best products I ever saw in this respect was a tiny, portable, heart-monitoring system, for postcoronary monitoring. Half the people who heard the presentation had already had coronaries!

The list of criteria could be extended *ad nauseum,* but by now you have the idea of what kinds of questions to ask. If you can answer yes to at least six of these eleven, go see your Aunt Hattie about some start-up money. If you ace all eleven, go see Goldman Sachs.

Venture Architecture

For any given business opportunity (new market or product) there are generally multiple modes for exploitation by the entrepreneur. For example, an incipient entrepreneur discovers that law firms are both numerous and poorly managed in a business sense. He realizes that a small computer for lawyers could process both their text and their business data. His primitive entrepreneurial instincts tell him, therefore, that he should raise money, set up a company, design the computer and software, set up a sales service organization, and revolutionize the legal industry—or should he? Let's consider some alternative ways of exploiting this same opportunity. He could:

1. Design a computer, have someone else build it, and concentrate on marketing it to the lawyers.

2. Buy out and turn around an existing firm in this field.

3. Buy computers, write some software, and resell the package to law firms (the so-called OEM or turnkey market).

4. Set up a service bureau and process information for law firms.

5. Set up a facilities-management company, to operate law firms' computer operations as an in-house basis.

6. Offer consulting and seminar services to lawyers, advising them on setting up their own information systems.

7. Become a salaried salesman for some firm already marketing a suitable product to lawyers.

8. Become an agent or distributor for such a firm, possibly adding other complementary products as well (supplies, books, accessories).

9. Set up a leasing company to finance the acquisition of such equipment by lawyers.

10. Start and operate a really efficient law firm, and put the others out of business.

The true entrepreneur probably adds more creativity and value to the venture at this stage than at any other—the venture architecture stage that must occur before the preparation of formal business plans can even begin.

To further generalize the venture architecture concept, let us adopt the following definition: Vendor architecture is the process of designing the new company. Therefore, not only must issues of product source and sales methods be addressed, but many others as well:

1. *Form:* Will it be partnership, single proprietorship, corporation, cooperative, real estate trust, or some other legal entity?

2. *Financial Structure:* How should it be financed? Some ventures, such as risky R&D efforts, will be largely figured by equity (i.e., stocks) sales. Others such as garment manufacturing can be financed by bank debt and receivables factoring. Agricultural and real estate ventures are most often debt-financed, with the land securing the notes and mortgages. And so there is generally a "best" financial structure for a given type of venture.

3. *Organization:* Will the company be steeply hierarchical, as a typical manufacturing firm might be, or will it be collegial, as might befit a consulting firm? How will the structure fit your management style? Will it be a holding company with specialized subsidiaries? Will it be acquiring other companies?

4. *Marketing Structure:* Should the product be sold by a company sales force, or by representatives, dealers, agents or other non-employees? What form of field support organization will be required? Will we start in one mode, with the intent of changing later?

5. *Product Supply:* Will we make or buy? Will we specify a product of our own design, or will we simply sell something already manufactured, tooled, and available? Will we buy something standard and modify it to meet our customers' needs (e.g., adding our software to a purchased computer)? Will we start out one way with the plan of switching over later as volume dictates?

6. *Technology:* Will we develop on our own, or license the technology of others? How large an engineering department do we really need?

7. *Locations:* Not all locations are equally suitable for sales, R&D, and marketing. Your location may *be* your business.

8. *Distribution of Ownership:* How many financial and operating partners are needed?

Obviously, a great many issues must be addressed in the architectural stage. A number of possible solutions should be explored for each issue, rather than just jumping on the obvious or the customary. Moreover, many of the solutions are certain to be interdependent. For example, if debt-financing is seen to be the optimal financial structure, the corporation is likely to be the preferred form to insulate shareholders against losses in excess of their investment.

What Characterizes Good Architecture?

As in selection of a first product, the entrepreneur selecting an architecture for his first venture must deal with more constraints than a more experienced businessman. When you have enumerated some alternative architectures for your new venture, you should then subject each to the following tests:

1. Does it provide a way of getting into business earlier than other strategies? (Time is still money.)

2. Does it provide a low-risk market entry opportunity? For example, a dealership for a proven product may be less risky than designing, building, and marketing a new product.

3. Does it build on my personal strengths? Can I make maximum use of my technical skills, selling abilities, industry contacts, personal capital?

4. Does it provide a growth path if it succeeds? For example, the Lanier Corporation was begun as a regional distributor of dictation equipment. A few years and several acquisitions later, they were one of the nation's major marketers and manufacturers of dictation and word processing equipment.

5. Does it make maximum use of other resources in the environment? Manufacturing might *in principle* be the best architecture but without the infrastructure of vendors, trained workers, and engineers, it might be a very poor architecture for you to adopt.

6. Does the architecture provide built-in hedges against failure? A consulting practice might be easy to reorient if the opportunity doesn't pan out, whereas a manufacturing plant may not be so easy to redeploy.

7. Can it result in the kind of company I want to own? Will it make a good living for me but be unsaleable (like many agencies and consulting firms)—or will it be a cash-eater that will later be saleable to a larger company?

8. Does it provide access to capital that might not be available otherwise? For example, if our make-or-buy decision is to manufacture, we may have access to financial and tax incentives to create jobs in particular regions of high unemployment.

9. Will it be consistent with the kind of life I want to lead? Though they may not admit or even realize it, many an entrepreneur would be miserable as manager of his own big company. Day-to-day operations, hiring and firing people, dealing with auditors, government agencies, stock analysts and other "non-productive" tasks can make life an agony for the free spirit who loves to design,

manufacture, or just sell things. Does the architecture, if the venture succeeds, really suit your life?

Some High-Growth Markets for the 1980s

I. Low Technology

Crafts/hobbies: services, instruction, supplies

Translation services

Courier services

Microcomputer retailing

Sportswear/sports equipment: manufacturing and marketing

Buyer protection: home and auto inspection, etc.

Energy-saving services: home audit, insulation, recommendations on alternative fuels, solar, etc.

Word processing/typesetting bureaus

Health/beauty/fat-farm salons

Local airlines, other common carriers

Contract training services

Specialty foods (low calorie, kosher)

Specialty restaurants

II. Medium Technology

Third-party maintenance

Solar heating: manufacturing and retailing

Wind power: manufacturing and retailing

Computer software: standard packages for wide marketing

Computer software: customized packages for specific users

Cable TV: retailing

Program material for home video consumption

Domestic security systems

Municipal waste management/recycling/energy recovery

Computer-aided design services (NC programming, auto drafting, etc.)

Specialized job-shops (microdrilling, laser cutting, laser inspections, etc.)

Recycling services for motor oil, asphalt waste, industrial solvents, dissolved precious metals

Medical monitoring: clinical and ambulatory

III. High Technology

Microcomputer systems, commercial applications

Home video terminals

Value-added datacom networks, buying satellite bandwidth

Specialized computer peripherals: voice recognition, bubble storage, etc.

Domestic energy storage (batteries, flywheels)

Office automation systems

Office automation components (intelligent copiers)

Low-pollution, small-scale coal-burning systems

Hazardous waste management

Data security/encryption systems

Computer aided design/manufacturing systems

Secondary oilfield recovery

Exotic batteries (lightweight, high energy density)

Efficient electric motors

Conventional Wisdom.   You need a technological breakthrough to start a successful company.

Reality.   Very few new ventures are based on completely new ideas. Most are based on extensions of proven old ideas.

References

1. Karger, D. W., and Murdick, R. G.: *New Product Venture Management,* N.Y., Gordon and Breach, 1972.

    This is the best all-around book on new product development going. It starts with evaluation of market needs and goes right through to public offering. The section on marketing and promotion is particularly good.

2. Smith, N. R.: *Entrepreneur and His Firm: The Relationship Between Type of Man and Type of Company,* Bureau of Business and Economic Research, Michigan State University, East Lansing, Mich., 1967.

3. Vesper, Karl: *New Venture Strategies,* Prentice-Hall, Englewood Cliffs, N.J., 1980.

    Excellent section on new venture ideas, criteria.

4. Siropolis, Nicholas C.: *Small Business Management: A Guide to Entrepreneurship,* Houghton-Mifflin Co., Boston, Mass., 1977.

Good discussion of specific industries and their suitability for small startups.

5. Karger, D. W., and Jack, A. B.: *Problems of Small Business in Developing and Exploiting New Products,* Rensselaer Polytechnic Institute, Troy, N.Y., November, 1963.

This is the proceedings of a conference on this subject. It includes some very interesting papers on why products run into problems. Excellent bibliography.

6. Cooper, A. C.: "Entrepreneurial Environment," *Industrial Research,* September, 1970.

Summarizes a study done on the impact of location on success or failure of new enterprises. Study focuses on the electronics industry in Palo Alto, and concludes that there is a right place as well as a right time to start a firm.

7. The Conference Board, Inc.: *Generating New-Product Ideas,* CB Report No. 546, N.Y., 1972.

A *very* pragmatic booklet on practical approaches, with references, checklists, sources, and sample company policies.

Chapter 4
MEASURING THE NEED

> *"Market demand for a* product *is the total* volume *that would be bought by a defined* customer group *in a defined* geographical area *in a defined* time period *under a defined* marketing program."*

> . . . Philip Kotler

It is probably true that entrepreneurs are worse at selling their own products than they are in any other area of endeavor within the business structure. Yet selling is the most *critical* area of activity in most companies. Its importance cannot be overemphasized, especially in the case of a new venture.

There are many ways of obtaining a product to sell: It can be designed, manufactured to order, imported, or assembled. The one thing which you *yourself* must do is sell it. Your merchandising methods may, in some cases, be the major "product" of your company (e.g., Colonel Sanders, Avon, Savings Bank Life Insurance).

Finally, a poor or unrealistic marketing program is one of the major weak spots for which prospective investors watch out. This chapter attempts to enumerate some of the major pitfalls present in the planning and execution of a market analysis program, so that you may, with luck, avoid them.

When you begin to develop a marketing program, the first step is the identification, measurement and documentation of the *need* for your *product*. The focus placed upon *need* and *product* is intentional.

Much of what passes for market research is actually generalized investigation of massive demographic markets. It is made up of guesses as to the share of the market which can be captured, and extrapolative projections of potential growth rates. This kind of cursory approach impresses no one, and introduces the risk that you will be deceiving yourself about the business opportunity. Here are some questions which you should ask yourself:

1. Will you be serving your customers' real needs? What are these needs? How much will your customer be willing to spend for your product? What is different about *your* product, which will cause him to choose it over that of your competitor?

2. To what industry will your sales efforts be directed? What is its size now, and at what rate is it growing? Who will your principal customers be? For what purposes will they use your product? How significant a competitor can you be in your industry?

3. How are selling and distribution usually handled by your competitors? What are the buying habits of your prospective customers? What will selling and distribution cost?

4. How many industries can you serve? Some entrepreneurs see so many potential applications for their product that they are unable to focus their initial energies upon developing *one major initial class* of customer. They try to reach all classes simultaneously, possibly with different distribution methods needed for each class. The results of such a practice can be disastrous!

5. What are the principal market segments which are reachable, and upon which one will you concentrate? For example, if you're selling electronic controls to machine tool builders, you will want to concentrate your sales efforts upon those companies which do not have in-house electronics capability. Who will the principal customers be, within your chosen segment? How much will each customer buy? At what price? What product is the customer presently using, which will be replaced by your product? What is its cost? What will it cost him to switch to your product, in terms of design change, tooling costs, changes in methods, etc.? What market segments, and in what order, do you wish to reach later on in your endeavor?

6. What are the major representative, distributor, and dealer firms within the industry, who now call on your prospective customers? Which ones would be most suitable for you to use in your sales effort?

7. Who are your present competitors? Who will they be in three years? What are the major characteristics of their products, their marketing methods, and the strengths and weaknesses of each? Are they planning the introduction of a new product, in the near

future, which would endanger your business? How large and how profitable are they? Are they making any money *in areas which would compete with yours?*

8. What will it cost you to sell to your proposed market segment over the next few years? How much money should you allocate for such things as salesmen's salaries, regional office expenses, representatives' commissions, field service organizations, applications engineering, customer training, warranty repairs, documentation, advertising, and promotion? Must we rent the product?

9. How long will it take to get your sales effort into full swing? Does the customer require a long cycle of need-evaluation, funds approval, and vendor selection? Is a long period of training on a unique new product required? Is intensive advertising over long periods of time necessary? Will use of your product force major changes in the way your customer runs his organization?

10. What are the names of the ten major customers who will be buying your product? (*Note:* General Electric Company is not a customer—Joe Snodgrass, equipment buyer for the General Electric Missile and Toaster Division, Houston Operations, may be.)

The final distillate of this information-gathering process is the top line of your *pro forma* profit and loss statement: Dollar Shipments per month. This is the great leap, the key assumption, the base of your entire business plan, the yardstick against which you and your business will be measured.

In general, it is easier to explain away the absence of profits than the absence of sales. If sales are materializing on schedule, investors tend to be more patient about profits which are below your stated target. Therefore, your chances of successfully financing and operating your business are increased by your knowing as much as possible about your product's users and your ability to present documented evidence regarding your market.

Where Do You Look for Information?

Once you have a business opportunity for which there appears to be good potential, your immediate aim should be researching and documenting that opportunity. In this way you will be able to convince others, as well as yourself, of its validity. There are many sources of data for any new product.

Your first task in the research process will be listing those sources which you will investigate, in their order of use to you. Some data sources, such as direct mail surveys, take a long time to complete and therefore should be begun at once. Others, such as literature searches, telephone interviews, and personal interviews, will produce almost immediate results and therefore can be scheduled on an *ad hoc* basis. In order to make the best use of your time, it is advisable to schedule them around other activities.

Some forms of research, such as library research, can be accomplished with little or no cost to you; others, such as hiring Dun and Bradstreet to analyze their market data base for you, are so costly that you may rule them out altogether. It is important to be sure that you proceed by exhausting those sources which will be least costly and most helpful at the outset of your research.

Some of the most common sources of information on potential markets for new products are as follows, in approximate order of descending cost-effectiveness:

1. *Library Research.*   This can be initiated in a university or large public library, and can be extended into technically oriented libraries or to the Library of Congress, National Technical Clearing-House, etc. You will make use of all the conventional methods and reference materials used in library research—abstracting services, specialized bibliographies, *Readers' Guide to Periodicals,* technical digest services, and, in some libraries, computer data-retrieval services.

Your research tools will, to a large extent, depend upon the field which you are researching. For example, if you were interested in a use for integrated circuits in automobiles, you could include such references as the electronics trade press, the end-user press (e.g., *Road and Track*); Government automotive research standards and perhaps patent documentation might also be useful to you.

If this form of research sounds endless to you, you might consider engaging the help of a diligent graduate student to aid in conducting the actual library research, under your close supervision.

2. *Questionnaire Surveys.*   The questionnaire survey is the mainstay of market research, whether it is conducted by mail, telephone, or personal interview. You are reaching your prospective customer *directly,* learning about his needs, problems, quantity requirements, and opinions regarding your proposed product. No form of indirect or inferential information is as up to date, helpful to you, or convincing to others. The questionnaire is always used (even if it's memorized) to ensure that the results are as comparable as possible.

There are perils, of course. A poorly structured questionnaire or an interview conducted with a weak format can result in your information being false and/or misleading. It is difficult, for example, for a customer to estimate his use of a product which he has never seen, which may be the first of its kind, and is possibly still nonexistent. Books have been written on survey techniques, questionnaire design, and interview psychology. By consulting one or more of these references, you may be able to avoid some of these perils.

3. *Existing Research Reports.* If the market which you wish to reach is growing, it has probably been studied by someone in the fairly recent past. The problem is discovering who has done it, and where to find the study. Many investor banking firms do such reports, or have them done by consultants for limited distribution to their customers. Various investment advisory services, such as Arthur D. Little's Service to Investors, do much the same thing. Consulting firms' livelihoods depend upon private studies of products and markets, both those which are potential in nature, and those which already exist. It is difficult, however, to obtain these reports unless you are in some way connected with the firm which commissioned them.

Some large studies, however, are syndicated by research firms, as well as other agencies, such as Stanford Research Institute or Batelle Memorial Institute. In such studies, which are directed towards many different clients, many copies may be available and your chances of obtaining one are better. In order to find out if any current study or report exists, ask your prospective customers, prospective competitors, and trade association personnel, as well as consulting/research firms themselves.

4. *Published Market Statistics.* There are two important sources of published market statistics: the U.S. Department of Commerce, and trade associations. The economic time series of the USDC are often criticized because of the tendency towards aggregation of figures; slow reporting; smallness of samples, and out-of-date SIC classifications. However, in some industries you will find the date to be quite current and detailed. Moreover, you can always contact the USDC directly, and tell them the information you need. They have much data at their disposal (some already published and some not) and they may be able to provide you with information that is more detailed and current than you would expect. There may be a charge, or they may do it for free, depending upon the complexity of your needs.

Trade associations usually publish gross industry sales, which are broken down into major product categories. Get in touch with those associations relevant to you, and find out what they publish. If you are able to get to know someone on their staff, at a national level, you may be able to obtain the information that they have, but don't publish. Such information is not necessarily secret, but may simply not be in demand. Your ultimate objective, of course, is to find out *who* is shipping *how much to whom,* and to find such information may require some persistence on your part.

5. *Trade Association Meetings and Trade Shows.* It is possible to obtain a lot of valuable information by attending the appropriate annual meetings or trade shows. You'll find out who your liveliest com-

petitors and customers are, who is spending the most money on promotion (at least on booths), what their newest products look like. You will be able to discover their major trends, what their literature and product documentation are like, and perhaps who their best sales people are. If you go to the technical sessions, you will find out about your competitors' *future* products, or at least about the technology they will embody. You may also hear something about what is happening in your field overseas. You might meet some potential offshore product sources, licensors, or distributors for your product. All this information can be yours for the price of a ticket to the annual meeting.

6. *"Experts."* Much valuable information may be gained from talking to experts in your field, such as trade magazine editors, consultants, university researchers, specialists in brokerage houses, and trade association staff. Aside from industry gossip and rumors, they can tell you about new technology which may soon revolutionize your field, some of your potential competitors who may be in trouble, and which products are good and which are bad. Aside from the facts that may be learned from them, they are generally interested in getting to know *you*, as an entrepreneur who is about to enter their world. Many of them will be happy to help you in any way they can, including paying for lunch occasionally.

7. *Phantom Products.* One method which is often used in order to obtain market data is the announcement of a nonexistent product (or one which has reached only the prototype stage). Then sit back and see who responds. This is sometimes done rather elaborately, with heavily airbrushed photographs of a mock-up product, or with artists' cutaways. A press release may be distributed to major journals, sometimes even using an assumed company name. When the direct mail results are analyzed and certain respondents contacted, you may find this to be a rather effective method of gathering information. Poorly handled, it may also backfire, and of course the ethical aspects may be considered questionable by some.

8. *Business and Credit Services.* Firms such as Dun and Bradstreet, NCO, and the American Bankers Association maintain extensive files of information on industries and companies. They can be excellent (although costly) sources of data. From them, one can gain knowledge of the size and geographical location of potential competitors, and specific classes of customers with whom they deal. Chilton Publishing Company and McGraw-Hill, for example, maintain files on several different industries. McGraw-Hill's *American Machinist* marketing service can tell you the location, type, and age of nearly every machine tool in the U.S.A. Other business publishers also offer market data services—again at a price.

9. *Professional Market Surveys.* The value of a report from a prestigious market research firm should not be underestimated as a tool in selling your proposal to investors. The length of such a report does not matter. The chances are slight that you will learn anything new by contracting for a market survey, if you have done tasks number one through eight of this section thoroughly. However, a corroborating report from a third party might be a source of extra confidence to you, as well as to investors. You will also learn from the process of negotiating questions of capability, scope, and cost with the market research firm. They must convince you of their experience and ability to deal with the question which you present. Therefore, you will have to meet their "expert" in your field, and they may well show you some nonclassified reports which they have done for other clients in your field, or in similar ones. It is entirely possible that they will suggest an "in-depth" study which will cost you $10,000–$20,000. What you really need from them, however, is a study costing somewhere between $1,000–$2,000, with you "helping" the researcher to understand what it is you need and want to know, and sharing your present information with him.

If done thoroughly, your market analysis will be beneficial to you in several different ways. It will provide you with quantification and documentation regarding the demand for your product. It will aid you in redefining the product (if redefinition is needed), and in modifying its specifications to fit the market more closely. You will be made more aware of what your competitors are doing, and of trends in distribution and promotion. It will give you a list of your first customers, and perhaps even yield one or two "letters of intent to purchase." On the other hand, your research may show that your technology is obsolete; that you will only have one-tenth of the market you originally expected; that there is already over-capacity in the business, forcing down profit margins; that there is some built-in reason why no one would buy your product, even if it were better than that of your competitor. (For example, for many years, "Buy American" had an extremely powerful influence on the use of imported parts and equipment, even though foreign-made products were often cheaper and frequently of better quality.) Avoiding just one massive blunder can more than justify the cost of the research.

Conventional Wisdom. The real entrepreneur will not be able to afford the time and money for fancy "market research"—and he probably won't need it anyway.

Reality. A little effort may yield enormous returns of information and increase credibility—both scarce commodities in most new ventures.

1. Dible, D. M.: *Up Your Own Organization*, Entrepreneur Press, Santa Clara, Calif., 1971.

   This book is a regular gold mine of practical information on sources of marketing data.

2. Aacker, David A. and Day, George S.: *Market Research*, John Wiley & Sons, N.Y., 1980.

   One of the newest and best references on all phases of market analysis.

3. Erdos, P. L.: *Professional Market Surveys*, McGraw-Hill Co., N.Y., 1970.

   This is a very practical treatment of the design, execution and interpretation of mail surveys—the principal tool available to entrepreneurs.

4. Smith, J. F.: *Interviewing in Market and Social Research*, Bosh, Routledge, & K. Paul, N.Y., 1972.

   Useful guidance to the techniques of interviewing.

5. Bolt, G. J.: *Market and Sales Forecasting: A Total Approach*, John Wiley & Sons, N.Y., 1972.

   A solid and very complete marketing text—oriented, however, more toward the larger firm.

6. Breen, George E.: *Do-It-Yourself Market Research*, McGraw-Hill, N.Y., 1977.

   Breezy, practical; 80 percent of all you'll ever need to conduct shirt-sleeves market analysis. Good section on questionnaire design.

7. Copulsky, W.: *Practical Sales Forecasting*, American Marketing Ass'n., N.Y., 1970.

   This is very practical, and useful to the large or small firm.

8. Anthony, E. L.: "Appraising the Market for the Services You Offer," *Small Marketers Aids, Annual No. 2*. Washington, D.C., Small Business Administration, 1967.

9. Clewett, R. M.: "Checking Your Marketing Channels," *Management Aids for Small Manufacturers, Annual No. 9*, Washington, D.C., Small Business Administration, 1963.

Chapter
5
SELECTION OF COHORTS

"Leadership is the ability to get men to do what they don't want to do and like it."

... Harry Truman

Companies are groups of people. Skillful management is fundamentally the ability to attract, train, motivate, and retain good, experienced people. However, your reasons for starting a new business may or may not include an exhibition of your superb managerial skill. The main objective should be to make money. This implies the retention of a maximum amount of equity for yourself, while raising the funds necessary for each ensuing stage of your company's growth.

Backers have a powerful and statistically well-founded preference for the founding *team*, as opposed to the individual founder. Both academic studies and venture capitalists' experience seem to confirm that a team effort is more likely to succeed than is the individual effort. The team, theoretically, should not be one-sided in its area of expertise, but should rather be a complementary group of people whose specialized skills cover the major, functional needs of a company of your kind.

Is a Team Really Necessary?

The question of the desirability and size of a team deserves some scrutiny, since there is an obvious conflict between having partners and retaining the majority of the stock for yourself. Whether a team is really necessary depends upon two major factors:

1. *The character of the venture.* Do you require a topnotch performer for every role, or can satisfactory people be hired, later, for the key roles?

2. *Your own personality, energy, and ability.* Are you the kind of person who is equally comfortable making technical, marketing, and business judgments? Or do you feel that it is essential to have a strong partner in one or more of these areas? Will you be comfortable in allowing your associates to tend the business while you're away, or is a real alter ego necessary to your peace of mind? Will you need a partner to share the day-to-day pressures and burdens, or do you function best when all decisions rest upon you?

The indications are that smaller founding teams work better than bigger ones. Despite the prevailing conventional wisdom of having teams share entrepreneurial efforts, it is the author's belief that the burden of proof is definitely on the larger team.

Common Team Problems

Teams, especially democratic ones, can create as many problems as they solve. This is especially true in cases where team members have not known one another before, or have not worked together under stress situations. On the other hand, people who *have* worked together tend either to be personal friends, or to be in the same specialty. Therefore, personal or noncomplementary relationships may tend to greatly dilute the alleged benefits of a team.

There also exist a number of potential sources of team conflict which are hard, if not impossible, to evaluate before the business is launched. People vary widely in the way they handle pressure, their willingness to work long hours, their ability to deal with ambiguity, their ethical standards, their sense of humor, and their innate intelligence. Serious mismatches in any of these areas can create conflicts of such magnitude that the presumed benefits of team effort will be negated.

Certain of these risks might be avoided by applying modern methods of psychological testing. Much is known about complementary and conflicting personalities. As a practical matter, however, it is unlikely that *your* team will consider it necessary to hire an agency for this purpose, however desirable the process may seem. Many will say, "That's just for other guys." And, of course, each person's sense of privacy may surface. Don't forget Oscar Wilde's bleak observation: "To be understood is to be found out."

The Question of Stock

A more important consideration at the outset will be: Who should have how much stock? Or, more bluntly, Why should I part with any of it? This is not a decision which should be made lightly, over a few beers with friends. It will have much to do with the future of the company. It greatly influences the direction which the company takes, how swiftly it can respond to changes in its environment, and how effectively its plans can be formulated and executed. Moreover, there is a tendency among teams to think of equal partnership as being, not only fair, but also the proper way of doing things. After all, if the company hasn't even gotten off the ground, why should anyone doubt that each partner will make an equal contribution?

In thinking about equity distribution, keep the following considerations in mind:

1. *Partners need not be equal partners.* Common stock makes unequal partnership both feasible and easily quantified.

2. *Do not take on a partner* if you can hire a person for the same role.

3. *Do not take on partners because you think having a "balanced team" will impress financial backers.* Responsible backers will be much more interested in knowing that the people who are *actually* responsible for the company's progress are the ones who hold the motivating stock.

4. *Do not allow your normal sense of democracy to cause you to part with more stock than is needed* to give your partner the motivation to use his full energies. Try to view the situation from *his* standpoint. What is he doing now? What are his prospects? Does he have a better opportunity?

5. *Do not allow the immediacy* of your present need, whatever it might be, *to bias your judgment* in favor of a partner versus an employee.

6. *Stay flexible in terms of compensation and motivation.* Consider stock options, or, preferably, bonus plans. Don't use stock when cash or IOU's will work as effectively. And don't make vague promises about stock when hiring.

7. *Do not approach potential partners* with tentative offers, in order to elicit their help in shaping your ideas, *until you have gone as far as you can go without them.* Get your initial business plan in order, incorporate, get an office, stationery, phone, and find a part-time accountant. In short, make sure that you have established the company as *yours*, so that anyone joining you will do so on *your* terms.

8. *If* your analysis shows that you can do it alone, don't be

afraid to try it. If you discover, as things progress, that you really *do* need a couple of partners, it's easier to get them later than it is doing it the other way around.

If the above seems to some to be rather Machiavellian, it will seem to others to be nothing more than obvious common sense. It may be that the team idea has been greatly overemphasized. One or two carefully selected and functioning partners can greatly smooth the road to success, but a team for team's sake is simply a source of more problems for the entrepreneur, at a time when he certainly has enough problems already. Contrary to the widely held view, the stock of a new company, rather than having zero value, is the only thing it *has* of value. Do not use it to compensate the janitor!

In presenting a business plan to potential backers, you will, of course, be expected to indicate the two or three key people who will be working with or for you. You should be able either to state who will fill the roles or to demonstrate convincingly that you understand the job requirements and possess the managerial competence to recruit and utilize people, when and if they are needed.

Ideally, the people you choose will have functioned in a small company before. Even an unsuccessful former entrepreneur may be a better bet than someone who has had no entrepreneurial experience whatsoever. If you need someone who has been a project manager from Collosus Aerospace Co., who has a brilliant record, but who has normally had three assistants and 100 engineers under him, consider making him a director or a consultant. The same is true for the marketing manager who functions only "first class," with huge advertising budgets, big staffs, and a nationwide direct sales force, replete with pep rallies in Bermuda. You will be better off with a bright young man who knows his way around in your industry, but whose mistakes are not going to destroy your company by their sheer magnitude. If he's had some entrepreneurial experience, perhaps as a rep, so much the better. He's the person who will get out of bed in the mornings and make his four sales calls and 20 phone calls. He's the person you need.

Hire people with the qualifications you need *now*. With luck, the man will grow with the job. If not, you can replace him at some later time. But don't make the error of hiring overqualified people, thinking that the company will fully utilize their skills when sales reach $3 million. Your job is to be sure those sales *get* to $3 million.

Offers made to prospective partners and employees before the company is on its feet have a somewhat surrealistic quality. The company has no money, no customers—in short, it is not a functioning company—*yet*. Realizing this, the prospective employee will expect some stock. But he will also expect market-rate compensation, even if it comes in the form of IOU's. *Don't make the mistake of hiring* *a man who is worth $20,000 for $15,000 and some stock.* Pay him what he is worth, even if it is partially deferred. Make the question of stock contingent upon performance.

The proper function of founders' stock is *not* compensation for past deeds. It is, rather, to provide motivation for deeds *yet to come.* The deferral of ownership privileges for a couple of years should not be viewed by the employee as the witholding of just compensation for two years of service. The two years should properly be considered as a probationary period, during which time the company must decide whether the person is worth having around for a longer time. During that period, the employee should receive full compensation, so that if for any reason the stock fails to materialize, he will have no basis for complaint against the firm. Your attorney will be able to help you in evaluating the various combinations of present and deferred salary and stock rights that are appropriate in different stages of corporate growth.

Equity Distribution: One Approach

There exist alternatives to the atavistic, keep-it-all philosophy of equity distribution. One such formula, for which White (1977) reports good results, is essentially an earn-in system. Under this plan, each founding member of the team agrees in advance to a schedule of values to be placed upon each major task that must be completed during the initial 1–2 years. For example:

Team Member	Task	Value (In Shares)
President	Write business plan	500
	Raise $100,000 seed capital	500
	Find facility	100
VP Marketing	Recruit 50 dealers	250
	Recruit and train three regional managers	200
	Write and print literature	100
	Obtain three letters of intent	300
Chief Engineer	Complete prototype development	400
	Complete production tooling	200
	Complete production documentation	100
	Complete User's Manual	100
	Hire software manager	100

As each task is completed on time, the shares are credited or distributed. Late or over-budget completion may be penalized. And, as tasks are added to the list, the founding team meets and agrees upon their value to the enterprise.

There are a number of obvious benefits to such a contractual approach to equity distribution:

1. It eliminates the arbitrariness and potential unfairness of simply giving most of the stock to the first one or two people in the boat.

2. By relating distribution to actual accomplished tasks, each partner has a special motivation to perform.

3. Since completed tasks trigger stock distribution, the nonperformer can be divested more easily than if he held a negotiated share of the company's equity.

However reasonable, the formula approach may contain the seeds of serious later problems for the company. This is because:

1. It is very hard to correctly gauge the relative difficulty of accomplishing specific goals. While we can easily estimate the effort needed to write a business plan, for example, it can be very risky to estimate what's required to raise capital—especially in a tight market.

2. The completion of a task is not necessarily the same as brilliant completion. Although the Chief Engineer has finished the working prototype, the design may be costly, inefficient, inflexible or unattractive. As always, quality of work is more elusive to measure than quantity.

3. It is likely that the future abilities and contributions of individual team members will be quite unequal. The person who was very good at getting start-up tasks done may prove later to be of much less value than a more managerial partner—yet they may both hold equal amounts of founders' stock.

Despite these and other pitfalls, the formal approach to equity distribution has considerable appeal and should certainly be considered by a founding team as an approach to solving this always sticky question.

Housecleaning

In the very early stages of forming a company, you are likely to discover that you have already made some mistakes in choosing your partners or employees. It's possible that your marketing manager will disappear to Cape Cod on the weekend he was supposed to finish his marketing plan. Your chief engineer may anguish for days over details which should be resolved within a few minutes. In short, for any number of reasons you may decide that you have hired the wrong person.

What do you do? He knows your plans. You've given him stock. You've told your prospective backers that he's nothing short of indispensable. He's given his employer notice, and his business cards are already printed. What can be done?

Well, maybe you should go ahead, raise the money, and keep the lid on. This problem can be dealt with later. Right? Wrong. *Get rid of him now*. Even though funding is in prospect, the stock has no "value," and it will take much longer than you had expected to get your money in the bank. Now is the time to level with him and make him an offer he can't refuse. Give him IOU's bearing interest for the estimated work hours he's put in. Offer to buy back his stock at a substantially higher price than he paid for it. Offer to reimburse his placement fees if he has to get another job. Offer to retain him as a director, or a consultant. Pay his price in the form of consulting fees if necessary. But *get him out*.

However friendly, forthright, and rational you try to be, however, you may expect the person to be hostile, irrational, and ungrateful. You have challenged his professional competence, trampled his self-esteem, and left him on a financial limb. If you were in that position you, too, would be upset. Expect some ugliness. Should it develop, your lawyer can suggest various alternatives. Hopefully it will not come to this, and it will be evident to both parties that the partnership just won't work. But if things do get worse, fight it out and remember that it's easier now, when the numbers are small, than it ever will be in the future. As far as your backers are concerned, they probably will not be dismayed by the disorder in your house. They halfway expected it anyway, and it will give them a good chance to size *you* up under pressure. After all, you were supposed to be a tough guy.

The initial stages, before you even reach the starting gate, are a lot of fun. This is the idea stage, when the creative architecture of your venture takes place. Seeds of eventual success or failure are planted. The real entrepreneur, however, is not swept along by the prevailing euphoria. He has the guts to correct early mistakes, before it is too late.

Conventional Wisdom.   Every venture needs a balanced team of pros with complementary skills in marketing, production, engineering, and operations.

Reality.   Every venture needs a founder who understands the need for supporting skills and knows where to find them, when needed.

References

1. White, Richard M.: *The Entrepreneur's Manual: Business Startups, Spinoffs, and Innovative Management*, Chilton Book Co., Radnor, Pa., 1977.

The author spells out his model for founder's equity distribution among team members. Recommended.

2. Steiner, Ivan D.: *Group Process and Productivity*, Academic Press, N.Y., 1972.

Discusses current research, relating task performance to size, composition, and motivation of groups.

3. Smith, P. B.: *Group Processes*, Penguin Books, Middlesex, England, 1970.

Discusses many of the things we now know about small group behavior. Presents research findings as well as theory.

Chapter 6

THE FETAL STAGE: FORM VERSUS SUBSTANCE

"Analysis, criticism are of no interest to me unless they are a path to constructive, action-bent thinking. Critical type of intelligence is boring and destructive and only satisfactory to those who indulge in it. Most new projects—I can even say every one of them—can be analyzed to destruction."

... Georges Doriot

Let us define the fetal stage of the enterprise as the time that lies between the fun of conception and the agonies of the birth of a corporation. This is by far the most ambiguous stage of the development of a new enterprise. Things may change radically in any direction during this period. You have your basic idea for a product, perhaps even a prototype. You have—or think you have—commitments from key people who will help you get off the ground. One or two of you are probably spending substantial time on the venture by now, even if you're still holding down a full-time job. The crude outline of a business plan exists, but you still don't know enough about the market to make any defensible sales projections or *pro forma* profitability estimates. You think you know a couple of investors who might be able to provide seed money, but you're not sure how to approach them. You're wondering whether to incorporate, how fast to move in product development, etc. In short you're asking yourself the question, hour by hour, "What do I do next?"

During the fetal stage everything is fluid. Nothing has become firm yet, and this fact amplifies every form of perturbation upon the incipient corporate baby. It is at this stage, for example, that you might discover that, instead of manufacturing, it would make a lot more sense to set up a sales or leasing company. Or, you might discover that your chief technical man is a phoney, and is a terrible engineer, and that the prototype that he has created doesn't work. Finally, you might discover that you can't enjoy the ambiguities of the new enterprise, that the lack of a structured work day is unbearable to you, and decide to give the whole thing up.

These are all radical influences, to say the least. It seems as though a million things need to be done, and a million questions must be resolved, all at the same time. Among these are:

What Form Should the Company Take?

Should it be a corporation, or a single proprietorship, or a partnership, a syndicate, or what? Each of these possibilities has its specific legal, tax, and debt liability consequences, which an attorney can help you to understand. However, unless some special circumstances dictate otherwise, you might as well incorporate right away. It is not an expensive process, and you do not need to have your permanent attorney selected at this point. Moreover, the very act of drawing up your corporate charter may help you in solidifying your vision of what you want your company to become, and the possible ranges of its activities. Other benefits include the following:

1. Incorporation forces you to choose a name and research it for prior claimants, thus eliminating the possible awkwardness of having to change the name six months after the inception of the company.

2. Being incorporated gives your venture, if nothing else, the illusion of permanence. This is a great help in recruiting partners on your terms, as well as in persuading suppliers, bankers, and customers that you're serious, and plan to be around for a while.

3. In a corporation, ownership is more equally divisable than in the common forms of partnership. This makes "uneven partnerships" more easily quantifiable.

4. It permits you to go ahead with a logo, permanent stationery, to have literature designed and produced, without risking the possibility of having to do the whole job twice.

Having decided to incorporate, you may ask yourself whether you should (as many big companies have) incorporate in Delaware. The answer is probably no. By the time you face the problems which incorporation in Delaware is supposed to solve, you will be able to afford to reincorporate there.

Secondly, you must decide what kind of corporation you want to have. There are some forms of incorporation in which special tax features are inherent. A *Subchapter S* incorporation will allow your financial backers to take as an ordinary loss any operating loss incurred by the corporation. A *Section 1244* incorporation permits them to take an ordinary loss, on their individual tax returns, from the sale of the company's stock, rather than a capital loss. Both these features operate in a similar way. They are intended to induce individuals with high incomes or a large net worth to invest in risky new ventures. These privileges are, however, limited to companies that fall below specified limits of total capital, number of investors, etc. Therefore, the principal benefits are available to the smallest and/or newest ventures. Since these features of corporate law exist, there is very little reason not to take advantage of them. Your attorney, however, should examine the particulars of your situation and make a firm recommendation.

What Kind of Facilities?

There are several reasons why it is desirable to have different addresses for your home and your business. In addition to having a place to which deliveries can be sent, where the phone can ring, and where prototypes can be developed, etc., it is a clear signal to prospective partners that this is *your* turf, and that any agreement made with them will be subject to *your* terms.

While ideas vary on the subject, you will probably be better off with an office of at least reasonable dignity. The want-ad section of the newspaper often contains information about space to share, along with secretarial help, office equipment, etc. This can be a better solution than renting an office immediately and hiring a secretary yourself. It can, however, be a bit costly. An alternative solution to this problem is to find a friend with an office or plant with the necessary overheads and ask him if you can share it, if not for free then on a deferred-rent basis. This might give you access to other desirable facilities, such as a shop, conference room, telephone board—maybe even a purchasing agent—all which would help you materially as well as enhancing your appearance. Remember: *appearances count*, especially at the beginning, when there is so little real substance with which to back it up. You must not, on the other hand, become one of those entrepreneurs who are so preoccupied with the form of the business that they forget all about its substance!

Directors, Pro and Con

Every corporation needs a board of directors, according to law. Such a board may be comprised of your wife and yourself, or of any number of other people. In theory, the board sets overall corporation policy and the executives execute it. In the small business venture, however, the board usually serves a somewhat different function. Many entrepreneurs use it as a kind of totem pole, made up of a maximum number of influential and impressive figures whose function is to impress the prospective investor. This is, in all probability, the major function of outside directors during the fetal stage of a company.

On the other hand, you should not allow the recruitment of important figures to become an obsession—you have other, more important things to do. Important people tend to be busy, and are therefore reluctant to become board members, especially if they perceive their function as being mainly one of decoration. As your plans and prospects develop it will become somewhat easier to find outside directors. Until then, however, too many outsiders may hamper your flexibility and become an encumbrance in your efforts. If you feel the need to have an outside officer, your attorney will probably be willing to be clerk. He has to do all the work, anyway.

It is often suggested that an outside mentor, or "godfather," can be extremely helpful in starting a new venture. This is true, especially if he is an experienced person, perhaps a retired executive, who has had first-hand entrepreneurial experience. He can serve as a sounding board for new ideas, as a reference for banks, attorneys, etc., and just as important, as a source of guidance and encouragement when you feel as though everything is falling apart. If you know any such persons, get them on board early. But note: They don't have to be directors.

Prototypes and Plausibility

You don't need a book to tell you that *the more fully developed your product is, the more easily you will be able to raise seed money for it* and get the project off the ground. There is, of course, a succession of stages in product development, running from idea, to design, to prototype, to preproduction prototype, to tooled production models, to sales of the actual product. You can show your product at any of these stages. It goes without saying, however, that the closer you are to the finished product the better.

In most instances the prototype stage is the earliest point at which you should seek investors. This is the point at which the venture begins to acquire momentum. Products which cannot be explained to prospective backers in technical terms *can* be demonstrated. The functioning entity can give your designers something concrete with which to work, as they begin to actually *see* ways in which the product can be radically improved while reducing the production costs. Most of all, the prototype is the first real evidence that your company *has* a product. Your statements about its marketability and profit-making potential increase in plausibility. In short, you'll probably be better off with a lower profile while the prototype is being built, in the fetal corporate stage.

Where Does Seed Money Come From?

Seed money—sometimes called *adventure* capital—must be differentiated from *venture* capital. Seed money is the money which goes into the company before it is actually functioning as such. Its purpose is to get the company from fetal to newborn status, and as much further as possible before outside financing and its accompanying ownership dilution occurs.

Seed money is most likely to come from the entrepreneur and his partners—at least the first few thousand dollars of it. If more is needed, the search widens. Studies show that virtually all initial outside funding for new technical enterprises comes from wealthy individuals. In practically every community, there are a few wealthy people who have an interest in entrepreneurial efforts. Seek them out when your prototype and business plan are in reasonable shape. Present your story as convincingly as possible, and sign them up. If there is a scarcity of wealthy businessmen or people who are themselves ex-entrepreneurs in your area, approach doctors, dentists, and lawyers. Such professionals often have large unsheltered incomes which might make them perk up their ears at an attractive "Subchapter S" offering. Failing this, try your Aunt Hattie, mortgage the house, sell the car, or do whatever else is needed in order to raise the necessary capital. Before you do that, however, stop for a moment and ask yourself whether the market is, perhaps, sending you a message.

Finally, *don't accept more seed capital than you need*. It is always flattering to have a high valuation placed on your company by even an unsophisticated outsider. However, the more you can achieve on a small amount of seed capital, the more impressive your results will be. It will also be healthier for your company in the long run. In the next round, money will be easier to find and will cost you a whole lot less stock ownership. Hold on to that stock!

What to do Until the Money Arrives

Whether or not you have reached your desired minimum level of seed capital, there are certain things which must be done immediately. Some are major, some minor, but all are important.

1. *Make sure that people are able to get in touch with you.* If there are times when the phone cannot be covered, get an answering service.

2. *Begin market research immediately*. This is essential if your information is to be of any value in shaping the product or the company. Since such research usually takes a good deal of time, the sooner you begin it, the better. Be prepared to spend some time travelling, because much of it will probably take the form of personal interviews. Questionnaire surveys can take a lot of time, too, and should probably be the first form of market research to be begun.

3. *Have a logo and letterhead designed*. Don't have your printer do it. Get an ad agency that specializes in that kind of work. It may cost you more money, but it is an investment in image and self-esteem. Then get your letterhead and cards printed, and don't sacrifice quality.

4. *Get the formal business plan moving*, even if there are large blank spaces to be filled in later. Try to get a feel for the figures, as well as for the sensitivity of your *pro forma* financial statements to variations in sales rate, price, materials costs, etc.

5. *Write some reasonable descriptions and specification sheets*, and have them set in type and neatly printed. You cannot afford to have sloppy literature, even if it is temporary. Have all line drawings, graphs, and cutaways done professionally, if at all possible. If you can afford it, use more than two colors in your literature. If you can find a free-lance professional artist to work with you, it is better than going to an ad agency. If you went to them, they'd probably send the job out to him anyway. Remember, your printed materials *are* your company to your prospective customers. The more you look like IBM, the better.

6. *Give your team enough work to do*. Maintain their level of enthusiasm. Get together with them at least twice a week to check results and keep everyone up to date. Don't forget that, as president of your venture, you are a combination of press agent, errand boy, cheerleader, and slave driver—it all depends upon what needs doing when.

7. *Don't stop meeting people*. If at all possible, keep widening your circle of contacts. Meet with bankers, investors, customers, consultants, other entrepreneurs, editors, professors, employees, and vendors. Try to have lunch with someone useful every day.

8. *Write some articles for the trade press*. Describe your product, discuss possible applications, work jointly with a user on a story, or, perhaps, do a comparative survey of existing products in your field. You'll discover that editors are willing and eager to find a source of new and fresh material, and that the by-line will aid you in spreading your fame and that of your company. Also, reprints make impressive-looking product literature and appendices for financial presentations.

9. *Set up a definite compensation* schedule for all your employ-

ees. Make sure that everyone's work hours are recorded and that the rate for each person's work has been agreed upon. Even if you have to issue IOU's, it is infinitely better than trying, a year from now, to distribute stock in proportion to services rendered. Or, even worse, trying to distribute it in proportion to "value contributed."

10. *Stay loose.* During the fetal stage, you should try to keep your ideas about your company and yourself as flexible as possible. You may discover a better opportunity. At the same time, you may come up against a complete roadblock which was invisible at an earlier stage. You are certain to learn things which you never knew about yourself, as well as discovering new facets of your partners' personalities. You may discover new markets or meet people with better ideas than yours, with which you would prefer to work. The fetal stage is immensely valuable, in that it allows things like this to happen without the danger of losing a lot of someone else's money or a great deal of personal credibility with the business and financial communities. Give it all you've got, but at the same time try to maintain a slightly Olympian viewpoint.

Conventional Wisdom. Get a million-dollar idea, find some venture capital, and *go.*

Reality. Venture capital companies are not interested in ideas. Get some seed money, make sure your prototype and your company are "debugged," and *then go.*

References

1. Mancuso, Joseph R.: *How to Start, Finance, and Manage Your Own Small Business*, Prentice-Hall, Englewood Cliffs, N.J., 1970.

    Excellent section on the typical role of directors.

2. Vesper, Karl: *New Venture Strategies*, Prentice–Hall, Englewood Cliffs, N.J., 1980.

    Vesper's description of various venture startup processes is required reading.

3. Richardson, C.T.: "How Directors Strengthen Small Firms," *Management Aids for Small Manufacturers, Annual No. 6*, Small Business Administration, Washington, D.C., 1960.

    Pragmatic advice, oriented toward the small and the growth company.

4. Anthony, E. L.: "Choosing the Legal Structure for your Firm," in *Management Aids for Small Manufacturers*, Annual No. 5, Small Business Administration, Washington, D.C., 1959, pp. 9–15.

5. Mace, Myles L.: *The Board of Directors in Small Companies*, Harvard University Printing Office, Cambridge, Mass., 1948.

6. Office of the General Counsel: "Steps in Incorporating a Business," in *Management Aids for Small Manufacturers*, Annual No. 8, Small Business Administration, Washington, D.C., 1962, pp. 60–65.

Chapter 7

LEAVING THE WOMB

"Companies are like babies—fun to conceive but hell to deliver."

. . . Anonymous

Gestation has run its course, and you feel that the time has come to cut the cord. You have a team, a product, a little capital (at least enough to make a start), and now you must make your first real commitment to the company's future by devoting your full energies to it. How best to proceed?

First, you should read (perhaps for the first time) the nondisclosure agreement which you signed when you joined your present organization. You may not think that your product competes with those of your present company. It may be inconceivable to you that it infringes upon that company's patents, or makes use of its trade secrets, or that it will be sold to the same customers. But take a hard look. It is just possible that your present employer might decide not to agree with you. Consult your lawyer, just to make sure. Courts are more and more frequently ruling in favor of firms holding such agreements, and the form that such agreements take is becoming more sophisticated and enforceable.

Should you decide that there is a possibility of your being challenged, take it seriously. Even if the challenge were frivolous, its mere possibility and the prospect of an impending court fight is enough to send prospective investors into permanent hibernation. Unfortunately, there is no sure way of discovering how your employer might view such a matter without letting him know that you are about to quit, and revealing rather fully the details of your venture. You might get some idea of his probable reaction from similar situations within the company, but this is far from a firm guide.

In addition to meeting your legal obligations to your employer (avoiding prosecution), you should reflect upon your other obligations as well. These can include:

1. Tying up the loose ends of projects on which you've been working.

2. Spending some time helping to orient and to train your replacement.

3. Taking whatever steps are necessary to ensure that your departure causes the minimum possible disruption in the company's business.

Remember, you're going to need all the friends you can get in your new role as entrepreneur. Your old company might be a future supplier, customer, or (God forbid) employer. In any case, he will be among the first sources to which bankers, financial backers, and prospective creditors will turn when they need to check on your personal integrity. Be sure that what they hear is good news.

Noncompetition Agreements

Such agreements are most often found in conjunction with employment contracts, and if you have signed one, go at once to your lawyer and have a long talk. While some agreements have defined competition so broadly as to be nonenforceable, the merits of the case would determine your actual exposure. If you are, in fact, going to compete with your ex-employer, you may have little choice but to accept the calculated risk of breaking the agreement. The law allows him to prevent you from competing; however, he *cannot* prevent you from making a living within your field of expertise. If yours is a borderline case, as many are, proceed—but with caution.

When to Split

From both a practical and a legal standpoint, it is time to resign *when you find that you are spending significant amounts of time on the new venture*. This will forestall the appearance of having worked on the project on company time, as well as the question of whether you have recruited company employees or customers while still employed at the firm. All of these are causes for possible legal action against you.

If (as is likely) your proposed business is something in which your present employer has a legitimate interest, you should consider discussing your plan with him. The benefits of such a course of action will probably outweigh the risks. If there are problems of proprietary products, patents, or trade secrets, they can be aired at the same time. Possible methods of circumventing problems can also be discussed (e.g., patent licensing, contract manufacture, or outright purchase of design rights for cash or stock).

The very fact of your giving up the security of your job to start your own company will force your employer to change his perception of you. You are no longer a hired hand, and he must decide whether to say goodbye and good luck, or, goodbye, see you in court; he must also decide whether to attempt to enlist your newly revealed entrepreneurial talents to the benefit of his company. The first two cases require no further comment. The third, however, could be interesting in that you might unexpectedly find yourself confronted with yet another career choice.

If your employer likes you or your idea a lot, he can react to your proffered resignation in a number of different ways:

1. He can offer you a large *compensation increase* to persuade you to stay.

2. He can offer to *create a new subsidiary* company to do what your own company is planning to do, with some possibility of equity for you, as president.

3. He can offer to *take a major equity position in your venture*, supplying capital and perhaps other resources. He could insist on a buy-out option, exclusive marketing rights, exclusive manufacturing contracts, etc.

4. He could *offer facilities*, manufacturing time, marketing capability, or other resources—for a price—in return for design rights, patent rights, manufacturing contracts, etc.

Such a proposition, depending upon its form and content, may turn out to be a better opportunity than your own company would be; or, it could be that you would simply be selling out your chance to build your own company, in exchange for a little security.

You must realize that your interests and those of your employer are somewhat different: You want eventual growth in your personal net worth, together with maximum flexibility to go public, merge, or sell out. Products or technology aside, he wants maximum earnings per share, plus whatever booster your glamorous little venture would give to his price-earnings ratio (assuming his stock is public). If, after reviewing all of these factors, his proposition seems to make more sense to you than your own, don't hesitate to take it. After a year or two, if the new situation proves to be less than you had expected, you may be in a stronger position than you are now to start your own company. *Caveat:* Don't discuss your plans with your employer in such a way that you seem to be *expecting* him to make a counterproposal. This situation puts you in an extremely unfavorable light, regardless of the outcome. Announce your departure and the formation of your new venture as a concrete *fait accompli.*

What to Take With You

What you take with you to your new venture should be limited to that which is in your head. What you should not take with you is any property of your employer, broadly construed: plans, blueprints, customer lists, vendor lists, research reports, market studies, competitive analyses, or any other documents which cost your employer time and money to acquire—even if you did them yourself, and even if you believe them to be of little value to your employer. Appropriation of such proprietary materials, even if it runs no risk of prosecution, places the formation of your new venture in a very poor ethical light, particularly in the view of your own people.

Raiding

As long as you are no longer employed by a firm, there is no legal constraint against recruiting its employees. Practically speaking, it may be very difficult to get a firm started *without* recruiting some of your former working associates. The financial community's preference for a team whose members have worked together previously is not without sound basis. (Of course, you, too, will prefer to have had direct experience with the first few employees of your company, whether they are your chief scientist or your secretary.)

Since raiding, however necessary, is not likely to enhance your popularity with your old employer, weigh the benefits carefully against the possible penalties. And under no circumstances should you begin recruiting until *after* you resign.

Parting Shot

Try to make your break with your employer as clean as possible, in every sense of the word. Then you'll have no reason to regret it.

Conventional Wisdom. Your old employer is a resource to be exploited.

Reality. Your old employer is a resource to be exploited at your peril.

1. Neumeyer, Frederick, and Stedman, John C.: *The Employed Inventor in the United States: R&D Policies, Law, and Practice.* The M.I.T. Press, Cambridge, Mass., 1971.
   Readable, competent, complete. This will tell you more than you want to know about your obligations to your employer.

2. Vesper, Karl: *New Venture Strategies.* Prentice–Hall, Englewood Cliffs, N.J., 1980.
   Excellent section on exit strategy.

3. Navin, W. J.: *Patents.* Practicing Law Institute, N.Y., 1966.
   A very good text, written in lay language. An excellent background book for any engineer-entrepreneur.

FINANCING AND FINANCES

II

INITIAL FINANCING

"Money is the seed of money, and the first guinea is sometimes more difficult to acquire than the second million."

. . . Jean Jacques Rousseau

Two distinct schools of thought exist regarding initial financing. The first maintains that the more money you can get into the venture at the beginning, the better. The arguments for this point of view are not without merit, and are as follows:[1]

1. Additional money permits you to survive unexpected setbacks, delays, and false starts in getting your product on the market.

2. It allows you additional flexibility in taking advantage of new opportunities, should they arise.

---

[1]Cohn, H.A., *Spin-off Organizations: A Study of Enterprises Spun-off from the MIT Community*, S.M. Thesis, Sloan School of Management, MIT, Cambridge, Mass., January, 1970. Cohen presents evidence that in a large sample of MIT spin-off firms, those with larger amounts of capital were statistically more successful. However, he also shows that those with large founder teams were also the most likely to raise substantial initial capital (i.e., the principal founder's equity was already spread thin at the start). It would be interesting to know how the *founder* fared financially in the companies with substantial versus less initial capital in the sample. It is also possible, of course, that some of the less successful companies sampled did not have enough capital for the venture—an extreme also to be avoided.

3. Visible working capital eases the problem of obtaining credit from suppliers, banks, etc.

4. It makes the entrepreneur feel secure, early in the game, to see that his net worth on paper is substantial.

The second school of thought maintains that, in the case of early financing, less is more. That is, you should raise only the amount of money which is absolutely essential for the operation of the company at each stage of growth. The following arguments support this point of view:

1. Limited capitalization prevents major losses, and also the loss of long-term credibility with the financial community, even though it increases the risk of failure, should a significant setback occur.

2. Close funding keeps attention and energies focused on the principal objectives and timetables of the company, rather than dissipating them by looking for better opportunities, further product refinements before introduction, etc.

3. Tight funding allows the first-time entrepreneur to gain some experience in cash management, operating on negative working capital, living off vendors, putting pressure on slow-paying customers—experience which will stand him in good stead in the future. Whether his company is very successful or very unsuccessful, it will be short of cash. Only mediocre or nongrowing companies have no cash shortages.

4. Finally, and most important: If you sell more stock than you need to sell, you are selling it too cheaply. You should consider the amount of money you will be able to make by selling the stock at future, higher prices. Be sure that you *need* every dollar you raise. "Reserve for contingency" is a prudent-sounding budget item for your business plan, but don't lose sight of what it may actually cost you—the entrepreneur—in the long run.

Selling stock in a brand new company is a little like cutting down a newly planted forest for lumber. It's worth far more left growing than it would be if it were used for wood now.

A secondary but important aspect of the issue is this: the type of person from whom one is able to raise initial capital may not be the kind of person whom you want to have heavy voting power, when and if the company gets off the ground. However, by the time financial institutions are ready to put major funding into your venture, it will cost too much to buy such a person out. Backers do not like to put money into a venture simply to buy out other stockholders. The money should be for growth.

Practically speaking, the questions confronting the entrepreneur when raising initial capital are: (a) How much money do we need to get by?, and, (b) How much control do I want to part with, in order to get that money?

These questions are related only remotely to asset values, net worth tests, or capitalized earnings streams. They are not at all sophisticated. Simply stated, you have no tangible assets, no net worth, no earnings. All you can present is your *pro forma* earnings projection, and investors do not credit such projections unduly. How, then, can you calculate and defend a price for your company's stock?

The answer is, of course, that you can't. Pricing a new company's stock is much like pricing any other glamour item (e.g., perfume, paintings, rare coins) where appeal is based on emotional, as well as analytical considerations. You must try to figure out what the market will pay, independent of analyzable worth. Your considerations include:

1. For what price has stock in similar ventures sold recently?

2. To what kinds of people do I hope to sell? What and how strong are their tax and other nonemotional incentives?

3. How glamorous will the offer appear? Is it presented in such a way as to take full advantage of a hot market, new technology, and proprietary product?

4. If things go as planned, what will the payoff be to initial investors? (If it really goes, they will be looking for something between 10-fold and 50-fold appreciation.)

This issue is not worth too many sleepless nights. Your price will turn out to be merely the opening shot in what is ultimately a negotiation. After you have tried to actually sell your stock, you will have a good idea of the extent to which it is overpriced. (On the other hand, should you get your money without earnest negotiation, you will never know to what extent it was *underpriced!*)

Venture Capital: What It Is and Isn't

In Chapter 5 we drew the distinction between venture and *adventure* (or seed) capital. Venture capital, despite its connotation, is most definitely not intended for the startup company. It is, rather, a term which is normally reserved for the first major outside financing. It is normally available only when: (a) the company is off the ground, (b) the team is functioning, (c) the product is on the market with demonstrated acceptance, and, (d) the company has demonstrated its potential for orderly growth and responsible management of other people's money.

If you make the rounds with the Venture Capital Directory in one hand and your business plan in the other, you are wasting credibility, time, and entrepreneurial energy. You should, instead, be talking to a few, carefully selected, affluent individuals. The principal share of your energy, however, should (at this stage) be put into the details of actually getting operations off the ground, many of which do not require much or any money.

Why Not Get a Loan?

In order to finance a new venture while keeping all the stock possible, a loan would seem to be the most logical way of getting money. The major problem is that you probably won't be able to get one—at least from banks. Banks require assets which can be used as collateral, together with the visible means of paying off the loan at a reasonable point in the future. They also want clear evidence that you will be able to produce the cash flow required to meet interest payments. Since few fetal ventures meet any, let alone all, of these conditions, the bank loan as a means of starting up a business will almost certainly not work.

However, this does not mean that you should not talk to bankers. Your principal criterion for choosing a banker should be his relative willingness to lend you money at some early point in the growth of your company (more on this in Chapter 19). Some banks, for example, are willing to lend money to companies whose balance sheets are disastrous, on the basis of pledged accounts receivable. So, if you have made a big shipment, by all means talk with the banker about a loan.

Banks *have* been known to waive orthodox lending standards, and lend substantial amounts of money to beginning ventures, on the basis of contracts (not accounts receivable) in hand, or even on the founder's signature alone. Other banks have Small Business Investment Companies, through which they try to work with new ventures. It is to your advantage to associate yourself with a good bank as soon as possible. The sooner you do it, the sooner you will be able to find out how much credit is actually available to you.

Of course, there are other sources of loans, besides lending institutions. Perhaps you will be able to borrow seed money from a relative or friend who does not want to become a stockholder in your company. In this case, you, not the company, are borrowing the money and are fully responsible for its repayment. However, a bank will want your personal signature, also, on any early loans which it makes to your company. In any case, you may prefer to have your

brother-in-law as a creditor, rather than as a stockholder with a
voice in the running of your company.

Other sources of seed money loans may include regional development agencies, mortgage brokers (using your house equity as
security), credit unions, the Small Business Administration, suppliers, and, in some cases, customers. Do not overlook the possibility
of negotiation for advance payment, progress payments, or other
advances which might be forthcoming from your customers. Depending on the industry, this may be the orthdox way of doing business, and they will expect such requests. Capital cost is, of course,
included in the negotiated price of the products or services you are
supplying, despite the fact that interest is seldom charged on such
prepayments.

Your particular situation may permit you to function either
partially or entirely on borrowed funds from the beginning, even
though it is usually necessary to sell at least some equity in order to
raise seed capital. Naturally, the feasibility and desirability of following such a course should be carefully investigated.

Operating Without Capital

As suggested above, there are many substitutes for permanent
equity capital available to the beginning venture. All of these possibilities should be carefully considered, not only because of the effects of early dilution discussed earlier, but also because there will,
sooner or later, come a cash crunch when you'll need to use them
anyway. Every tightly run company reaches this point.

Earlier in this chapter, we listed some sources of cash loans.
Other sources of borrowed value exist, however, to an extent which
is not readily appreciated by the new entrepreneur. These sources
include:

Your Vendors. A new venture's suppliers can be among its
most valuable friends. If such a relationship is not excessively
abused, one's suppliers can be among the most important sources of
short-term capital. Most firms will offer 30 days credit even to a new
company, with a penalty for running over 30 days. Other companies
charge the penalty indirectly, by denying an early payment discount
to thirty-day accounts. Even if such an arrangement costs you
money, however, at least the credit and the materials are available to
you. You will discover, practically speaking, that you can *occasionally*
run considerably over the 30-day limit—as long as you reach a current status again, as quickly as possible.

Your Capital Equipment Suppliers. Suppliers will often make
very favorable terms available, even to new companies, in their desire to sell equipment. This is possible because the equipment itself

secures the loan. The contract may be a lease, held by the seller or a leasing company, or (usually cheaper) a conditional sales agreement whereby the seller retains a lien or title until the last installment payment is made and received. Generally, capital equipment and plant facilities are easier to finance than are ordinary working capital requirements.

Your Employees.   Nobody has a greater stake in the health of your firm than your own employees. For the more mature firm the Employees Stock Ownership Plan (ESOP) may provide an investment vehicle for the employees. For the smaller firm struggling for survival, however, the employees may be an obvious source of aid. The financing can come in the form of loans (interest-bearing debentures), stock purchases, or even deferred compensation, backed by interest-bearing notes. The employee may be your best possible investor since you can pay him substantially higher interest than he could get elsewhere and, in the case of stock purchase, he acquires a whole new stake in the success of the firm.

Export Banks.   If your company either imports or exports significant amounts of product, you should know of the existence of export banks. Every industrial country has some such organization, designed to promote the export of its products. Such export banks, including the U.S. Export-Import Bank, are empowered to offer attractive credit terms to domestic manufacturers and foreign buyers of their goods. This function is also performed to a degree by the large trading companies of Japan and the Eastern Bloc nations. They all represent a source of capital over and above that available from normal financial institutions.

Leasing Companies.   Such companies can, as noted previously, make it possible for you to buy capital equipment. It can, however, work the other way around if *you make* capital equipment. In such a case, your capital equipment suppliers can make it possible for your customer to buy the equipment, on a prepaid basis, before it is even built—especially if it is custom-designed, one-of-a-kind equipment.

Receivables Factors.   These institutions, instead of lending money against accounts receivable, buy the receivables outright, at a discount. Thus you are relieved of the delay and cost of collection efforts. However, factors are usually geared to specialized customers, and typically serve firms which have a seasonal or cyclic business pattern. Unless your venture falls into this category, you may find it either difficult or excessively expensive to work through factors.

Deferral of Payables in General.   When money is tight, most companies (including very large ones) lag behind in their payment of bills. There will be times when you must avail yourself of this source of short-term financing. Also, don't overlook the fact that

certain of your employees (especially professional employees) might
be willing to defer portions of their salary, or take notes, either as a
gesture of bonhomie, or as a practical measure taken to avoid being
laid off.

One person from whom you should *not* borrow short-term capital is Uncle Sam. Make your withholding payments on time, or you
are in for a lot of trouble.

In addition to these possible funding sources, there are other
ways in which you can save valuable cash while getting your no-cap-
ital venture off the ground. These include:

1. Sharing office and shop space (and thus overhead) with
another company.

2. Doing any carpentry and painting which needs to be done
yourself, in order to create offices, a lobby, etc., in low-rent space.
(If Digital Equipment Corp. could do it, why can't you?)

3. Using other firms' capital equipment during off hours.
This could include their machine shop, printing equipment, test
equipment, data processing machines, or anything else that has low
incremental cost of operation.

4. Purchase used office and plant equipment wherever possible. Preferably, buy it at auctions or bankruptcy sales. Such a practice can save you 50 to 90 percent of new equipment costs.

5. Use part-time specialists. Engineers, technical writers, layout artists, and technical typists can all be hired on a part-time,
moonlighting basis—often at a much lower cost per hour than their
own employer pays, since he covers their benefits. In some cases,
you may be able to avoid witholding taxes—if the person qualifies as
a "consultant." Check with your accountant on this point.

6. Begin your sales effort by using reps or agents, rather than
hiring a full-time sales force. Although most new companies haven't
much of a choice, try to evaluate the use of reps thoroughly before
hiring direct salesmen.

7. Have your product manufactured wholly outside your
company. This can avoid many headaches and is, in many cases,
cheaper, due to the economies of scale which are inherent in most
manufacturing efforts. In some areas, competition among vendors
is so great that you might be able to arrange to have your vendor
stock your finished goods at no carrying charge. This is, of course,
a reversible decision. You can, when you wish, bring prime manufacturing efforts back in-house, while subcontracting any overflow to
your (by this time well-debugged) vendor.

8. Try to make use of free public relations, instead of paid
advertising. Send out a news release to your trade press at least once
a month. Write stories for the trade press, arrange to be interviewed

about your product, company, and prospects. Hold a press conference in a decent hotel suite to launch your new product. Avoid ad agencies, and the big advertising budget which goes with them, like the plague.

9. Arrange to buy materials, at cost, from a larger user who commands a large amount of purchasing power. You will both benefit, since it is possible that your volume will add to his clout with vendors.

10. Push your customers hard for prompt payment. Convince them that it is better to pay you on time and let their other creditors wait. Frequent contact with the accounts payable department at your customer's office will, eventually, have its effect. Unfortunately, most entrepreneurs regard the collection of bills as at least uninteresting, if not degrading. They would much rather spend their time and energies in getting a new order or in filling one which already exists, rather than in collecting money for one which is already completed. But, unless you get paid—on time—all of your other efforts will be in vain. If you can't stand this work, get someone who can. However, make sure that you personally keep a sharp eye on the receivables problems.

11. Above all, stay cool. Don't panic, even if ten suppliers have called in the last hour, demanding payment. If you find that it will take 90 days instead of 40 to pay them, even after all your planning, go to the head of the supplier firm and talk to him. Work out a schedule of partial payments, and then stick to it. Nothing else which you can do will go further in bolstering his confidence in you. And—when all of this gets *too* depressing—go make some sales calls.

The Magic of Initial Sales

On the day that you make your first sale, your baby becomes a business. Up until that point, everything is preparation and hope. Once the first sale is made, you know that you can not only get your product to market, but that there is someone out there who will pay money for it. Symbolically, the importance of the first few initial sales cannot be over-stated. It may be the ounce of proof outside backers are looking for, the signal to bankers that a modest loan may be in order, the indication to suppliers that they will probably get paid—sooner or later—and that they might even be justified in increasing your credit limits. It also does fantastic things for your morale and that of your team. You're finally *shipping products*! Put your concentrated efforts into reaching this goal as early as possible, with little or no outside financing. Such an achievement will go far toward ensuring a healthy start and a successful first financing.

Conventional Wisdom. The failure of most new companies can be attributed to inadequate initial financing.

Reality. Many of those companies which fail are adequately, if not overly, financed. Most of these failures can be traced to inept management, of which "inadequate financing" is one symptom.

References

1. Summers, George W.: *Financing and Initial Operations of New Firms*, Prentice–Hall Inc., Englewood Cliffs, N.J., 1962.

   A good practical guide to getting off the ground, financially and otherwise.

2. Baty, G. B.: *Initial Financing of the New Research-Based Enterprise in New England*, Federal Reserve Bank of Boston, 1963.

   Verifies the widely held suspicion that rich people provide most of the seed capital for new technology companies.

3. Wayne, William: *How to Succeed in Business When the Chips are Down*, McGraw-Hill, N.Y., 1972.

   This gritty little book is full of suggestions on operating without cash, infighting with the bank, chopping costs, etc.

Chapter
9
EQUITY SOURCES: A RANGE
OF MOTIVATIONS

"For the engine that drives enterprise is not Thrift, but Profit."

. . . John Maynard Keynes

Your seed money is beginning to sprout. Most of the early problems with your product have been ironed out, and the team has survived the initial stresses inherent in any startup venture. The first few sales have been made. People are beginning to hear about your company and your product, and to get excited about it. The time has come for you to find and use the first serious chunk of outside capital. Where do you go from here?

Unless your company is very unusual, this is the stage at which some equity financing is required. There are several different reasons for this. First, it is extremely difficult to borrow for such purposes as market development, research, and product development. These are investments, but they do not normally appear as assets on your balance sheet.

Second, borrowing would place undesirable strain on your cash flow during this critical growth stage, due to interest payments.

Third, a layer of long-term equity money will give your company the financial strength required to borrow strategically.

And fourth, you don't want to be faced with the necessity of paying loans back, just as the company begins to move. This is especially true if there is a tight money market, or if more funds are unavailable for refinancing. Such leverage multiplies the risk of failure.

Your basic need at this point is for *permanent equity capital*, even though the financing may include a component of debt—possibly convertible into stock.

Venture capital sources to which you will probably turn can be grouped roughly into five significant categories:

1. Private individuals, or a syndicates of individuals

2. Closed-end investment funds (e.g., Venroc, Payson-Trask, Heizer Co.)

3. Publicly-held venture capital companies (e.g., the larger SBICs)

4. Fiduciary funds managers (e.g., insurance, pension fund managers)

5. Industrial corporations

All of these are or have been significant sources of venture capital for beginning enterprises. All are similar, superficially, in that they invest reasonable amounts of equity monies in risky enterprises, hoping for substantial capital gains. However, each one has its distinct motivations for being in the business. Consequently, each has distinct attitudes and policies of operation. It is important that you, as an entrepreneur, have some appreciation of these differences, in order to ensure that the capital search is as efficient as possible, and to maximize the chances that the new partnership will work out as hoped, in the future.

Private Individuals or Syndicated Investors

Private individual or syndicated investors will sometimes be the same individual who invests seed money in a startup venture. He is likely to be either a self-made, entrepreneurial businessman or a member of the investment banking fraternity who may or may not have come up from industry. In either case, this individual is likely to act pretty much on his own. He is also likely to have strong confidence in his instincts and his ability to size people up. Sometimes, he will *syndicate* a large deal. Even then, however, his friends may play a secondary role, depending largely upon his judgment.

Aside from large capital gains, this individual has other motives for venture investment, which differentiate him from institutional sources of capital. First, his principal business probably gives him a large taxable income. Therefore a "Subchapter S" shelter may be a significant inducement for him, although seldom, if ever, a deciding one.

More important is the fact that the individual may simply enjoy associations with entrepreneurs and with the business growth process. He may see great social usefulness in the product being developed, or he may feel that the economy of the region will benefit from the new company. The private investor has both the funds and the autonomy to pursue his inclinations, for whatever nonfinancial reasons. He has always been, and undoubtedly always will be, a major source of venture capital.

Such a person's operating policies often include a willingness to become involved at an early stage of the growth process. Occasionally, he will desire to become involved more or less actively in the management of the venture as consultant, director, or godfather.

Usually the private investor will be more willing to accept high risk than will the institutions. Often he also has a lower economic investment size. Both of these facts make him a good partner for the beginning entrepreneur. He is sometimes willing to invest further in the company. Such investment, however, is likely to take the form of nonequity commitments (e.g., cosignature on bank loans). His waiting period may be somewhat less than that of institutions—perhaps two to four years.

It is not difficult to find prospective investors within this category. Your lawyer, banker, and other entrepreneurs are good sources of names, and you will probably be able to turn up a number of prospects through them, since your strongest prospect is the person who has already invested in similar ventures.

Recent reductions in the effective capital gains tax rate, together with certain other measures before Congress to make investments in small companies more attractive, tend to suggest that the importance of the wealthy private investor will only become greater in the 1980's.

Syndicated R&D Funding

A new and novel form of venture financing has begun to find favor among high-income investors. It is in essence a tax shelter, comparable in some ways to the more familiar oil-drilling and cattle-feeding shelters. It provides a way in which your company can obtain funding for specific R&D programs without either assuming additional debt or incurring additional stock dilution.

In a typical R&D shelter, the company is usually the general partner, the investors limited partners, in a limited partnership formed just to perform the specific R&D task. Then, if successful, the innovation is licensed to a manufacturer (usually the general partner), and the partners are paid a royalty off the top of sales, when and if the product is produced.

From the investor's viewpoint, the shelter is a good investment, because he can write off almost the entire amount of his investment in the year of investment, and there is a good chance that his royalties will qualify for capital gains treatment. Usually there is a very generous royalty to the investors until their investment is recouped, after which the royalty rate drops. Even so, however, the investor's upside gain may be unlimited, and could be quite high.

Although most such partnerships have, at time of writing, been circulated by private syndication without fanfare, some of the larger Wall Street houses, including Oppenheimer and Co., Shearson Loeb Rhodes, Smith Barney, Harris Upham, and Bache and Co. are reputed to be structuring R&D shelters. R&D shelters represent one of the more innovative fund-raising developments to appear in the last several years and deserve your careful investigation, if your product development effort involves very heavy expenditures. It should be noted that this investment form would not normally be suitable for a startup, but would be used by a firm that has already demonstrated the ability to manufacture and market a product profitably, i.e., a second-round investment company.

The "special situations" desk in a major brokerage firm may also provide contacts. Once you have found one person, even if he doesn't agree to provide financing, he can become a source of referrals to similar people who may be willing to help you.

Investment bankers often play a role at this stage, even though your company is not ready to go public. If they think your proposal is feasible, investment banking firms may syndicate a private placement of your stock to a small group of sophisticated investors. They get a substantial fee for this work, although they do not underwrite the offer, and proceed only on a best-efforts basis. This can be an extremely good way of raising private equity, as well as guaranteeing that there will be an interested underwriter, when the time comes to go public.

Closed-End Investment Funds

Closed-end investment funds existed even before the term *venture capital* came into common usage. Firms such as Venroc (Rockefeller Brothers), Payson Trask, and American Research and Development were on the scene long before the SBICs. Some of the newer venture capital partnerships, such as Charles River Partnership and the Palmer Organization, have operating standards and policies similar to the older firms. They have had much experience in their field—albeit with mixed results. Unlike the publicly held SBIC, the private closed-end fund is normally not dependent for current investment upon its portfolio firms. Unlike the individual investor, it requires no tax shelter from its portfolio. Moreover, this kind of investment firm is reputed to be about the most patient class of investor. In this sector, willingness to invest two or three rounds of money and wait for repayment for as long as ten years is not unheard of.

Such firms exhibit unusually high managerial standards. On the other hand, they tend not to become heavily involved with their portfolio companies' operations. The principal firms in this category are not difficult to identify. Before approaching them for capital, however, their distinct preferences as to the type of market should be considered. These preferences are catalogued in *Reubel* and *Kelly*, referenced at the end of this chapter.

As of mid-1980 these venture funds are probably more liquid and aggressive in seeking opportunities that at any time since the mid-1960s. Moreover, many firms are now looking at earlier-stage projects than would have been considered a decade ago.

This situation is a marked contrast to the circumstances that prevailed at the bottom of the last recession, in mid-1974. At that time, the funds were illiquid, and those that had money were investing in 12 percent commercial paper—then considered an outstanding yield (and in fact it probably was better than the overall rate of return of many of the venture portfolios). An entrepreneur with his cap in his hand, especially one with a startup venture, was pretty much out of luck.

Paradoxically, one explanation for today's new thrust in the venture capital market may be that old enemy of capitalism, inflation. The rate of inflation today is such that ordinary prudently managed portfolios have a hard time keeping their principal intact, let alone showing a return to the investor. Hence, the search for a few very high-return investment opportunities even at the cost of palpably higher risk. These forces make it easier for the venture fund managers to raise the necessary capital to invest.

Another factor contributing to the liquidity of the funds has been a modest recovery of the public market for new issues. This has enabled a number of funds to cash out mature investments, and to recycle their winnings into new firms.

All of this makes the present era a very unusual and exciting time for the entrepreneur. A good business plan in one of the emerging areas will receive careful attention from the capital markets.

Publicly Held Venture Capital Companies

Such companies are usually larger, publicly held SBICs, and would include such names as Narragansett Capital Corporation and La Salle Street Capital Corporation. Enabled by the Small Business Investment Act of 1958, these companies function, with loans from the U.S. government, on a leveraged capital basis. They most often invest in the form of mixed equity and convertible debt/debt-with-warrants, or on the basis of debt exclusively. Their use of debt is based on several factors—most importantly, upon their need for current income to service their government loans, as well as their administrative costs.

Their stock price is a strong function of current income and only a weak function of asset value, as in other public companies. Although there are about 325 SBICs in operation, it has been asserted that only about two dozen of them are active in the venture capital business; these two dozen are, for the most part, publicly held. The rest are simply in the business of making orthodox small business loans. Many are subsidiaries of banks.

One significant advantage that the publicly held venture capital companies offer to the entrepreneur is that their portfolios and investment records are public information. One can easily gain access to facts regarding specific case histories of companies in which the firms have invested, thereby simplifying analysis. The ventures in which they have done well and/or poorly are readily visible, and you can contact the entrepreneurs with whom the firm has invested in *either* category, and find out how they regard the firm.

These firms differ greatly in the amount of management involvement, with the portfolio company, which they desire. Some require management consulting revenues to meet current expenses, so it is advisable to ask (in advance) about their policies toward such involvement in general, and specifically in regard to your venture.

On the average, according to Faucett[1], these firms remain invested on an average of 2.7 years. In Faucett's study of 13 publicly held SBICs, he discovered that, while most of his sample firms did not as a rule invest heavily in the earliest stages of company growth, the early investments were more profitable, statistically, than were the later ones. This finding may foretell a shift in attitude toward early investment or even investment at startup stages, on the part of some SBICs. Faucett also discovered that the firms in which the investments had been primarily of an equity nature fared better than those in which it was mostly debt. One may assume that the cash outflow for debt service may have adversely affected performance of the company, in at least some cases. The areas of investment preference for these firms are also catalogued in *Kelly* and *Reubel*, in the references at the end of this chapter.

Fiduciary Funds Managers

This category (although the nomenclature is not completely correct) would include insurance company managers, university endowment funds, large pension funds, and other funds held more or

---

[1]Faucett, Russell B., "The Management of Venture Capital Investment Companies" (Thesis, Massachusetts Institute of Technology, 1971).

less in trust for other people. Venture investment never represents more than a minute sideline for the managers of such funds. The possibility of substantial capital gains compared to other, more orthodox investments has, however, attracted a number of such institutions into the venture capital business.

These investors' policies are far from uniform, and it is dangerous to generalize about them. Some of the larger insurance companies have been involved in venture capital investments for many years, and have evolved a professional investment approach. Other institutions, who have entered the field more recently, may still be experimenting with variables in policy such as the size of the deal, desired markets, time horizon, and level of risk.

The portfolios and investment records of such institutions are not, for the most part, public knowledge. It is not easy, therefore, for the entrepreneur to have advance knowledge of exactly what he is dealing with. Nonetheless, fiduciary funds would appear to continue to be a significant source of risk capital, and the institutions themselves may take further steps to attract better deals for their consideration.

Industrial Corporations

There is some evidence to suggest that industrial corporations are a significant and growing segment of the venture capital scene. A number of industrial corporations flirted with the idea of venture capital in the early '60s, both as a source of new subsidiaries and as a "window" through which they could view new technologies not readily developed in their own laboratories. A number of companies later withdrew from venture capitalism, somewhat the poorer for their experience; others withdrew without having made a single investment. Still others, such as Exxon; Textron; Time, Inc.; and Union Carbide have stayed in the market, presumably with good reason, and others are entering.

The entrepreneur must realize that the industrial corporations have different objectives from those of other venture capital sources. Their main interest is in building and strengthening their basic business to the maximum degree possible. Statistical expected value of capital gains is much less important to them as a rule, than is the idea of finding entrepreneurial, highly motivated people to work on problems which are of interest to the corporation. If such an investment can lead to a new division for the corporation, so much the better.

Certain other corporations seem to invest in the hope that the technological glamour of the new enterprise will provide a newsworthy kicker for their own stock, with the result that the firm's overall price-earnings ratio will be raised. One suspects that the results of this tactic have, at best, been temporary.

For certain types of new ventures, industrial firms may be the best financial partners to be found. Often they can offer management assistance, ready-made marketing or distribution channels, manufacturing services, and, in some cases, a large, built-in demand for your product. Often they understand the business problems which you encounter much more fully than would a straight financial investor. Hence they may be more disposed towards patience and calm. Also, they may present a ready market for any or all of the founders' stock, when the entrepreneurs wish to cash out.

On the negative side, however, you must keep several factors in mind which may be more or less important, depending upon your particular case:

1. Industrial corporations are usually not anxious to see the new venture go public. They are more disposed towards the acquisition of new divisions and/or subsidiaries.

2. For this reason, you may find yourself tied in, either with a buyout formula based upon performance or, at the very least, a right of first refusal to buy any founders' stock. In the first case you may actually end up donating your stock to the corporation, if the performance test is not met.

3. Your affiliation with one major corporation may, in effect, stop you from selling your product to its competitors. This could cut off a major portion of your potential market.

4. If your deal is poorly structured, your business may be required to adopt certain operating policies, banks, accounting conventions, etc., of the investing corporation from which you are borrowing. You may also be required to share research results, to use the corporation's facilities (whether or not they are the lowest cost), or meet other requirements which further reduce your autonomy. Such requirements may go against the reasons why you began a company of your own in the first place.

5. It is harder to fool an industrial corporation than it is to fool other financing sources.

Balance the pros against the cons. If the pros win, find the biggest and best firm which might have an interest in your field, and approach it.

Table 9–1 provides a quick summary of the principal distinctions among the various categories of venture capitalists. Naturally, large variations exist *within* each category as well, and the table is merely indicative of tendency, in the author's view. Individual sources within the category may be radically different on one or more characteristics from the central tendency of the group.

In summary, you will never be able to find out all you need to know in advance about a particular funding source you may be approaching. But the more you know, the better will be your negoti-

Table 9–1
Equity Sources Motivation And Other Characteristics

Motivation	Private Individual or Syndicate	Closely Held Invest- ment Co.	Publicly Held V.C. Companies	Fiduciary Funds Managers	Industrial Corporations
Nonfinancial: excitement of new venture, regional development, socially desirable product, etc.	H	H	L	L	H
Tax shelter for ordinary income	M	M	L	L	L
Long-term capital gains	H	H	H	H	M
Current income from dividends, interest, management fees	L	L	H	L	L
Desire for future subsidiary, technology, new markets	L	L	L	L	H
Other Characteristics					
Desired waiting period, in years	1–3	3–10	1–5	2–7	2–5
Willingness to invest further	H	H	M	M	H
Minimum economic investment	$10,000	$200,000	$100,000	$200,000	$100,000
Risk acceptance	H	H	M	M	H
Management involvement	L to H	L	M	L	H
Early investment preference	H	M	L	L	H

Code: H—High degree
M—Moderate degree
L—Low degree

ating position (in that you will know what concessions are of most value to *them*), and the better will be the chances that, once made, the deal will be comfortable for all concerned for several years.

The Only Game in Town?

Most first-time entrepreneurs focus more or less exclusively on the normal individual and institutional equity financing sources, while overlooking other, less conventional ways of getting the company off the ground. This focus on the conventional channels is understandable, due to the high visibility of the venture capital firms. However, in his rush to get into their game, the entrepreneur may be overlooking some very good alternatives. A very partial list might include the following:

Internally Generated Funds. The possibility exists that the company can generate enough cash and credit to supply its own needs. This is not the usual case, but is common enough to justify some serious analysis of your venture before heading down the venture capital trail. A combination of high margins, fast collections, and intensive use of short-term capital and operating tactics *could* get you to the point where you're ready to go public, with *all* the stock in your possession.

State and Regional Development Agencies. The U.S. and Canada have numerous agencies, charged with the responsibility of increasing job opportunities in particular areas. In some areas you can obtain long-term, low-cost loans for plant and equipment—forgiveable in some instances. Outright grants of money for each job created in such a way are not unusual. Attracting working capital loans can often be arranged through banks with the guarantee of the public agency. Grants for the training of new employees abound. Other schemes and inducements to entrepreneurs are offered by regional development agencies. If your venture has the potential of employing reasonable numbers of people, be sure to investigate these opportunities in all areas in which you would consider locating.

Technology Development Agencies. The U.S. and Canada both have a variety of programs aimed at development of commercially significant technology, to bolster the economy, create jobs, taxes, and export opportunities. In Canada, government programs offer outright grants for the development of new commercial products, processes, and technologies. In the U.S., the emphasis is on technology transfer—getting technology originally developed at government cost into commercial markets. Pilot programs have been funded in both the National Science Foundation and the Bureau of Standards for this and related purposes.

While such funds are normally not available to startup ventures, once your enterprise is off the ground with proven capability in an appropriate area of product development, you may well qualify for such a grant.

The National Science Foundation's Small Business Innovation Research (SBIR) program was started in 1979 to fund quality research proposals. Their main criterion is that, if successful, the research have "significant public benefit." Secondly, they hope to convert publicly funded R&D to privately funded commercialization. This program provides up to $25,000 for feasibility research, up to $200,000 to conduct the research, and an open-ended phase-three funding by the private company sponsoring the work.

As of February 1980, 96 phase one proposals and 21 phase-two proposals had been funded with firms of ten or fewer employees receiving 52 percent of the awards. Thus, the chances of the entrepreneur obtaining his R&D seed capital from this source may be relatively good.

R&D Contracts. The emphasis on the "venture capital scenario"—garage-to-SBIC-to-Wall Street—tends to obscure the fact that a *very* large fraction of today's high technology companies got started on the basis of a fat government research or development contract. Usually such contracts originate in the same agency which funded the founder's work while in his previous job. The benefits of building a technology company on this basis are:

1. You are working at the frontiers of the art.

2. You immediately have a cash flow which will permit building up the professional staff and overheads which are necessary to attract private work or to develop products.

3. Your work will be recognized and you will have a chance to establish your firm as a leader in its field.

4. You may obtain access to expensive government-owned equipment and facilities which would otherwise be inaccessible.

The drawbacks include, of course, all those inherent in any single-customer firm:

1. Slow collections (sometimes).

2. Dependence on contract funding, vicissitudes of Congressional spending, etc.

3. Negotiated or limited profit margins.

4. Detailed government financial reporting procedures and other red tape.

5. Lack of pressure to develop a marketing capability.

These perils notwithstanding, government R&D contracts have launched many fine technology companies, providing the base from which commercial research and product development have grown. It is probably true that this route was easier in the past, when defense-oriented contracts were relatively easy to obtain. Nonetheless, there are still many opportunities and there will continue to be so in the future. However, they usually are visible mainly to the entrepreneur who has already been actively engaged in the field, working with his future research sponsors.

Consulting. Often a competent professional will decide to start a company on the basis of his or his team's ability to attract consulting contracts, with the ultimate objective of developing products as the company gathers financial momentum. This has worked well in many cases. Consulting provides the cash flow to pay the team, support facilities, and maintain technical prominence. However, this route is not without its perils. Often the necessity of getting a number of successive consulting contracts just to say alive totally diverts the energy and resources of the firm away from product development—with the result that ten years later the venture is still a small consulting firm hoping to get around to developing some product some day. The product, the staff, the marketing orientation, simply do not seem to develop spontaneously from a consulting environment.

An alternative approach has been adopted by some other consultant-entrepreneurs, with mixed success. This approach envisions the consulting group as the R&D team for a succession of new companies. The reasoning is, that by developing and spinning off a succession of new product-oriented companies, the consulting firm can maintain an equity position in each and still support a much better engineering capability than any of the individual spinoffs. Eventually, in theory, the consulting firm develops a portfolio of new venture stocks not unlike that of any other venture capital firm.

There are other ways in addition to the five listed above to get your company rolling without selling *any* of your stock. Be sure you investigate a few of the more promising ones before committing yourself to the venture capital scenario.

Conventional Wisdom. Every new firm needs equity venture capital to get it through the early growth stages.

Reality. Most new companies need outside financing from somewhere, but not all have to sell stock in order to get it.

References

1. Reubel, Stanley M., and Novotny, E. G.: *How to Raise and Invest Venture Capital,* Presidents Publishing House, N.Y., 1971.

   This is about the best book in print on the venture equity markets. It is very much an insider's view of the industry and is recommended reading to anyone seeking venture capital.

2. Dominquez, John R.: *Venture Capital,* Lexington Books (D. C. Heath), Lexington, Mass., 1974.

   Outstanding structural study of U.S. venture capital industry. In-depth recommendations to entrepreneur. Contains directory of venture capital firms, organized by preferred investment size.

3. Morner, Aimee L.: "Shelters for the Venturesome Rich," *Fortune.* July 28, 1980.

   Describes the new R&D shelter industry.

4. Bylinsky, G.: "General Doriot's Dream Factory," *Fortune,* Aug. 1967.

   A fascinating look at the career and philosophy of Georges Doriot, senior statesman of the venture capital industry.

5. Kelly, A. J., et al.: *Venture Capital, A Guidebook for New Enterprises,* New England Regional Commission, Boston, 1971.

   This is the best free venture capital directory around. Lists firms, together with their areas of investment preference and other data.

Chapter 10

PUBLIC OR PRIVATE: WHAT'S THE DIFFERENCE?

"There are plenty of public companies that should be trying to go private."

. . . V. J. Ryan, Venture Capitalist

It is impossible to watch the equity markets over a few years without amazement at a phenomenon, the predictability of whose recurrence rivals Halley's Comet. That phenomenon is the hot new issue market—the recurrent wave of gullibility that prompts the public to buy the shares of startup of even fetal companies. The hot new issue markets usually seem to accelerate in the latter phases of a sustained bull market. One was running in late 1961; it collapsed, along with everything else, in May, 1962. Another was roaring in 1968–69. What happened to it in May, 1970 is also history.

As of mid-1980, a modest new issue market has begun to show some evidence of vigor. While it may not rival its predecessor of a decade ago in volume or furor, it clearly suggests that there is again an opportunity for at least certain types of young ventures to raise public money.

Without question, there are periods during which it is possible for a totally unseasoned company to go public, to obtain public money, a broad market for its stock, and the other (presumed) benefits of public ownership. If that is so, why not sidestep the lengthy venture capital step which, after all, only leads to a public issue anyway? This is a reasonable question.

Hot new issue markets are usually characterized by at least some of the following phenomena:

1. New underwriting firms spring up as though by magic. Their disappearance from the market after the inevitable bust is equally magical.

2. Established investment banking houses also get caught up in the excitement, and begin to relax their standards for marketing companies, in order to get some of the action.

3. A form of recruiting begins, with representatives of small and not-so-small underwriting firms sitting in the lobbies of small companies, singing the siren song of registered stock, yachts, and trips to the Bahamas.

4. "Deal packagers" roam the back streets of Palo Alto and the parking lots of Route 128, looking for disgruntled engineers, unhappy division managers, and unappreciated marketing vice presidents, to be set up in business, for the purpose of selling some stock.

The siren song of the fast buck artist is everywhere, and nothing could be more dreary and discordant than the legitimate venture capitalist's carping about sales performance, budgets, meeting profit and cash projections, and all that.

From the venture capitalists you will get a list of reasons for not going public prematurely that goes something like this:

1. It costs too much for a tiny company to go public. Even with a Reg. A. (short form) registration, the costs of legal, audit, and placement services can be upwards of 20 percent of the total issue proceeds.

2. It diverts too much of the young company's energies to establish and maintain the status of a public company. Stockholder relations, SEC relations, stringent reporting and disclosure requirements, all divert entrepreneurial energy from the company's main business.

3. An unseasoned company probably cannot attract a good, reputable investment banking house (whatever *that* may be). It will, instead, be taken public by Blitzkreig Securities, which, as everyone knows, won't even be around two years from now, let alone able to raise additional capital for you. And, of course, Morgan, Stanley isn't going to take over any of Blitzkreig's former deals, are they?

4. If your company doesn't perform as expected—loses too much money, fails to realize sales projections, is unable to debug the product—*then* there is no big brother to turn to for a second, third, or *n*th round of venture capital. The show is over.

5. Everyone knows the record overall of unseasoned public offerings is pretty lousy.

Is this an impressive list of prudent arguments, or merely self-serving ad copy from the equity capital club? Nobody knows for sure, but one thing *is* sure: This elixir shouldn't be swallowed neat. It does deserve some critical scrutiny before you dismiss the possibility of taking your deal public in the next hot new issue market. Some of the counterarguments could be posed as follows:

1. A public issue is "too expensive," but compared to what? Even after all expenses, companies going public under these circumstances often raise more net cash for less equity than they could ever get from venture capital firms. And don't forget that even a nice dignified private placement by a "reputable" investment banking house can cost you over 15 percent of the gross proceeds, plus warrants.

2. Unquestionably a public company has more overhead and more clients than a private one. However, the overhead costs of working with private backers are not exactly zero, either. They also will require the audits, stockholder and directors' meetings, monthly reports, full disclosure and general good practice that one would expect of a public company. Moreover, if round one private money is insufficient for all but the initial stage of growth, the entrepreneur will quickly find his time being eaten up making further negotiation with the old backers, trying to enlist some new ones, and ultimately parting with perhaps more equity than he ever intended.

3. While you *probably* cannot attract a "reputable" investment banking house to handle your deal, *maybe* you *can*. As noted earlier, a lot of the long-established houses get pretty excited when they see all that action on the street. A look at the registration statements for 1968–69 will verify this. (A review of the brokerage failures and SEC rules violations in 1970 suggests also that a redefinition of "reputable" may be in order.) Also, a self-underwritten Reg. A. offering may not be out of the question.

4. It is almost certainly true that a public company that performs miserably is more or less out of luck—unless, of course, it happens to have an investment banker with sufficient clout and guts to stand by and, if warranted, support the stock. But it is equally true that a lousy performer—even one with great prospects—arouses rather limited enthusiasm from the private equity sector. Among the least enthusiastic are the backers who have already lost a bundle on the deal. Neither private nor public money is any guarantee of continued largess for the company whose performance, whether through bad management or bad luck, is poor.

5. It is easier to assert than it is to prove that unseasoned companies raising public money in hot markets always fare poorly. The author is unaware of any systematic study that shows that they

either fare poorly, or fare more poorly than their privately financed counterparts. Many companies have gone public earlier than the conventional wisdom would dictate, and have done extremely well.

None of the above can be taken as a conclusive case for or against going public immediately. It is intended merely to show that the case is far from closed, and that there is room for reasonable disagreement with the orthodox cant on the subject.

If you find yourself on the threshold of growth during a hot new issue market, you should definitely weigh the costs and benefits to the company and to yourself of going public. And, if the net benefits seem to exceed those of the private route, go to it.

Sizing Up the Market

Short of actually prancing into Morgan, Stanley with your prospectus smoking, you ought to get answers to the following questions:

1. Can you get somebody (anybody) to take you public?

2. Can you get a "reputable" house to take you?

3. Can you raise as much money as you need for as much equity as you're willing to part with?

4. What are the costs of the issue likely to be?

5. Can you get an underwriting or only a "best efforts" deal?

The best way to answer these questions is to take a look at some offerings recently undertaken (so you can see how they sold and later traded) and in registration (so you can see what investment bankers *think* they can sell in the near future). A good starting place is the *OTC Review* which summarizes both. You can then call or write the underwriter or the management of interesting-looking companies, requesting a copy of the final prospectus or, alternatively, the Red Herring interim prospectus. If you get prospecti from companies whose scale, markets, and prospects seem comparable to your own, you can get answers, or at least evidence, on the several above-mentioned issues. Some further conversation with the companies' presidents can give you a further feel for the markets, the alternatives that they examined, and the considerations that led to their choice of investment bankers.

If you are encouraged by what you find out and decide to take the next exploratory step, you already have your list of three or four initial contacts to make in the investment banking community. Go at them with a *brief* (two-page) mini-plan and get their reactions. You'll find out fast if your plan is a salable commodity. And if it isn't, they may make a few friendly referrals, so you can only win.

The Public Route: Some Additional Considerations

Going public is more than merely one of five ways to raise capital for your new venture. More than any other financing option, it sets the style for your future corporate and personal operations. It may foreclose or encumber certain options that are open to the privately held venture. These include:

1. The possibility of selling out on more favorable terms or cashing out earlier, to an industrial corporation or other buyer.

2. The possibility of maintaining the privacy of certain types of information the disclosure of which would be otherwise required by the SEC.

3. The possibility of learning, innovating, making some mistakes at relatively low risk in the early stages. After all, even Polaroid didn't spring on the scene with an instant camera on Day 1. *Your* big winner may be your third or fourth product.

4. The possibility of knowing your backers personally, and obtaining nonfinancial assistance from them.

5. The possibility that you discover you aren't the hot shot you thought you were and that you can't or don't enjoy running a company. It is possible that your exit may be more graceful from a lower-profile enterprise (assuming you're concerned with grace).

The list could be extended, but the point is this: There are many considerations other than feasibility that should determine the desirability of an early public issue. We are not proposing prolonged breast-beating on this question—but merely that all of the important issues get examined before a decision is made for wrong or insufficient reasons.

Conventional Wisdom. Before going public, a firm should have net profit after taxes of half a million, five years of operating experience, and, above all, a "reputable" investment banker.

Reality. Before going public, a firm should decide if this will net the necessary capital on more desirable overall terms than the private route.

Reference

1. Hutchinson, G. S.: *Why, When and How to Go Public,* Presidents Publishing House, N.Y., 1970.

   This is the best thing in print on the practical issues of a public offering. "Must" reading for entrepreneurs.

Chapter 11

THE BUSINESS PLAN

"Only one thing is certain about a new venture: it's going to turn out very different from its business plan."

. . . William Congleton, Venture Capitalist

Your business plan is the essential piece of software that makes your whole machine function. It is your means of communication with the outside world to help you attract talent and money into the enterprise. It is your internal control mechanism, against which actual performance is measured and to which corrections are made. It is, or ought to be, your regularly updated battle plan, providing the bridge between distant objectives and present deployment of men and material.

A Variety of Purposes

Your business plan is a central and detailed statement of what your business is going to do. A checklist for what business plans should include is provided in Table 11–1. Although the common core of assumptions stays the same, there are different uses for business plans. Consequently, the form of documentation, the emphasis, the depth of background support, the statistical bounding (best/worst/expected), the line-item detail of financial projections, the sampling rate (weekly, monthly, or yearly) of projections, and other features may vary according to intended use.

Table 10–1
What to Put in Your Business Plan

	Fund-Raising Plan	Operating Plan
1. Miniplan: One-page summary of *essential* facts. Should be usable alone.	Essential. This is all that many people will read.	Not needed.
2. Background of Plan: Origins of product, identification of business opportunity, reasons for market need.	Essential. One to five pages.	Include for future recollection.
3. The Team: Description of individual qualifications. Why will it function as a *team?* Present organization chart. Identify directors.	Make it convincing. Some investors will turn here first.	Detailed job descriptions and organization chart.
4. Product Description: What it is, what it does, why it's better than competitors, proprietary features. Family-of-products implications. Customer benefits.	This is where the glamour is. Do a good job, illustrated if possible.	Include.
5. Ownership: Before proposed financing. Description of any stock options, warrants, other commitments.	Include.	Include, with formal criteria for distributing employ stock or options.
6. The Market: Present *documented* evidence of market growth, trends in price, need for your product. Include names of key customers, reps and agents. State all assumptions.	Present graphically. Include corroborating opinions of industry leaders, prestigious consulting firms, trade associations, government agencies.	Include backup statistics and data, plus segmentation of market.
7. Marketing Strategy: Detail sales channels, sales costs, sales calls/ salesmen/year. Unique promotional, delivery, other features. Line-item schedules and milestones.	Some detail and evident grasp of *costs* of marketing is essential.	Full detail, including budgets and schedules.

Table 10–1 (Continued)
What to Put in Your Business Plan

	Fund-Raising Plan	Operating Plan
8. Operations: How to make it, learning curves, economies of scale; key vendors, make-or-buy decision points. Facilities, inventory costs.	Go lightly. Investors tend to assume you can make things.	Full detail, schedules back up detail. Projected unit costs. State assumptions.
9. R&D: Objectives, costs, and schedules.	Stress the D. Investors hate paying for R.	Make sure *you* can justify. Include all detail.
10. Staffing: Timetable, skills needed, availability & cost.	Be brief. Investors are usually willing to assume people can be hired.	Reasonable detail. Try to predict what organization chart will look like in two years.
11. Financial Strategy: What cash needed when, for what purposes? Sources of long- and short-term financing. Narrative rationale for each. When and why go public? Leasing plans.	Apparent understanding of cash flow *most* desirable. Also present *pro forma* statements in best/expected/worst case forms. Be honest. Have reviewed by CPA.	Full details, including cash flow by month for six months. Graphic format desirable, as well as numerical.
12. Contingency Plans: Outline general plan for dealing with two or three probable crises.	Detail not essential. Evidence of serious consideration adequate.	Include whatever detail is readily available.
13. Concluding Summary: Benefits to investor. Identify major risks.	One page, but quantify if possible. How will risks be *minimized?* Why is *this* a desirable investment, relative to others?	Section on risk most essential.
APPENDICES		
A. Backup, market analysis data, independent studies, etc.	Summarize data, reproduce complete study if feasible.	Include full backup.
B. Biographies of key personnel.	Keep it short. Full resumes are a bit clumsy.	Not needed.
C. Key articles written by personnel.	Include if feasible, for benefit of outside consultants.	Not needed.
D. Table of competitors and their product specs. Establish sales in relevant products.	Simplifies evaluation of proposal.	Include *all* detail, plus intelligence reports on plans, key personnel.

The uses to which business plans are put include the following:

1. To raise capital.

2. To provide an internal operating plan upon which to base day-to-day operations.

3. To provide a source of preestablished contingency plans for certain events.

4. To create, through scheduled review and updating, a semi-formal mechanism for management planning.

5. To communicate with directors, attorneys, bankers, and prospective employees the plans and progress of the company.

The Fund-Raising Plan

This is usually and unfortunately the first of the two plans put together and is all too often the only one. Logically, the basic work and detail for the Operating Plan should be done initially, and summarized, extracted, and supplemented to create the Fund-Raising version.

It is all too easy to be carried away by the fund-raising plan. Documentary overkill may be responsible for as many fund-raising problems as underdocumentation. Don't forget that those who read such things are people—not information-processing machines. The purpose of the fund-raising plan is *to get them interested*—not fully informed on every last detail of your proposition. They want to see evidence that the detail, the backup, the field work have been done—but if they *want* the detail, they'll ask you. A concise, attractive 20-page plan is about 50 times more likely to get read and comprehended than a detailed, gray 200-page job.

Remember your audience. Where possible, tailor the material to the knowledge, interests, and needs of the person whose O.K. is necessary for your deal to move ahead. Is he an engineer? Then summarize the market data and financial plans in graphs, and beef up technical areas. Is your target reader an SBIC officer? Then show how your cash flow allows for servicing of convertible debt and, possibly, for some management consulting services from you-know-who. Is his background security analysis? Better have a CPA, or better, a security analyst, check your pro-formas for out-of-whack ratios, etc.

Don't forget that, besides being a specialist of some sort, your reader is also a human being. Business plans by engineers often sound like first attempts at English prose. Keep it readable. Don't make it so interlocking that every preceding page must have been read before the present one makes sense. Include graphs, diagrams.

Avoid grandiloquent adjectives when describing your product and market.

Make it attractive. It need not be elaborate, but it must be neat. If diagrams, drawings, and artwork are needed, spend a few bucks and have them done professionally. Get the final version set in IBM Executive or cold type. Get a first-rate printing job done on good stock, and use GBC or equivalent binding so that the thing will stay open on the reader's desk. Design a decent cover. Where product photos are indicated, use half-tones instead of glossies, in case your reader wants to copy the thing on his office copier.

Before final type and printing, plan to pretest the plan on a few knowledgeable friends. Get their comments on appearance, content, form of financials, believability, etc. They may spot some problems that you can easily correct.

Above all, try to keep ever before you the picture of your reader: A busy guy with eight other business plans on his desk, plus both phones ringing. He doesn't need vast detail. What he needs is a fast overall view of what your business is all about, and enough corroborating *outside* evidence (consultants, market data, etc.) to suggest that you know what you're talking about. Don't spell out the deal for him—just tell him how much money is needed.

Final note: Write the plan yourself. There are consultants who will offer to write your business plan, stressing that you are an amateur while *they* are professionals. Forget it. Your plan will be better if you do it. Moreover, since you'll know all the assumptions that went into it, you won't get crossed up while discussing specific aspects of it with investors.

How Much Money?

It is a well-known fact that many entrepreneurs simply begin with the amount of money (large) that might possibly be available from the funding source, then back into a business plan that seems to justify this investment. This is a highly refined art, to which this book has nothing to add.

However, if you are a member of the majority of entrepreneurs who are sincerely trying to size their deals optimally, then there will be a definite question as to how much money you should attempt to raise this round of financing. As General Georges Doriot, founder of American Research and Development, is fond of pointing out, there are two times to raise money: the first (now), when the beautiful dream is almost to be realized—all the elements are ready to go when the money arrives. The second is eons from now: When the product is proven, the company is healthy, growing, and outrageously profitable. Between those two points in time there will be innumerable problems, refinancings, struggles, reversals of direction, and zero-crossings in the cash balance. These will be times when getting additional money will be difficult, costly, and perhaps impossible. What General Doriot is saying indirectly, then, is get plenty of money the first trip to the well. Or at least get a substantial enough commitment, based on performance, so that you don't have to spend the next two years in constant negotiation for capital.

In the fetal stage, the shoestring financial philosophy is valid. Now, in stage one, it is not. Stock sold in the fetal condition will be virtually given away; now, it has a demonstrable worth and will bring the company meaningful amounts of working capital. Adequate funding, a cash reserve of some sort, and a downstream commitment for further funds as warranted are definitely desirable now.

There are several ways to calculate the appropriate magnitude of funding for your company at this stage:

1. *Financial Projections.* Your *pro forma* P&L statement, based on the best possible sales forecasts, is the starting point. Developing this into a cash-flow projection will reveal the amount of cash theoretically required at each stage of the company's growth. However, a little simulation using your accounting model will show you just how treacherous such cash prediction can be. Your future cash balance is unbelievably sensitive to minor variations in assumed growth rate, seasonality, product cost, overhead costs, and collection and billing times. Trying to develop meaningful best/worst cases from this sort of simulation is mindblowing. If you vary *all* factors against you at once, your cash requirements will look like the national debt. About the best you can do is to have an expected, a best and a worst case sales forecast, and work out the cash consequences of each, holding other assumptions constant. However, you should privately realize how slippery these cash requirements projections really are. Don't start believing them too much. For a planning period use the length of time it will take you in the expected case to get to a condition where a public offering is clearly feasible and desirable. This could be when, for example, annual aftertax profits exceed $200,000. Do not be abashed to include a moderate allowance for contingencies. This could be 10 to 15 percent of the total requirement.

From this exercise you will also learn another interesting number: The absolute minimum amount on which your venture can move ahead for, say, one year.[1]

---

[1] One reason why entrepreneurs get fooled by their own numbers is that realistic amounts of simulation on a sales driven model are just too laborious. Changing one assumption (e.g., collection period from 45 to 80 days) can require a whole day's

2. *Outside Observations.* What sorts of money has your prospective backer been putting into comparable deals, and for how much equity? What have comparable firms been able to command in the recent past from other sources? Other entrepreneurs will often be willing to discuss their experience with you.

3. *What Timing of Funding Is Necessary?* Obviously, even if you get all your money tomorrow, it will be some time before it can all be put to use by the company. Therefore, some venture capitalists make it a point to stagger the input of funds, often based upon the attainment by management of certain milestones in operations. Your cash flow analysis will help you to develop a schedule of requirements, to have in case the negotiations head in this direction. The future funding may take the form of equity, convertible debt, or even a cosigned line of bank credit. There is, incidently, a case for negotiating a higher price for stock bought by investors at a later date, since the attainment of milestones and operating experience lessens the risk that will be taken then by the investing group.

After you have analyzed the financial projections, the outside factors, and possible deal timing, then think about how hard it's going to be to raise money when and if everything goes wrong in a couple of years. Don't go after too much, but be damned sure you're asking for *enough,* and that you can justify to the investors what you're asking.

The Operating Business Plan

In addition to its secondary function as the backup for your Fund-Raising Plan, the Operating Plan should be the blueprint to running your business. Management consultants and business school professors emphasize the importance of a formal operating plan and, to some extent, they are right. However the plan must be your servant, not your master. It is not something to be followed slavishly because you think someone expects you to use it. To the extent that it is useful for *your* management style, you should use it, update it, and modify it in a series of midcourse corrections. File the thing in half a dozen looseleaf binders, and keep it in a place where

---

recalculation of balance sheet, cash flow and operating statement (P&L). One solution to this problem is the personal computer. There are now several small computers which can run a software package designed for just this type of simulation; one such program is called Visicalc⊖, which runs on various personal computers. Such a package permits you to input your entire P&L, balance sheet and cash flow models. The parameters may then be quickly adjusted, and the resulting column and row values instantly recalculated, saving you endless grunt work. The results may be quickly reaggregated, by week, month, quarter, or year. Then, when you get a set that makes sense, it can be quickly printed out, saving a laborious typing/proofreading/retyping job. Also, respectable word processing software is available for these small machines, further streamlining the task of business plan preparation.

it's accessible to all the key people in your group, and get them accustomed to using it, too.

Try to think of the plan as a sort of hairy organic creature, not as a tidy finished document. Keep adding your quarterly sales projections to it, but don't throw out the old ones (however great the temptation). Ditto, of course, for budgets. Have a place to plot actual versus planned results. Have a volume for market data, and keep adding to and updating industry projections and shipments. Plan every six months to spend a day or weekend with your key people updating, or at least reviewing, their sections of the plan.

Use the document when briefing directors on progress. Use it to help bring new management personnel up to speed, so they understand not only where you are, but also how you got there, at what rate, and with what mistakes along the way.

Although your plan really won't be much use until you actually have your money and are able to function as planned, you should get it together right away and enlist the aid of your partners in the chore. Then, as you move ahead, the thing becomes a good place to file reports, idea summaries, acquisition possibilities, and any number of other things with major bearing on the company's direction. And eventually you may find that the plan is worth the trouble. If you don't, kill it.

Conventional Wisdom.   You only get one whack at the venture capitalist, so better tell the whole story the first time.

Reality.   If you hand him the complete unabridged edition, he won't even read the dedication.

References

1. Mancuso, Joseph R.: *How to Start, Finance, and Manage Your Own Small Business,* Prentice-Hall, Englewood Cliffs, N.J., 1978.

   This book should be called, *How to Write a Business Plan.* It is the outstanding reference on the subject. Appendix includes several actual model plans. Mancuso appears to be the only author who has ever asked venture capitalists what they actually do with business plans.

2. Dible, Donald: *Up Your Own Organization,* The Entrepreneur Press, Santa Clara, Calif., 1971.

   This gives several very useful checklists and general ideas on creating business plans.

Chapter 12

SHOPPING AND NEGOTIATING

"Let every eye negotiate for itself and trust no agent."

. . . Shakespeare

The moment has come. Your business plan is shaped up, the company is now able to survive a few afternoons without you, and it's time to raise that money. You've evaluated the *pros* and *cons*, and the private venture capital route looks the least bad. How do you proceed?

Sizing Up Investors

First, you should do a little investigation within the class of investors you have selected (see Chapter 9), and find answers to as many of the following questions as possible:

1. Who likes ventures in your general field? Who will look at anything?

2. Who presently has cash and is looking for deals? Firms who have just raised a lot of capital or realized large capital gains may be under a bit more pressure to invest than others.

3. What kinds of financings are being done currently by these firms? Is there *any* chance that you will get what you want?

4. What are the operating policies of the more promising firms? Do they want more management participation than you want

to give them? Will they want heavy debt? Will they stay in long enough? Will they put in the additional cash needed between first round and public issue?

5. What is their track record? Are their portfolio companies happy? Are they competent? Ethical? Reasonable?

It is not easy to answer all these questions in advance of actually contacting the firms. However, one very good source of data on most of them is another entrepreneur who is currently making the rounds or has just finished. If you can find somebody who has recently financed his company (or failed to, for that matter), he will be your most valuable source of current data.

When you feel you know about 80 percent of all you're ever going to know, stop and make up your list of about four top prospects. This is where you'll be concentrating your energy, starting with the *least* likely candidate, so that your story has been tested, modified, and refined by the time you get to the top prospect's door.

A Note on Finders

At nearly any stage of a fund-raising effort, someone may emerge from the woodwork, representing himself as a financial consultant. He thinks your company is fantastic, he has some *unbelievable* (literally) contacts, and for a reasonable fee (say, 5 percent of the total offering proceeds) he will introduce you to some of his high-level contacts, who will take it from there. This gentleman is known in the trade as a finder, or a packager. He may, indeed, have some good contacts; then again, he may merely lead you down the street to introduce you to firms you could have found in the yellow pages. Since most legitimate sources of venture capital will make you warrant in the contract that no finder or broker is involved, isn't it a little foolish to start out with one? He may have use later in the search, but then only if he has been checked out thoroughly, and you understand what he really is.

Folklore: Don't Shop the Deal

This is the cant one hears from the financial world. Translated, it means that if they like your deal they want to be sure they're the only ones who have heard about it, so that competition, or anything resembling it, can be avoided. However, one suspects that very few serious venture capitalists would wish to back a businessman so naive as to not get at least three bids for the largest purchase he'll make for some time: his operating capital. There are, of course, perils at both extremes. If you do a mailing of your business plan to everybody in the Venture Capital Directory, you will quickly find yourself the butt of some uncharitable jokes. Nobody wishes to feel he's being shown a "shopworn" deal—even if it's a good one. The logical strategy, then *is* to shop the deal—discreetly. If possible, pick firms in different towns whose officers don't each lunch together. Try to let each firm know *they're* the one you really want to get in bed with. If pressed, however, be honest and acknowledge that a couple of other firms have seen your plan.

Your Initial Approach

Most venture capital firms consider it a bit gauche for a president to march in, unintroduced, with his business plan under his arm. Etiquette aside, there is good reason why an introduction may be helpful at this stage. If you have done your homework well, you will know that in each target firm there is one man you should reach first. He is the one who is interested in your kind of deal. He is the guy who is going to become your champion before, during, and after serious financial negotiations. You should know his name and something about him before you approach the firm.

Your next problem is to find someone who can introduce you to him, and set you up to be a hell of a guy. You can begin by asking your banker and lawyer if they know anyone in the firm. If not, whom can they suggest? Try some of your "expert" friends, or the president of a portfolio company of the firm. All you really need is a phone call, letting them know what your deal is and that you will be contacting them in a couple of days to set up an appointment. Then it's up to you. When you phone, the target man may turn you over to somebody else, but at least he knows his company is talking to you. He may ask you to come in, or to send in your business plan, or miniplan. At this point, you're rolling.

The Pitch

Assuming your business plan didn't end up in the garbage immediately, you'll be asked to come in and make a presentation of your deal. You'll be selling yourself as well as your enterprise at this meeting, so a little planning is in order. Remember, they will be looking beyond the numbers and the glamour, and will be much more interested in the man behind it all. They'll be evaluating your apparent ability to sell, your intelligence, integrity, and capacity for thinking on your feet. They will be trying to decide whether you're going to be their next big winner, or a crook.

Avoiding overkill, the presentation can be polished to some degree. Flip charts of key financial data, sales curves, etc., can be much more effective than referring people to their individual documents, or struggling at a blackboard. If you can bring along a prototype, or at least some photographs of the product, you will add visual interest. Slides or vue-graphs can help. A little rehearsal may be in order.

Bring along your Operating Business Plan, too, because they are going to probe your assumptions about market size and customer needs. They are going to want to know where the data came from, how the surveys were conducted. They may want backup schedules for capital equipment budgets, product cost breakdown, or other supporting information. Every question you can field on the spot without having to say "I'll have to send you that," wins you double points. An effective presentation at this point makes your in-house champion look good, too, and will help move your deal up in the firm's work-order priorities.

Rank Your Targets

There is reasonable disagreement on how many parties one should be negotiating with at once. The author's experience suggests that three is about the optimal number. More than that, and you begin to forget what you've told to whom, or what information each is still expecting from you, and for whom that consultant who called you was working. Don't underestimate the strain of doing all this while keeping the company running and the shipments going out the door. However, *do* initiate discussions in parallel, because for any single discussion to come to a conclusion—favorable or unfavorable—can be a matter of weeks or months. If it falls through, it may be pretty late to be starting at ground zero with another firm. Moreover, one firm may offer a lot better deal than another. A logical gamesman will merely rank his top prospects and start working them as promptly as conditions permit.

Some firms pride themselves on the promptness with which they can get back to a company president with a "no" or a tentative proposition. Others, however, appear to pride themselves on the opposite. They can keep you hanging forever, waiting for a "market study" to be completed, or with some equally transparent excuse. What they may *really* be doing is waiting to see if the big sale you said was pending actually materializes, or waiting to see if you have any alternatives, and how desperate for cash you really are, or procrastinating and doing nothing.

If you suspect that any of these apply, you have a strong signal that it's time to redouble your efforts to find other capital sources more interested in your deal. Don't deliver any ultimatum or deadline—just put them on the back burner. You may need them yet.

What Is In a Financing Agreement?

If you are fortunate enough to get a preliminary offer from one of your target investment firms, it will include at least some of the following elements:

1. A reasonable amount of equity, that is, money paid for stock. In general, the greater the percentage of equity money, the better for the entrepreneur (although study suggests it may be more profitable for the investor, too).

2. A component of straight or convertible debt, ranging from zero to 100 percent of the financing. As explained earlier, many investment firms rely upon interest to help cover their operating costs; others prefer it because, in case of disaster, a bad debt may be written off against ordinary income, rather than becoming a capital loss. Still others seem to enjoy the illusion of control that the borrowing covenants offer. In any case, you may expect the debt to be convertible to stock at the lender's option, or that you will be asked for options (or warrants) which will permit purchase of your stock in the future at a low price. These may be detachable from the debt instrument, depending on the form used. The debt money you raise will normally be subordinated, to permit banks and trade creditors to provide additional short-term capital.

There is nothing wrong with convertible-debt financing *per se*, but a higher dollar amount of it is required (relative to straight equity) to ensure that you will have resources to avoid defaulting on interest payments.

3. An employment contract for each key member of the team. This will spell out maximum salary, benefits, term, and various non-competition provisions.

4. Provision for life insurance on key team members, with the investor as beneficiary.

5. A fractional investor ownership probably ranging between 20 and 75 percent, depending on how early and how risky the deal is. Most investment firms don't require control, but will expect roughly proportional representation on the board.

6. Some sort of consulting agreement. This is not too common, but it can become part of the initial agreement. It will oblige you to buy a certain amount of consulting time per year from the investor.

7. Miscellaneous other provisions, including right of first refusal on any sale of management stock, right of "piggy back" registration of investor shares in any future stock registration, right to veto any new financing, preemptive stock purchase rights to maintain their fraction of ownership, etc.

You should also not be surprised if the investor comes back with an offer from two, three, or more investors, combined in a "syndication." The purpose of this is either to spread the risk around, or to repay favors to other investment firms, or, in the case of SBICs, to permit investment beyond their statutory percentage ownership limits. One firm will generally be the lead investor, putting up most of the money and handling relations with your company. This is a fairly good arrangement from the entrepreneur's viewpoint, although it does leave him with more stockholders to satisfy in negotiating any future offering or financing.

The initial offer will normally be quite informal, probably in the form of a letter. It will form the basis for negotiation of the specific points, and you can probably improve some aspects of the deal if you are prepared to yield on others. Do not in any case regard the initial offer as the final one; both parties realize that it is merely the opening gambit in a process of negotiation. This negotiation gives the investors a further chance to size up your negotiating skills, maturity, and experience. If this experience turns them off, they can find an excuse to withdraw their offer. No deal is ever final until the check has been deposited in your bank.

Assuming that the basic agreement is at last negotiated to your satisfaction (this may take several meetings, strung over many weeks), you then have the problem of selling it to your own stockholders. If you are the only stockholder, your job is simplified. If you have a number of stockholders, including present and past employees, suppliers of seed capital, etc., you may anticipate some problems. Some are going to feel that the resulting dilution of their ownership is too great. Some will feel that the stock is being sold too cheaply. Others will resent the fact that restrictions will be placed on the transfer of their stock.

In general, you will have better luck with your stockholders at this point if you have kept them informed over the weeks of fund raising with a series of memoranda. Let them know how tough it is to raise capital now, what hard deals are being driven, and how many firms you have approached who had no interest at all, etc. When you do come through, the deal will look a lot more attractive if they know what went into getting it. If you do have some holdouts, you should be aware that minority stockholders have well-defined rights under the law. Discuss your possible tactics with your attorney before doing anything.

The Document

Once all parties have agreed in principle, the investor will give you a draft of the document—a two-inch-thick monster of legal and financial detail. You will be horrified when you read it, because you thought those people at the investment company were so *friendly*. Now they give you a document which apparently strips all rights from you, encumbers the company under endless borrowing covenants, operating rules, restrictions, reporting conventions, endless personal warranties, and all sorts of other unpleasantries that never came up in the meetings. This will all be dismissed as mere "required formality" by the investor, but in fact many new issues of substance are always introduced in the document. Go over it with care, since it may be necessary to initiate an entire new round of negotiation to get it acceptable to you, your investor, and your other stockholders. This can take weeks more, plus endless hours of your attorney's and accountant's expensive time, and greatly dilute your efforts in company operation. It is this stage— when patience grows thin, when seemingly endless haggling over small points and what may seem to you as very petty sharpshooting on the part of your investor—that may totally undermine what seemed like a pleasant business association, and cloud the purpose of the financing itself. Many deals fall apart at this late stage.

The Problem with Bridge Capital

Assuming you were short of operating cash when you started the negotiation, you may be in even worse shape after weeks of searching, negotiating, travelling, haggling with stockholders, and paying those endless legal, accounting, and Xerox bills. Your investing firm may acknowledge this and offer to lend your company some "bridge capital" to tide you over until the last details are complete and the final money comes in. Very generous, you think. However, unless you are *very* sure the deal is going through, and *completely* sure of the integrity of the investor, avoid the bridge capital if possible. Cut whatever corners are necessary to keep the company going without it (see Chapter 7). The reasons are:

1. You probably will have to pledge your stock as security for the loan, since everything else is already pledged. This means that legally *any* default condition, however minor (e.g., late interest payment, or inability to meet net-worth tests) and the company is theirs—for a tiny fraction of its value.

2. If the deal falls through, the note is probably due and payable in full, with perhaps a 30-day grace period. *Then* where is the money going to come from? This puts tremendous pressure on you to concede negotiating points you shouldn't, just to keep the deal from falling apart. At that point, in fact, there ceases to be a negotiation—it is fundamentally a dictation of terms by the investor.

Perhaps if you are an exceptionally strong negotiator, or are dealing with an unusually cooperative investor, such provisions will not be attached to the bridge capital note. Otherwise, look out.

The Negotiation Process

Your negotiation with your prospective investors will probably leave you with a heightened sense of humility. It may be the first time that you were ever confronted with the fact that negotiating itself is both a science and an art—one at which the investor has an immeasurable advantage, because he is negotiating deals constantly. You, on the other hand, may negotiate only two or three major financings in your company's existence. What can you do to protect yourself? Here are some possibilities (more on negotiating tactics and strategy in Chapter 14):

1. Get a lawyer who is a good negotiator. This is hard to do without having been through a negotiation with him, but it is a key selection criterion. Have him with you, if possible, at any significant negotiating meeting. He will be able to give a dozen legal and tax reasons why some point you don't wish to concede *can't* be conceded. Conversely, he can attack the legal arguments of the other side as to why they can't do what *you* want. He will be able to help shape the deal in a tax-minimizing form, and provide the foresight and necessary safeguards against problems you could never imagine. He will give you an excuse to caucus when the going gets heavy, yet can often maintain the semblance of a friendly rapport with the other side's attorneys. In general, the adversary process is second nature to lawyers, while it probably isn't to you.

2. Learn as much as possible about the man you're facing. What is his background, education, reputation? What kinds of deals has he been signing? What are *his* real goals and needs, as opposed to the manifest one of driving the toughest possible bargain for his company?

3. Try to list all the issues that will surface in the negotiation. Then decide which are negotiable and which nonnegotiable for the other side. How far are you prepared to move on your negotiable issues? Remember, a point that may be very important to the other side to win may be a concession of little significance to you—and *vice versa*. If you've thought this through in advance, the process of making these tradeoffs at the bargaining table will be much less agonizing.

4. Try to maintain an atmosphere of openness and bonhomie during the sessions. Some occasional jokes and levity help to relieve the tension and make it easier for both sides to concede points that should be conceded. When the going gets really heavy and you know you're being clobbered, just call a recess for some hours or days. Tell them you have to talk *that* one over with your auditors, your directors, your stockholders, your priest, etc. If this isn't possible, at least suggest sending out for some sandwiches—anything to break the momentum of the meeting.

5. Remember, the objective of negotiation is not to beat the other side. It is to strike a deal that is better for everybody than the initial conditions. Each side should concede points of lesser value to

it for points of greater value. Naturally, your adversary may not take this Olympian view of matters, but you should enter the process with this attitude, nonetheless.

Sometimes, for no apparent reason, a negotiation will bog down. The investor just seems to lose interest in the deal, is always out of town, or in some other way permits the momentum to die. At this point you must ask yourself if the loss of interest is real, or merely a negotiating tactic to make you more "reasonable." If this happens well along in the process, it is clearly serious. You should take the initiative and try to find out what the trouble is. At the same time, it may be timely to introduce yourself to some additional prospective investors, to help reduce the psychological pressure on yourself to close *this* deal. Since you will now have a long process of education behind you, as well as calibration on the value of your deal, the next negotiation with the new investor may go much more smoothly and swiftly than the first.

You may gain a little insight into the way venture capitalists think from the following epigrams of Fred Adler, a leading venture capitalist. He calls them Adler's Laws:

1. The probability of a company's succeeding is inversely proportional to the amount of publicity it receives before it manufactures its first product.

2. An investor's ability to talk about his winners is an order of magnitude greater than his ability to remember his losers.

3. If you don't think you have a problem, you have a big problem.

4. Happiness is positive cash flow. Everything else will come later.

5. The probability of success of a small company is inversely proportional to the size of the president's office.

6. Would-be entrepreneurs who pick up the check after luncheon discussions are usually losers.

7. The longer the investment proposal, the shorter the odds of success.

8. There is no such thing as an overfinanced company.

9. Managers who worry a lot about voting control usually have nothing worth controlling.

10. There's no limit on what a man can do or where he can go, if he doesn't mind who gets the credit.

Conventional Wisdom. Don't shop the deal.

Reality. You *have* to shop the deal.

References

1. Nierenberg, Gerard I.: *The Art of Negotiating*, Hawthorne Books, N.Y., 1968.

   The original negotiation book. Spells out Nierenberg's needs theory.

2. Levin, Edward: *Levin's Laws: Tactics for Winning Without Intimidation*, M. Evans & Co., N.Y., 1980.

3. Nierenberg, Gerard I., and Calero, Henry A.: *Meta–talk:—Guide to Hidden Meanings in Conversations*, Trident–Press, N.Y., 1973.

   Guidelines for interpreting behavior in negotiating settings.

4. Karrass, Chester Louis: *The Negotiating Game*, World Publishing Co., N.Y., 1970.

ACCOUNTING—INSIDE
AND OUT

"President-and-Treasurer disease is corporate cancer. The president's job is to take the assets of the corporation and drive them forward as fast as he can. And it is the treasurer's job to say, 'Yes, but . . . ' These two qualities do not rest easily in the mind of one man."

. . . Arthur Snyder, Banker, Venture Capitalist

It is hard for entrepreneurs to fully appreciate accounting and what it can do for them. In fact, many tend to view the accountant as a bean counter, a sort of scorekeeper sitting at the sidelines, rather than as a player on the field with the first team. This is a great mistake.

Every business organization has need for orderly collection and deployment of quantitative information. This information has two broad uses: *inside uses*, to give the manager the data he requires in order to run the company, and *outside uses*, to permit reporting the results of the operation to the outside world, including stockholders, directors, IRS, regulatory bodies, and research organizations. These two functions, while proceeding from the same data base, are really quite different. The former looks ahead, tries to show the manager where he's going, how to control future costs, and what problems to anticipate. The second is largely historical, generated by the book, for the record. While you will have some latitude for experimentation and innovation in the first area, you must conform to rather orthodox forms in the second. In both, you need competent help.

Accounting as a Language

Accounting is much more than a function; it is a language, a means of communication among all segments of the business community. It assumes a reference base called the *accounting model of the enterprise*. While several other models of the enterprise are, of course, possible, the accounting model is the accepted form, and is likely to be for some time. To the extent that the entrepreneur does not speak the language of accounting and feel intuitively comfortable with the accounting model, he is at a severe disadvantage in the business world. He must be *literally* as facile with accounting concepts as the physicist is with mathematical ideas. It is a fundamental tool of the trade.

For the entrepreneur to rely solely on common sense and hired hands to get him through is unnecessarily risky. To understand what you're asking your accountant to do, let alone evaluate his work, *you* require some basic accounting knowledge. This knowledge may come from reading (see the references) or, better, from some formal training in accounting. Nearly every town and city has some sort of college, university extension, adult education, or commercial school where the basics of accounting are taught. The entrepreneur who has had no accounting, or who has not had it since early college, should seriously consider enrolling in such a program. You don't have to pass the CPA exam, but you *do* need the basics. In addition to basic courses, you may be able to find, as well, a somewhat more advanced offering of an appropriate character, in cost accounting and control. Consider taking it as well.

Accounting Help: How Much and What Kind?

In the fetal stages of your venture, you probably found it necessary to obtain some part-time accounting help to set up your books, do posting, reconcile the bank statement, and, perhaps, prepare a few monthly financial reports. Now, with some capital in the venture and shipping dates approaching, the problems change in kind as well as in size. You may find that your brother-in-law's accountant working on Saturdays simply can't keep up with the volume any longer. What you need is an accountant, possibly a part-time one, but certainly one with the experience and energy to do what needs doing. There are bills to verify and to post, checks to write, invoices to be issued, collections to be pushed, suppliers to be cajoled, deposits to be made, checkbooks to be balanced, operating statements to be prepared, tax returns to be filed, and a myriad of other tasks, large and small, that are custodial in nature but which must be pursued with diligence.

In addition, there is a creative side to the job, for which your accountant must have some time and energy. You must have his assistance in developing cash-flow projections, budgets, standard costs, and cost accounting systems. These are all tasks for which text book models are inadequate. Your systems must be designed to fit the context of your company, and to accommodate the needs of the people who will use them.

You do not need Albert Einstein to do all this. What you do need is a solid accounting person who has actually set up systems in the past—not merely posted the books and turned the crank on an inherited accounting mechanism. You need somebody who is fundamentally methodical, orderly, and neat. If your workload will permit part-time personnel (say, afternoons only), you may very well be filling this role with an experienced woman with school-aged children or with a retired person. In hiring, don't worry about keeping him or her for ten years; it's help to get you through the next two years that you need now. In locating such a person, some newspaper ads, or a few inquiries through your auditing firm, should net you some candidates.

As the company grows, the duties of the accountant become both more numerous and more demanding. The need for cost accounting and budgets becomes more pressing, and there are additional interfaces with suppliers, bankers, and customers to be managed professionally. At this point, your accountant will probably come to you and tell you he or she needs some more help—more billing clerks, a cost accounting clerk, another secretary. This, however, is a very critical moment, and you should not act immediately on the advice of your accountant. This is very likely the juncture at which you should instead hire a controller, to reorganize your accounting and control function for the next stage of growth, to oversee your accounting staff, and to raise the entire professional level of the activity. There will, of course, be the possibility of promoting the accountant to controller: however, this is rarely a good idea. The person you were able to hire 18 months ago to do all the detail work would, had he the qualifications to be a controller, never have taken your job offer. Do not mistake ambition for talent in this area. Enlist your auditing firm in recruiting for this job; it is an extremely critical role. A good controller can make a company, to the extent that probably few other employees can. For a poor one, the reverse applies with a vengeance.

Auditors

There is often misunderstanding as to what, actually, the auditing firm does. It is not the FBI. It does not come into your firm and go over every last transaction with a fine-tooth comb. Your auditor probably cannot tell you if you have a thief in the stockroom or an embezzler in the accounts receivable office. His function is to examine your accounting and control *procedures* and determine whether they are adequate and whether they are being followed. In the process of so doing, some sampling of accounts payable and receivable is necessary, as well as a detailed check on very large accounts with customers and suppliers. In addition, in an audit he will require that a physical inventory be taken under his observation, during the course of which he will investigate both the condition and the value of this asset. He will want to see any contracts of a major nature, stockholder lists, certificates of indebtedness, and other documents with significant bearing on the company's worth.

Needless to say, this is a rather long and sometimes arduous process for the entrepreneur and his accountant. Normally it is done only once per year, although additional partial-year audits may be necessary in connection with financing efforts. The result of this effort is the certified statement, in which the auditing firm certifies that it has examined the accounts and accounting methods of the firm and found them in accordance with "generally accepted accounting practice." However, you will eventually discover that these practices are far from universal, and that there is broad latitude and flexibility in their application. Some businesses try to exploit this flexibility, with the acquiescence of their auditors, to mislead the readers of their financial statements.

Significance of Certified Statements

There are, roughly speaking, three levels of "quality" in year-end statements:

1. *Unaudited*. These statements, even though they may be prepared by your auditor, have little weight with outside persons, because they are merely prepared from the books of account without benefit of auditing.

2. *Audited, Uncertified*. These statements are the result of a partial audit, in which most but not all of the steps may have been taken. For example, it may be that the auditor was unable to witness the taking of inventory, although the other tests have been performed.

3. *Certified*. This is the most believable, because it means that all steps have been taken, and the auditing firm has stuck its neck out as far as possible.

Young firms sometimes fail to obtain certification of statements in the early years, either to save auditing fees or because the managers don't appreciate its significance. However, if in later years you decide to take the public financing route, you must be able to supply certified statements for the last five years to the SEC. This can be rather clumsy, because it is very difficult for the auditor to certify the activities of five years ago—or even five days ago—if he did not witness your inventory–taking. For this reason, and simply because more people will believe them, be sure *all* your year-end statements are certified.

Selection of an Auditing Firm

This is rather easy, as there are only eight firms in the country that you should consider, provided you are a firm with national growth aspirations. These are the "Big Eight" public accounting firms. They are: Arthur Anderson and Co.; Coopers and Lybrand; Ernst and Ernst; Arthur Young and Co.; Haskins and Sells; Peat, Marwick, and Mitchell; Price Waterhouse and Co.; and Touche Ross and Co.

There are many persuasive arguments for the use of smaller, highly competent local accounting firms. Their advocates will argue that you get more personalized service; that you are more likely to get a senior man on your account; that you can later switch to a Big Eight firm if necessary; that the rates are lower; that you will have the same man year after year on your audit.

Countering this, however, is the central fact that out-of-town people simply will not *believe* the statements prepared by an obscure accounting firm whose reputation they know nothing about. Investment bankers in particular have what amounts to a horror of small local firms. If you enlist one of the Big Eight on Day One, the issue will simply never arise.

It is possible that the Big Eight firm will charge somewhat more than the local firm. However, it is also possible that they may have more to offer, in terms of backup services over and above auditing. Most have small business sections, designed to help entrepreneurs in setting up systems and in other types of business problems. All have management consulting sections, which may or may not be capable of in-depth work on some specific problem you may have. It is also true that if you object to the man assigned to your firm, the large firm will have the depth to send in someone more suitable.

The Big Eight are all similar in that they are large and nationally recognized. However, there are significant differences among them in terms of size, operating policies, and clout. One may be much better in your area, while another may have the stronger office in a different location. Ask your attorney, banker, and any other businessman who they like in the area; then go call on the top two or three prospects, and see which one you prefer.

The Audit

The auditing firm you select is your big friend—until the day of your first audit. From that point forward they may seem to become your adversary. They will criticize your cash control system will wish to create reserves for bad debts in excess of anything you can imagine, and also to reserve for specific accounts which may be a bit slow in collecting. They will raise Cain with your inventory, insisting that at least half of it is obsolete and should be written off at once. They will find your cost accounting inadequate to determine the actual labor and materials content of your work-in-process. They will want you to write off your capitalized development costs. They will discover that a couple of your accounts receivable claim never to have seen an invoice from your firm. In short, they will appear to be doing everything possible to reduce your bottom line profit, for which you have labored so long and hard.

This experience, repeated annually, tends to produce a mild paranoia among company presidents. However, you should remember that they are, ultimately, only your hired hands. If you disagree with their stand on important issues, take them to task; special circumstances may justify your view in their minds. If not, you can still do as you please anyway, and let them note their objection in a footnote to the certified statement. If difficulties persist, you may be justified in changing auditors. The great umbrella of "generally accepted accounting practice" may, in the hands of a different firm, cover you, too.

Budgets and Control

The budget is a key tool in your effort to operate your company. It is, in essence, the connecting linkage between your business plan and your organization; the piston rod connecting your power source with your drive wheels. Formal budgets serve a lot of useful purposes, and only a very foolish president would try to function for long without them. The budget is:

1. *A Tool for Implementing Plans.* In this role, the budget states, in detail, how much money and time is to be allocated for each purpose in the pursuit of the business plan. It states who will spend the monies, what his authorization will be, and for what materials and services they will be spent. To this extent, the company's budgets are more or less an elaboration of the financial projections of the Business Plan.

2. *A Tool for Communication.* The budget and the process which produces it is one of the principal means of communicating the exact plan of operation throughout the organization. As finally published, the budget will tell everyone precisely what his spending limits will be for accomplishing each task. It is your *only quantitative statement* of corporate priorities. To the extent that your managers submit budgetary proposals for consideration, they are communicating in a most quantitative form their plans and priorities for carrying out their functions.

3. *A Tool for Cost Control.* By considering in advance the necessary amounts for each class of expenditure, and getting each manager committed to that statement of expenditures, you have the rudiments for achieving financial control. By reporting actual expenditures against budget, you have a monthly historical record of (a) how good your budget was, and (b) how good a job your people have done in controlling costs. Where tighter control is indicated, and to permit the *prevention* (as opposed to reporting) of overbudget expenditures, you may wish to have your accountant maintain *daily* tallies of expenditure requests, purchase orders cut, etc., and notify the appropriate parties when the budget for a particular item is *about* to be exceeded. It is only at this level that you actually have control of costs. The monthly budgets versus actual profit and loss statement will only highlight major areas of overrun or underrun for future management action, but the money is already gone. *Caution:* Budgets can also hide a good deal of information. For example, a department that is consistently within its overall budget may be using savings in one area to hide gross inefficiency or other problems in another. Be sure your budget has enough detail to pinpoint the reality of the situation.

4. *A Tool for Assessment of Employee Performance.* Sad to say, the ability to meet goals on budget is among the few quantitative measures of employee performance available to presidents. For this reason it is probably overstressed, but unsatisfactory performance in the spending area usually connotes problems. Each manager must assume responsibility for the controllable (i.e., nonoverhead or distributed) costs of his area of the business. To the extent that he helps to set his own goals and budgets, he must be responsible for meeting them—not merely for mounting a forensic attack on the "unrealistic" budget. Unless every manager accepts this fundamental responsibility, your business plan, your cash projections, and your intended profits will all be meaningless.

For all of these reasons, it is imperative that even startup ventures establish some form of formal budgeting as early as feasible. When resources are limited, there will be hard tradeoffs to be made, and everyone on the team should have a voice in how these are made and implemented. Probably once per quarter is adequate for a full budget update. Procedurally, one starts with an updated sales forecast, and works down through the P&L line items entering costs as they *will be* (as opposed to have been) during the next four quarters. Avoid the temptation to merely insert last quarter's estimates; challenge each line item, and be sure that it deserves all that is being spent on it. Where could cuts be made if necessary? Improvements postponed, capital equipment deferred? For which jobs are we overspecifying skills? These are the sorts of questions that should be asked, at least every quarter, of each operating manager.

Your first few budgets will probably be terrible; they will evoke a hue and cry from their victims, and the results may be rather discouraging to you. Don't quit trying, however; keep refining, improving categories, pushing for compliance, and creating an attitude of recognition for the people who achieve their targets. This is the only way that your costs will come under your control and stay there.

Final Note. Don't overdo it. Too much detail, too much frequency can drown a budget system in its own paperwork. Be sure the system is your servant—not your master.

Conventional Wisdom. The accountant should sit on the sidelines and keep score.

Reality. A good accountant will be right out there on the field with you.

References

1. Heckert, J. B., and Willson, J. D.: *Business Budgeting and Control,* 3rd ed., The Roland Press, N.Y., 1967.

   This is an excellent work, showing in some detail how to develop business plans into budgets, then controlling the firm through the budgets. Takes up where accounting texts leave off.

2. Myer, John N.: *Accounting for Nonaccountants,* New York University Press, N.Y., 1st ed., 1947.

   This is oriented toward understanding, rather than how-to-do-it detail. A good substitute for a course in beginning accounting.

3. Lasser, J. K.: *Handbook of Accounting Methods,* 3rd ed., D. Van Nostrand Co., Inc., N.Y., 1964.

   This books gives suggested forms and methods on an industry-by-industry basis. Also has good sections on electronic data processing in accounting, stock registration, and other practical issues. A fine reference book.

4. Overmyer, W. S.: "Picking an Auditor for your Firm," *Small Marketers Aids Annual No. 4,* Small Business Administration, Washington, D.C., 1962.

   Practical advice for the small businessman, rather than the growth-oriented president. Not bad, though.

5. Witschey, R. E.: "Public Accounting Services for Small Manufacturers," *Small Business Management Series, No. 5,* Small Business Administration, Washington, D.C., 1954.

CARE AND FEEDING OF BANKERS

"A banker is a fellow who offers to lend you his umbrella when it isn't raining."

. . . Anonymous

It is common currency among entrepreneurs that bankers are parsimonious, hidebound, unimaginative, and timid to the point of irrationality. However, it is time the truth was bared: *Some are not.* It is incumbent on the entrepreneur bent on survival to find a bank in that small category, and cultivate a relationship as one would cultivate a garden of beautiful flowers.

Differences Among Banks

To the outsider looking in, most banks look alike. They all offer about the same services, pay about the same interest on deposits, charge about the same on comparable loans. However there are differences among banks. Some of the more obvious gross differences are in asset size (general clout), net worth (stability), region served, number of specialized departments, and general prestige. However, most of these don't make too much difference to the entrepreneur. The differences that *do* matter include:

1. Source of income. If you are dealing with a bank that depends mainly on mortgages for income, your loan requirements aren't going to get much priority.

2. Capacity for working with small firms. Banks vary radically in this regard. Some regard a startup company as just one more bad risk; others see it as an opportunity. Some have departments or SBIC connections for dealing with the smaller enterprise. Has the bank you're considering made unsecured loans to small firms lately?

3. Reputation for staying in when the going gets rough. Did they call their small business demand notes (or fail to renew) in 1970, when even their old, established customers were crying for cash, or did they hang in there? You can get some interesting insight into bank behavior by talking to entrepreneurs who have been in business since, say, 1968.

4. General creativity of approach. Do they just look at your balance sheet and faint, or do they try to suggest constructive financial alternatives—e.g., rotating receivables financing, factoring, leasing, or negotiating contract advances? Some banks are more adept at this than others. Also, within a given bank, individual officers tend to vary widely in level of creativity. As a New England bank is fond of saying, "The man you talk to *is* the bank."

Selecting a Bank

Bank selection, though not so irreversible as many other business decisions, is a very important step for the entrepreneur. You begin investing in a good relationship, starting on Day One. If your choice is a poor one and you have to switch after two years, that's two years of effort and investment in credibility down the drain. Select the right bank early, and begin grooming it against the day you really need it; when your cash crunch finally comes, it will be too late to start shopping.

Following are some guidelines for bank selection:

1. Develop a list of criteria, then refine them into questions you will put to the various bank officers you interview.

2. Ask other entrepreneurs to describe their experiences with their banks. After you've talked with a few people, a general pattern may begin to emerge. Be sure to find out who their lending officer is at each candidate bank.

3. Ask your accounting firm, your lawyer, and your godfather for suggestions on banking connections.

4. Talk to a few different banks, even if you're convinced you know where you ought to be banking. Try to calibrate the differences for yourself.

5. In interviewing the officer, be sure to ask for some small business customer references.

In the selection process, keep in mind that institutions are only agglomerations of people and that, as their personnel makeup changes, so do their policies and attitudes. For example, a bank with a long record of working with smaller firms may have lost one or two sparkplug officers who emphasized and championed that part of the business—and not be, therefore, too strong or interested in more new venture business. Or, they may just have attracted so much of it that they are not seeking more. Or, money may be so tight at the moment that they are not seeking any but the very highest quality lending opportunities. Thus, what you must search out is a bank and officer that you can work with *now* and *over the next several years*. What it did in the past is important, but not of itself decisive.

Grooming the Relationship

To the extent that your side of the banking relationship is active rather than passive, you will be maximizing your chances of long-term cooperation. Some of the steps you can take without investing much energy include the following:

1. Keep your banker informed. This applies *whether or not* you have a loan outstanding. Place him on your P.R. mailing list, your key customer newsletter list, etc. Be sure he gets a set of operating statements monthly, and the audited annual statements while they're still fresh.

2. See him in person. Bankers are big believers in pressing the flesh. Once a month is probably too often, but once per quarter might be about right. Have him come to your office and review the operating results and the projections, have a look at the plant, and review R&D in progress. Fill him in on key customers and prospects, and get his subconscious working on possible other business sources for you. Have lunch, and establish some human contact. Get him *interested* in what the company and you are doing. Remember, if you do a good job now, you'll want to take your banker with you in your *next* company. Likewise, if he changes banks, it may be beneficial to move your account with him. Banking is fundamentally a business of people, of mutual confidence and assumed integrity.

3. Start borrowing. Even if your company has $500,000 cash from fund-raising, now is the time to begin establishing a record for businesslike borrowing and on-time repayment. It is also time to let the bank start making a few dollars on your account, which they will be only too happy to do—if you have a bundle of cash. If you don't, then you probably need a bank loan, and it's high time to start learning to use bank credit constructively.

4. Meet your targets. Everything said in Chapter 12 about meeting targets applies to the banking relationship. If you acquire a reputation for sloppy cash management, poor planning, or feeble follow-through on your plans, your bank will be lukewarm on your account—*even if you're growing and profitable*. A few minor targets met *on time, on budget* early in the game will let the banker stop worrying so much about you. Be sure he (and everyone else) knows about it when goals are reached.

Miscellaneous Services of Banks

There are a number of formal and informal services which your bank can render once you're rolling together. These can be worth a lot of money and should be used:

1. Credit checks. You probably won't be able to justify the annual fees for credit agencies such as Dun and Bradstreet at first, and maybe you'll never need to. Your bank has access to all of them. This can also be a useful route for sizing up prospective customers and competition.

2. Equity financing. Banks with SBICs can work directly with you; others can often put you in touch with investors or investment bankers who would not otherwise be accessible to you.

3. Product leasing. If you sell capital equipment, the bank may be willing to help you develop a leasing plan to offer to your customers.

4. Equipment financing. When you need capital equipment, your banker may be able to show you how to afford it earlier than you thought.

5. Export-related services. Banks with strong foreign contacts can advise you on letters of credit, export credit insurance, foreign bank drafts, and other details of international finance.

6. Payroll and other accounting. Banks increasingly offer data processing services to their customers; their rates are of necessity competitive with outside data processing services.

7. Tax advice and services. Certain banks are set up to do a substantial amount of tax-related work for company clients.

8. General business advice. Your officer may prove to be a valuable sounding board and source of advice on business problems. You may get suggestions as to possible sources of business, ways to deal with particular delinquent accounts, methods for setting up payroll and other labor intensive accounts. Besides knowing sources for additional capital, he may know firms that might be interested in acquiring or being acquired.

It may be desirable to maintain a small account with a local bank with offices near by. This will not be for the purpose of borrowing (although don't rule them out) but for the convenience of your employees. They need a place to cash their paychecks and do personal banking. Your accountant will occasionally need a certified or cashier's check on short notice, and a safe deposit box for certain documents. Your petty cash box will need refreshing periodically. These are all functions for which you want a nearby bank. In addition to this bank, you may wish at some point to establish a discreet account with a *third* bank, in which to keep a portion of the company assets to protect them against being frozen by a creditors' committee or a court action. Such an action, brought to make you do something you don't want to do, can be extremely awkward if you have not anticipated it.

Parting Shot. Remember, your banker is the fellow who's going to rent you working capital that you'd otherwise have to buy with undervalued stock. He's going to do a lot, therefore, toward making you rich. Treat your relationship accordingly.

Conventional Wisdom. All banks are pretty much alike.

Reality. All banks are pretty much alike—until you ask for a loan.

References

1. Reiter, E. F.: "How to Choose Your Banker Wisely," *Management Aids for Small Business, Annual No. 2,* Small Business Administration, Washington, D.C., 1958.

   Practical ideas, but relating more to the small business person than the president of a high-growth firm.

2. Wayne, William. *How to Succeed in Business When the Chips are Down:* McGraw-Hill, N.Y., 1972.

   This book, written by someone who has obviously been through the mill, is full of advice on dealing under duress with bankers.

Chapter 15

THAT NEXT ROUND OF FINANCING

"Take the money and run."

. . . Woody Allen

Financing Future Growth

Raising money for a small, growing firm is seldom easy. But raising money to *continue the growth of sales and profits* is a snap compared to raising money to finance past losses.

The company that has met its targets and has the firm support of its stockholders, bankers, and employees has a variety of choices. It may seek additional capital from its old stockholders, it may seek out funding from venture capital firms, it may arrange a private placement of stock through an investment banker, or may elect to go public. Possibly it will be attractive enough at this point to elicit acquisition interest from another company. Its optimal strategy at this point is to maximize the net worth of the existing stockholders, given the total scenario of events that each choice implies.

The course of action with the highest present value (future revenues discounted back to the present) would, normally, be the one selected. This may or may not be the same course of action that yields the highest *immediate* return. For example, you may receive an offer to buy the entire company for $1 million ($1.00/share, assuming one million shares exist). The founders and the original investors walk away with a pocket full of cash and a handsome capital gain. You may also have the alternative, however, of selling one-third of the company for $250,000 in working capital. Not too attractive, you say. Not only is the value per share lower, but neither you nor the other stockholders get any cash. Plus the old investors grumble that they paid as much, but took all the risk. However, based on present growth, you think that the $250,000 would carry the firm another 10 months, by which time a public offering could be arranged. In such an offering, the company could raise perhaps $1 million for 20 percent of the stock; thereafter a secondary issue could perhaps be arranged to generate some working capital and stockholder liquidity, perhaps in 12 more months. Let us then compare two possible cases, with some illustrative numbers.

Case 1: Sell Out for $1 Million

	Number of Shares Owned	Cost Basis	Sale Price	Net Gain
Founders @ $.01	$750,000	$ 7,500	$750,000	$742,500
Original Investors @ $.50	250,000	125,000	250,000	125,000

In this case, the founders will probably be required to stay and operate the company for two to five years, depending on the buyer.

Case 2: Sell one-third of Company for $250,000, then go public for $1 million = 20%

	Number of Shares Owned	Cost Basis	Sale Price	Net Gain
Founders @ $.01	$750,000	$ 7,500	$3,000,000*	$2,992,500
Original Investors @ .50	250,000	125,000	1,000,000	875,000
New Investors @ .50	500,000	250,000	2,000,000	1,750,000
Public @ 2.67	375,000	1,000,000	1,500,000	500,000

*Assumes that a secondary offering at $4.00 is possible. However, this value will be only a paper gain for a substantial period of time for the founders.

It is to be acknowledged that the foregoing example contains some heroic assumptions: To wit, that the management and original stockholders had perfect knowledge of some unknowables:

1. The price and time when the company could go public.

2. The price and time when a secondary offering and registration of letter stock would be feasible.

3. The ability of the management and initial investors to sell all their stock in the secondary offering. However, this is not necessary, if we simply take the market price of $4.00 as a reasonable basis for computing "gain."

The principal point is that decisions based on the relative "dilution" of capital value, loss of "control," or immediacy of cashout can be very poor decisions. The public issue remains the major avenue for realization of the full rewards of entrepreneurship. If you relinquish the possibility too early or too cheaply, you will have lost the ball game in the final inning. In the illustration, our founders quadrupled their gains over the sellout case; moreover, had they sold out they would have relinquished their opportunity to go entrepreneuring again for the next several years, due to their employment agreements. Thus the opportunity cost of the sellout is probably even in excess of the loss in sale price. A little simulation along these lines, looking at various assumptions about the future, can help a great deal in clearing up your own thinking.

An on-target company seeking Round Two capital has a rather broader range of choices available than it had for Round One. Many venture capital and other institutions invest *only* in Round Two situations; most venture capitalists are more comfortable with this situation. You may also be able to entice in funds from insurance companies, college endowments or other quasi-fiduciary institutions, once you have a winning track record.

Who Needs Those Guys?

A peculiar phenomenon occurs in Round Two financing with sufficient frequency to warrant some comment. It is the "Who-needs-those-guys" effect—"those guys" being the old investors. It often happens that, after struggling with the entrepreneur through the pains and risks of startup and the agonizing initial couple of years of operations, the original investors cannot or will not put up the Round Two money. They may be fully invested by then in other ventures; they may have specific preference for startup or Round One investments; or, they may simply have reached what they consider a prudent limit for investment in one deal.

At this stage then, the entrepreneur starts looking for new sources of money. Enter Mr. Round Two Deal Man. He looks at the company and likes it—*except* for one thing: those old stockholders hold "too much" of the company. *Who needs those guys?* he asks you. After all, *they* aren't going to contribute any further to the company's progress. *They* will simply be sitting on a pile of cheap stock that rightfully ought to be in the hands of management and new investors. *They* are just going to be a pain in the neck, a source of trouble, and a possible veto on later financial dealings. Let's get them out.

Herein lie the seeds of a great error. When Mr. Round Two says, "Let's you and them fight," he is setting forces in motion which could tear your fragile new company apart, literally. If he makes an offer contingent on forcing out the old stockholders (e.g., by offering them an unreasonably low price and insisting everyone sell), he will be pitting you against them, with nothing to lose himself. If the deal falls through, he walks away to another one. Meanwhile, he has convinced you that the old backers are a bunch of mendacious parasites, while they are now convinced that you are a thief and a bounder, trying to deny them a reasonable reward for taking the front-end risk and hanging on with you. The damage that is thereby inflicted on the company may be irreparable. You will no longer be partners and the emphasis will shift from a joint seeking of corporate goals to one of maneuvering, one-upsmanship, and defense of personal interest. It is now impossible, because of the suspicions created, to approach *any* new investor with a united front, and no investor wants to buy into a fratricidal family struggle. Moreover, your manifest willingness to dump your old investors over the side will permit the prospective Mr. Round Two to vividly project himself into their position two years hence.

This is not to say that there is never cause to take out some old investors in seeking new capital. Some may want out; others may be willing to get out, if they feel that it is in the company's best interest. However, if they feel you attempted to cheat them or to force them out on unfair terms, they will always resent it, and it will come back to haunt you. You personally have nothing to lose by pressing Mr. Round Two for a fairer deal for your old investors. He may not agree, but he should at least respect your commitment to treating investors fairly.

Financing Past Losses

Any reasonably intelligent entrepreneur can probably find ample capital for Rounds Two and Three and Four, if his company is growing, profitable, and reasonably near target. The real test of entrepreneurial skill, however, comes when you are in some combination of the following circumstances:

1. You are out of cash.
2. You are losing money.
3. You are far behind sales targets, and other company goals.
4. Capital intended for market development and production facilities has been eaten up by development delays and operating losses.

If this is your situation, you have your work cut out for you.

The first thing to do is to take a hard look at the next few months' cash flow and determine whether you can keep the doors open; there is nothing so certain to sabotage any negotiation for capital than the joint recognition that the company is in utterly desperate straits. It is, in fact, no longer a negotiation, but a unilateral dictation of terms.

If you see that the company is headed full speed for a cash

cliff, take immediate steps to alleviate it. Drastic measures may be warranted, even though they may be somewhat embarrassing to your "growth company" image. It is vitally important to get the cash flow positive and be negotiating from a viable position. It will also vastly enhance your position to be able to show that the company is currently in the black (temporarily) in addition to having a positive cash flow.

The measures you will take will be the obvious ones: Cut personnel expenses by discharging some people, furloughing the more valuable people, and asking the key people to accept some deferral and temporary cut in salary. Try a four-day week (32 hours) in the shop for a while; if people sense that it is only temporary you may not lose anybody. Cut all other discretionary expenses, and consider various forms of postponement buying (e.g., on operating supplies, expendable tools, and materials). Stretch out your vendors, and arrange financing on any unpledged assets. Try selling off underutilized equipment and inventory. Try subleasing some plant space. In addition, you must consider lending the company some money yourself, and obtaining short-term loans from whatever source possible.

When your business plan has been fully updated for selling purposes, you should take to the road. In addition, try putting your stockholders to work, exercising their contacts and making pitches to possible investors.

Your selling posture is in essence:

1. The company is about to take off and realize its multimillion-dollar potential.

2. The heavy risks and expenses are all behind now, and the bill was footed by someone else.

3. The commitment and determination of the management team have been amply demonstrated by the tough times you've ground through.

4. The adverse market conditions (if any) have been as tough on the competition as on you. In fact, your competitors may be about to throw in the towel.

5. The prolonged development cycle, with its attendant expense, has resulted in a far better product than originally conceived.

6. There's still time for an astute investor to get in on the ground floor (indeed—you haven't even left it yet).

Acquiring an Acquirer

You may discover after some exposure to the investment community that the money you need at this stage simply is not available on any kind of reasonable terms. If so, it may be time to start looking for a company with some logical reason for wanting to acquire you. There are, of course, many noninvestment reasons why a going concern would be interested in buying you, despite your past record and current distress:

1. Quick entry into a new (your) market.

2. Expansion of their present market by annexing your customers.

3. A cheaper, faster way into a new technology or product than designing it.

4. A source of supply for some needed products or capability (vertical integration).

5. A captive customer for some of *their* products.

6. A means of absorbing existing overheads (factory space, machine time, sales force, dealer base).

7. A P.R. tool for asserting their support of minority enterprise (if applicable).

8. A source of some pizzazz to get their stock moving.

Armed with this list of possible motives, start your search for possible corporate partners, first on a local basis, then widening the circle. This may not be the point at which you would normally have wanted to be bought out—but acquisition may be the right answer. The acquiring company may be able to add a lot of things besides money to make your venture go, and the personal risks to you may be diminished a full order of magnitude.

Other routes may be open to you at this point. One is Chapter XI reorganization, discussed in a later chapter. Another is government lending agencies designed more or less specifically for the firm in temporary or reversible straits. The SBA offers direct loans (often unavailable due to lack of funds) as well as bank loan guarantees for firms unable to meet normal bank lending standards. State or regional agencies (e.g., Massachusetts Business Development Corporation) make loans to struggling firms. Your chances with these people are best if you're a substantial employer, but let them judge that. Go see anybody whom you even suspect is in the economic development business. Your state legislator may be a good man to steer you to the right doors and help you to kick them open. If a federal program appears to have some glimmer of salvation, you should also keep your Congressman or Senator aware of your activities. Don't forget that they have a big stake in the economic welfare of their constituents.

For you, the entrepreneur, the toughest part of this whole business may be in keeping your own faith alive. With it, anything is possible (if improbable); without it, you won't be able to convince anybody. You may at times have to indulge in a little autohypnosis to keep on going, but a confident, enthusiastic and optimistic attitude is essential—and contagious. You must evince the belief that the hurdle you confront is the last major one between the company and the Big Apple.

Conventional Wisdom. Each round of financing is easier than the last.

Reality. Each round of financing is easier than the last, *if* you're on plan.

References

1. Hutchinson, G. S.: *Why, When, and How to Go Public,* Presidents Publishing House, N.Y., 1970.

   This offers prudent, if somewhat orthodox, advice and procedures for going public. Best book I've found on the subject.

2. Mancuso, Joseph R.: *How to Start, Finance, and Manage Your Own Small Business,* Prentice-Hall, Englewood Cliffs, N.J., 1978.

   See Chapter 6 on raising new money.

3. Sears, G. A.: *"Public Offerings for Smaller Companies," Harvard Business Review,* September–October, 1968.

4. *A Summary of Financial Assistance Programs,* Small Business Administration, Washington, D.C., 1966.

   There may be a later edition. Lists a surprising number of government-backed financial assistance programs for small business, most of which are still around.

PEOPLE III

Chapter 16

PEOPLE IN SMALL FIRMS— GENERAL CONSIDERATIONS

"Youth gets together his materials to build a bridge to the moon, or perchance a palace or temple on earth, and, at length, the middle-aged man concludes to build a woodshed with them."

. . . Henry David Thoreau

The most important resource of any company is its people. As an entrepreneur, one of your most important jobs for the next several years will be the recruiting, training, motivating, and, where necessary, thinning out of your staff. Much of your energy will be consumed with such issues as training new salespeople, creating compensation and incentive packages, struggling with rivalries and conflicts within your team, trying to maintain a creative climate, and getting rid of people who don't work out. To the extent that you are efficient and successful in these tasks, you will probably be efficient and successful in building your company.

The Fallacy of Hiring for Future Needs

In Chapter 5 we addressed the issue of overspecification of partners in the fetal and startup phases of the enterprise. The same general point can be made for any employee, however. You are doing a disservice to both the person and the company to hire somebody who is overqualified for the job at hand.

The practice of overhiring is sometimes justified by the argument that, while the person's talents aren't needed now, in a year or two he will be fully utilized. Using this justification, many firms have exploited recessionary conditions in hiring $25,000 per year people to do junior engineering for $12,000—with very disappointing results for all concerned. Hiring an overqualified man can result in several problems:

1. In hiring the top person for the job, you will normally be overpaying, relative to what it would otherwise cost to get the job done.

2. If you take advantage of unusual market conditions to hire an individual for less than his normal worth, you will invest money and effort in training, only to lose him as soon as a normal job market returns.

3. In the very early stages, before the company has significant substance, you will have to pay more in terms of salary, options, stock, and other nonsalary incentives to attract a top person than you will later.

4. If the individual is from a larger company (which is likely), he will be accustomed to staff, clerical help, substantial budgets, and other trappings of office. He may function poorly in the spartan environment you offer—or worse, persuade you to add the overheads long before you should.

5. If he's bored by the detail and do-it-yourself drudgery inherent in a new-company job, he may quit long before his talents are actually needed by the company.

As an entrepreneur, your responsibility is to survive the first couple of years—not to "build for the future" with people who won't be needed until year three. Therefore, match your hiring to the actual job, as it will be for the next one and a half to two years. The future can take care of itself.

The Outgrown Employee

In one version of *The Peter Principle*,[1] a man gets successive promotions until he reaches his "level of incompetence," after which he advances no further, and prevents the further progress of the organization in his area. In the new enterprise context, however, *The Peter Principle* works somewhat differently. Instead of the individual being promoted up the pyramid, the pyramid grows under the individual. The resulting situation, however, is the same. In the new enterprise it is more serious, though, in that the person who does not grow with his job can effectively block the progress of the entire

---

[1] Apologies to Lawrence J. Peter.

company. You don't *have* the option of working around him—you must usually get rid of him, or subordinate him to a new manager from outside. Either can present some unpleasantness.

For example, assume you have hired a manufacturing manager who is hard working, loyal, and extremely competent—as long as he only has about 25 employees, whom he can oversee directly. He enjoys first-line contact, and trains and motivates workers beautifully. But now your organization has grown. You now have 100 workers, and three foremen. Your old manufacturing manager, however, is not thriving on his success. He dislikes supervising foremen, he misses the direct contact with the workers, and feels that the foremen are doing a poor job of training and supervising them. Production is falling more or less permanently behind schedule, quality is slipping a bit, and firedrills and confrontations have begun to replace planning as a management method. What do you do now?

The simplest answer might be to get rid of the man. However, he is a good man, a friend by now, and has been with the company virtually from startup. He will walk out with some stock which can no longer motivate the performance of another employee. Moreover, he's well liked by the team and his ejection could have a devastating effect on morale.

A second answer is to bring in a higher-power manufacturing manager, and make the old one a foreman under him. This might work, but the old manager is likely to feel humiliated by his demotion, and to resent the fact that he no longer reports directly to the president. These factors may undermine his efficiency greatly.

A third course is to create a sinecure (e.g., Vice President for Manufacturing Coordination), but this is costly and will arouse the resentment of everyone.

There is no single correct answer to such a situation. Your best bet overall is likely to be to get rid of the guy, even though it's painful. At least, once it's over it will eventually be forgotten. If you keep him on, your may just be buying yourself a future of trouble and lost opportunity. Change the scenario a bit, and substitute Chief Engineer, Controller, or Sales Manager for Manufacturing Manager, and you have a drama that occurs in just about every small company sooner or later.

Talent versus Experience

A different consequence of the overhiring dilemma arises from the entrepreneur's own tendency toward insecurity in a new marketplace. It always seems like a surer bet to hire somebody who has been in the industry awhile, or who has a reasonable track record. This applies with particular emphasis to hiring sales personnel.

Your alternative, of course, is simply to hire a very good junior person and hope that he will grow into the position quickly enough to compensate for his lack of experience. If, of course, it were possible to hire someone with both talent *and* experience, the dilemma would never arise. However, in the general case you will be obliged to settle for one or the other.

If it comes to a showdown between talent and experience, you will always be better off to err on the side of talent. The older, more experienced hand may be ideal for some jobs. However, it is more often the case that in the new enterprise his experience becomes a liability, rather than an asset. His previous success may have been a function of the market dominance of his former employer, or of an early product advantage, or of some market condition that no longer applies. To be effective, he may require a full product line, an applications engineering staff, a big ad budget, and a big-company reputation to back up product credibility. You will be unable to support him fully in any of these areas. The junior person, on the other hand, will be out to make his mark. He will be willing to pour in the energy and time needed to develop *your* product, *your* market, *your* company. He will be more disposed to innovate, and to work around the resource limitations inherent in the situation. Finally, even though there may be significant age difference between you, there is likely to be a much better impedance match between employee and president. Both will be in a learning experience. Both will be innovating and improvising. Both should be capable of taking a fresh look at what the competition is doing well and poorly, and at what the market really needs. To avoid creating a case of the blind leading the blind, both should be looking outside the company for some experienced guidance. This can come from directors, from the company godfather, from professional associations or elsewhere. Via this route, hiring a bright junior person can sometimes be much less risky for the company than taking on the person with "many years of experience."

Creating Creative Environments

Endless books, articles, and dissertations have been written on the problem of establishing and maintaining a climate of creativity in the business enterprise. A few of the better examples are to be found in the references to this chapter. However, most begin with the assumption that where creativity is concerned, the more the better. A few irreverent words on this subject may therefore be in order.

Creativity is to the organization what food is to an organism. With too little, it will anguish and die of malnutrition. With too much, it will become bloated, arteriosclerotic, immobile, and will die. As with nourishment in organisms, there is a range of creativity that is somewhat near optimum for a given organization. Business enterprises vary drastically in their capacity to utilize creativity. An aerospace firm, developing space-flight hardware, for example, inherently requires and consumes more ideas than a firm making plumbing supplies. In the former, the ratio of scientists and engineers to direct workers may be one to one. In the latter it may be one to one thousand. (This is not to imply that only scientists and engineers are creative, but merely to indicate a tendency).

In the earliest stages of your venture you will not be troubled with the need to strike this balance. Everyone on the team will be innovating, setting up areas of functional responsibility, and trying to relate them to the needs of the company. Everyone is excited, working hard, and highly motivated. It is precisely this atmosphere of heady involvement, in fact, which permits you to attract still more first-class people. The excitement, involvement, and creativity substitute for the security of the larger employer.

However, as the orders begin to come in, as delivery pressure mounts, and as day-to-day operating problems begin to replace the yeasty excitement of a year ago, you will begin to confront the first real challenge: To maintain an atmosphere of creativity without overdoing it. Your methods for accomplishing this will of necessity change as the company expands in size and changes in character. In general, the larger you get, the harder the task will get.

In a creative environment, ideas are sincerely elicited, evaluated impartially and implemented as warranted, to prove themselves. There is an openness of communication, a minimum of perceptible hierarchy, and a willingness to suspend judgment of the ideas of others until they are fully explained and understood. There is a sharing of power among staff, and a willingness to become involved in problem solution that, strictly speaking, falls outside one's range of immediate responsibility. There is recognition and perhaps tangible reward for the inventor (who thought up the idea) and the innovator (who implemented it).

At the opposite end of the spectrum, the noncreative environment is often characterized by authoritarian innovation from the top down; by an attitude among subordinates that says, "I don't get paid to think about that"; by defensive tactics, not-invented-here attitudes and contests to see who can shoot down the other person's idea first (perhaps in retaliation for the shooting down of one's own pet idea). There is little effort to elicit ideas, and lack of recognition for even those whose ideas are implemented. Efforts to elicit ideas on a single problem in this environment are likely to be regarded as being manipulative.

We will not provide here a long checklist of all the things you can do to maintain a climate of creativity in your firm. The context and personalities dictate almost entirely what will work in a given organization. For hourly people, you may wish to try a suggestion system with cash awards. For professional personnel, try leaving your door open to everybody. Try brainstorming sessions for specific problems (e.g., new product definition). When an idea is implemented, make sure everybody knows about it. Keep criticism for lost sales, missed delivery dates, etc., to a low level—attack your problems, not your people. Try to keep creativity focused on real problems, and on solutions that are affordable and which can realistically be implemented.

The overcreative environment is occasionally found in technology companies—especially those trying to make a transition from consulting or R&D to products. There is positive competition to see who can be the most "creative"; emphasis upon generation of myriads of clever ideas rather than evaluation and practical implementation makes it impossible for anyone to focus on any common objective. The resources of the company become dissipated in the pursuit of too many ideas and as a consequence, none gets carried to complete fruition.

Small-business Types We Can Do Without

The Dead Founder.   Made quite a contribution a few years ago as cofounder, fundraiser, and general go-getter. However, the years and the security of a steady paycheck seem to have robbed him of the vitality and push needed in his area. He's more interested in his boat or his roses than in his company. Subordinates must work around the dead founder to get anything done.

The Empire Builder. Was hired as an expert on some problem area (e.g., quality control), but tends to see his function as the central reason for the company's existence. He is constantly jockeying for more staff, newer equipment, and an enlarged sphere of power. He writes a flood of memos depicting the shortcomings of other departments and underscoring the efficiency and value of his own.

Dragon-Person.   Often a legacy from the past, found in some accounting or administration capacity, wherein his efforts to collect receivables, approve expense accounts, and police budgets seldom fail to patronize and offend customers and coworkers alike. Frequently invokes the old startup days when he and the boss were a real team.

The Sales Eagle.   Came recommended as the top sales executive in the industry. Commands highest salary and incentive package in the firm (including yours). Never fails to speculate on how far he would be now with Collossus Computers, if only he'd stayed there. No shortage of complaints about lack of staff, and budget, our high prices, cheap-looking literature, etc., all of which are adduced in explaining why the sales forecast is consistently missed.

The Technical Wunderkind. Conceptual genius, hired to beef up the original engineering department. Misses no opportunity to show up the incompetence of whoever designed the original product. Frequently throws up hands in despair, refuses to go on with the old design, insisting that a clean new design is the only answer. New design materializes, generally one year late, over budget, and with the meagerest of documentation. Old design still selling well and carrying the company. Old engineers now work for competition.

The Good Hard-Nosed Businessman. When things aren't going well, the normal instinct of investors and directors is to send in the "good hard-nosed businessman," someone of "mature judgment" and "sound principles" (generally someone who knows absolutely nothing about your business). You will be appointed Vice-Chairman. He will join up and within about three days will have cut out the deadwood (i.e., your best young people from the engineering and sales staff). He will then impose daily budget review meetings to get costs under control. He will raise all prices 20 percent to the delight of your competition, and double the service contract fee, to the dismay of your customers. The product will be cheapened up, sales commissions will be reduced, and the ad budget eliminated. If the company survives, it may be due only to his predictably early departure.

Conventional Wisdom. The new firm needs all the creativity it can get—the more the better.

Reality. As with any resource, there is an appropriate level of creativity for every firm.

References

1. Carlin, G. S.: *How to Motivate and Persuade People*, Parker Publishing Co., West Nyack, N.Y., 1964.

   Practical, usable ideas on the entrepreneur's No. 1 problem: Motivating and persuading employees, customers, suppliers, and financial backers.
2. Taylor, Jack W.: *How to Select and Develop Leaders*, McGraw-Hill Co., N.Y., 1962.

This is a fairly good, pragmatic guide to identifying and developing leadership and other talents in your associates and employees.

3. Exton, William, Jr.: *Motivational Leverage: A New Approach to Managing People*, Parker Publishing Co., West Nyack, N.Y., 1975.

Lots of things besides money motivate your people. Find out what.

4. Crosby, Andrew C.: *Creativity and Performance in Industrial Organizations*, Tavistock Publications, N.Y., 1977.

5. Prince, George M.: *The Practice of Creativity: A Manual for Dynamic Group Problem Solving*, Harper and Row, N.Y., 1973.

ACQUIRING AND DIVESTING PEOPLE

"Hell is—other people!"

. . . Jean Paul Sartre

A considerable amount of your personal energies during the first several quarters of operation will be consumed by the establishment and implementation of policies and practices for dealing with personnel. Acquiring and divesting people can be considered among the most highly entrepreneurial of your tasks. To the extent that it is done reasonably well, every other task in the new enterprise will be just that much easier to do. This chapter focuses on some practical considerations to help you do the job well.

Compensation Packages

Beyond the privilege of working in your exciting, creative environment, your prospective employee will be looking for a few other things, including salary, vacation, holidays, sick leave, insurance, stock purchase plans, profit sharing, commissions, bonuses, and perhaps education payment. A few words may be in order on each.

Salary

In establishing an offering salary, do not attempt to induce the employee to accept a salary lower than his market worth by relying on the glamour of the new enterprise or stressing vague future stock benefits. Pay each his full market worth, then use the other intangibles, like stock, to get twice the effort from him for the money. It's O.K. for the founding group to operate on partial salaries for a while to conserve cash or enhance operating profits, but it's totally unrealistic to expect a first-rate man to come on board as an employee for less than his worth. Various state manpower surveys, as well as personnel managers of other firms, can give you guidance in setting salaries, if you're in doubt.

Vacation, sick leave, holidays

Your vacation policy will probably be dictated for you by the practices of the region you're in. At the outset, forget about plans that increase the vacation time as tenure reaches 10, then 20 years. Your principal decision in this regard will be whether to have a two-week plant shutdown each year, or whether to permit staggered or partial vacations for your people. Holidays and sick leave policies will also be dictated to a large degree by the practices of the area in which you're recruiting.

Insurance

The immediate need is for some form of group medical coverage, just as soon as you qualify. It is much better to start at least a modest plan with high deductibles and minimal benefits than risk having anybody wiped out financially by medical costs. Start out with the company paying only a fraction of the cost, then build up this fraction (with suitable fanfare) as the company matures. Many medical packages can be supplemented with a small amount of life insurance (say, one year's salary). Such term life insurance is rather inexpensive and should be considered, since many of your non-professional people will have no other personal life insurance.

It may be that your group is too small to qualify for attractive rates of group insurance plans. If this is the case, you may be able to find trade associations, professional societies, local business associations or even pooled-insurance groups who, by offering coverage to all their members, can themselves qualify for group rates from the insurer. However obtained, this coverage is the most fundamental obligation of the employer, and should be obtained as promptly as circumstances permit.

Stock Purchase Plans

Where small companies are concerned, everybody wants a piece of the action. Since the subject is going to come up virtually every time you interview somebody for a professional job, it is desirable to have the policy for nonfounder stock purchase worked out and committed to writing in advance of recruiting. Stock purchase and stock option plans abound, but they have only one purpose: To motivate *those within the company.* They act as an incentive to those who are working to earn them; they act as a double incentive to those who already have them. Your attorney will be able to review for you the several types of restricted stock option plans, their business benefits and tax characteristics.

Try to design a plan sufficiently flexible that you will not have to abandon it in the first exceptional situation. Make sure that each new employee "earns" his way in—don't include stock as part of an initial offer.

Be concrete on the subject of stock. Don't make vague promises that you would be unwilling to put in writing, and be certain that stock purchase privileges are related to performance in an agreed-upon way.

Profit-Sharing Plan

Forget it. It will be a long time before there are any profits to share. It will be longer yet before there is excess cash to pay out on a plan. Therefore, its existence will only create disappointed employees.

Bonuses and Commissions

Bonuses may be among the best managerial tools available to the small-company president. The bonus may be cash or merchandise (which should, nonetheless, be declared as income by its recipient). It should be offered to motivate accomplishment of a specific task outside the employee's normal job expectations: i.e., getting 20 new dealers reunited by June; solving the electrical interface problem in the system; reducing accounts receivable from 80 to 40 days. Avoid getting trapped by paying a Christmas or year-end bonus to all employees. Today's privilege has a way of becoming tomorrow's birthright. Concentrate on task-specific achievements.

The awarding of a bonus should be accompanied by recognition and fanfare as an example to all.

Commissions are the classical way to motivate performance among salespeople, and of keeping your costs variable. The smaller company should have high commission rates with the lowest tolerable salary structure.

Finally, a suggestion system, together with cash bonuses related to the savings from the suggestion, can be an excellent way to maintain morale in the operating departments, while taking advantage of people's inherent creativity. Even the sweeper probably has some idea that could save you plenty.

Education Payments

In a new company, especially a technology venture, some of your employees will be disposed toward continuing their education in work-related fields. Even small companies find that the cost of partial or complete tuition reimbursement is often justified as a recruiting incentive and as a way of upgrading the abilities of people on the job. In some geographic areas it may, in fact, be a virtual competitive necessity.

Other Benefits

You may find that certain other employee benefits may be very popular without adding much actual cost. These include vesting savings plans, credit unions, sports, parties, and luncheon facilities. It is very easy to go overboard in this department—especially when you, the boss, are expected to show up for the bowling tournament! However, don't underestimate the importance of these things to your people, especially among the nonprofessionals of the company. In this area, it is often best for everyone if the initiatives come from the employees themselves.

One area in which you can compete with large local firms very favorably is in the area of workhours. Increasingly, people want to control their work schedules, and you may be able to accommodate this desire at little or no cost. You should consider:

1. *Four-Day Week.* Typically, this involves a ten-hour workday, with half the firm getting off Fridays and half Mondays. And, if some employees prefer the five-day week, you can readily accommodate them, too.

2. *Flextime.* Flextime has been pioneered in Europe. It permits the employee to set his own starting and quitting times, provided he is present during a five-hour "core period." This is especially popular among those with long commutes.

3. *Mothers' Hours.* Consider a short day, say five hours, permitting employees to leave home after the children have left for school and to arrive home before they do. This is also a help for one-car families, as it permits one spouse to drive the other to and from work.

4. *Employ Retired People.* One of the best sources of talent and experience in any community is retired people. A retired inspector, draftsman, toolmaker, bookkeeper, or other skilled person can work a few hours per week and contribute a great deal to the growing firm and at very modest cost.

Recruiting

Now you have it all together: a hot company, a creative working environment, and a well-thought-out compensation package. Now, how do you find a prospective employee?

Your tactics in finding good prospects will, of course, depend upon the job to be filled. However, try to exercise the lowest-cost sources first, as recruitment *can* be very costly. The following are places you can advertise for employees, in order of ascending cost:

1. *School Placement Bureaus.* Colleges, technical institutes, secretarial schools, and vocational high schools all maintain offices both for the placement of new graduates and for alumni changing jobs. If you're looking for technicians, don't overlook Job Corps and similar community or government-sponsored training and retraining programs.

2. *Signs.* A conspicuous sign on your plant for nonprofessional help may net you some candidates, and it is an indication of company growth to outsiders.

3. *Professional Societies.* A low-cost notice in the society journal, newsletter, or bulletin board at the annual convention can net you many prospective employees. There are also, at time of writing, some loose federations of unemployed technical professionals, which may become permanent placement agencies.

4. *Government Employment Agencies.* State governments offer placement services for both professional and nonprofessional people, at no cost to users.

5. *Firms Known to be Laying Off.* The placement director of such firms will be glad to hear from you, although you must realize that the best employees are not the first to be let go. This nonetheless can be a good source of leads.

6. *Newspaper Advertising.* This is not inexpensive, especially when pursued in national publications such as the *Wall Street Journal*, *Electronic News*, etc. However, it can be quite effective, since the newspaper is the first place a person looking around will look at—it costs him nothing in effort or commitment to anybody to look at the paper. Even if he's still employed, your ad may just spark the desire to make a change. You need not be splashy with your ad, but it should be large enough to convey a reasonable amount of information and the impression of substance.

7. *Personnel Agencies.* Private agencies vary in quality from lousy to excellent. They also vary in the types of personnel they are effective at recruiting. One way in which they are alike, however, is expense. None is cheap. For a secretary, the fee might be two weeks' salary; for an engineer or a manager, it could be one to two months'

salary. As soon as you run an advertisement in the papers, you may be beseiged by agencies who have "just the man for the job." Your best strategy is to keep them at bay until you're sure the other sources are not going to come through for you. Then, do some inquiring and visit the agency. Some will engage in some limited search in your behalf—others will just fire off resumes of everybody in their files. Instead of a mechanical engineer, you may end up reading the resume of a locomotive engineer!

8. *Personnel Search Agencies.* Now you're talking about real money. The professional headhunters usually don't operate on a results basis—they generally want a retainer fee, and maybe a commission, too. They are normally employed by larger companies in filling the higher management posts. The headhunter tries to find the top three or four people in the field, then approaches them discreetly in behalf of his unnamed client. This probably is not a recruitment channel available or appropriate to most new ventures.

Interviewing

Once you've lavished money, energy, and time in trying to find suitable candidates, it's a pity to blow it all in the interview. Yet this is precisely what happens in an unnecessarily large number of instances. The prospect gets rejected for the wrong reasons, hired for the wrong reasons, or gets an offer that is not accepted.

Employment interviewing is a subject about which a good deal is known. A couple of better references on the subject are listed at the end of this chapter. It is probably well worth your while as a company president to spend a long evening reading some of this material, and developing a more or less formal interview strategy. By so doing, you'll learn a lot more about the candidate, you'll avoid missing any critical areas, and you'll do a much better job of selling your company to the person you want.

The New Employee

In addition to the normal procedural details of signing up for health plans, withholding, etc., your new employee should be asked to sign an invention disclosure agreement. If this is not among the first things he signs coming on board, you will have great difficulty in getting him to sign it later—especially if he has been working in your firm's R&D function and has made some valuable discovery! One of the first actions of the startup company president should be to work with the attorney and develop a suitable agreement of this type for all appropriate employees. To delay it is an invitation to downstream problems.

Although few new companies have a formal training program

of any sort, there should be a single individual responsible for the training of the new recruit, and you should commit to writing the exact steps which will be taken to integrate the new employee into the organization. For a production person, this might include familiarization with company rules, policy, production methods, workmanship standards, and related information. For a new controller, it would perhaps include exposure to the Operating Business Plan, familiarization with the existing accounting system and financial history of the company, and orientation with regard to major customers and vendors.

In small companies, it is often difficult to write satisfactory job descriptions, because after a while in the firm people tend to structure the job to suit themselves. One of the strengths of the small business environment is, in fact, the ability to accommodate itself to the skills and interests of the individual employees, to a degree not possible in the large firm. Nonetheless, it is very necessary that the president be sure that a job description is in fact written for *every* position to be filled. This description, in addition to describing the job to be done immediately, should describe the directions of growth, the responsibilities and functions which might be added to the job. It should specify the minimum, desired, and optimal qualifications that a successful candidate should have. Although it may need modification in the future, such a description is absolutely necessary for several obvious reasons: It helps management decide if an employee is needed at all (a question that sometimes doesn't even get asked!), how to budget for the job, how to advertise the position, and how to communicate about the job with the candidate. It also helps to establish the performance criteria for the new employee.

Divesting People

One of the least pleasant experiences of the entrepreneur is getting rid of people who (a) haven't performed as expected, or (b) must be jettisoned in a company cutback. Most entrepreneurs encounter the first case fairly often, and the second at least once in the first two to four years of operation. These two cases are sufficiently different to warrant some individual comment.

The Low Performer

Most entrepreneurs seem to put off the inevitable long past the point where it is obvious that a particular person is not going to make it. There may be pressure to "give Joe just one more chance." There may be extenuating circumstances which could "explain" his lack of performance. There may be some areas in which he's doing a good job, and with some more help he may improve. Forget it. You're only kidding yourself. You are telling yourself that you're being humane, being fair. However, in reality, you *know* the guy isn't going to make it. So you're only sparing yourself the discomfort of acting.

When you do act, it should be decisive and clean. Repeated warnings, probationary periods, etc., probably just prolong the agony. If a visibly low performer stays around, you damage the morale of the entire team and, worse, handicap the functional area for which he is responsible. Give him his notice (usually two weeks), but tell him that he should use the two weeks to look for a job. (You do *not* want a person who's been fired around the plant or office for two weeks.)

In your termination interview, try to be fair. Tell him why he's being terminated. Spare the soft soap (e.g., "You're just overqualified for our job."). Help him to understand where he went off the track, so he can find a more appropriate opening or operational method in the future. He won't be grateful, but at least he won't spend the rest of his life wondering why he was fired. To help ease the transition, you should make sure that his medical insurance is extended to cover his interval of unemployment. You should steer him toward state agencies for personnel placement, unemployment insurance, and other benefits to which he may be entitled. You may be able to suggest companies you are aware are hiring, or job training programs that can help him in his areas of weakness. In short, by helping to make the best of his opportunities, you are doing him a much bigger favor than you would by keeping him on for a few more months.

The Cutback

This situation is much worse than the low performer. The company has hit some rough sailing—maybe a business recession. Now you are obliged to terminate not only some marginal people, but also some people who have been doing a good job. And you may be putting them on the street at the very time that other firms are laying off, too (as, for example, during the recession of 1969–70). This is the sort of thing ulcers are made of.

Just deciding who's going to be thrown out of the boat to lighten the load is a difficult process. You should probably not even discuss it with your partners in the office, since rumors have a way of starting—particularly when business conditions have everyone apprehensive anyway—and of undermining morale and performance, thereby worsening a bad situation. Your main job is to make the cuts without demolishing the morale of the remaining troops. This is a challenge, to say the least.

While emerging business conditions may make this impossible, you should strive to make your total cut at once, as opposed to a few every Friday. The effect will be stunning, but will challenge those remaining to close ranks and try to get the job done without the people who have gone. In the other case, everyone will be wondering all week if he's going to be the next to go. Your less effective people will start digging in and mounting defensive tactics. Your better people will start looking around, and some of them may find other jobs and leave. The net result is that the initiative is taken away from you, the morale of the team is undermined, and the best people leave or wish they could. Make your blood-letting as clean, brief, and complete as possible.

You can take the same steps to assist the victims as you did for the low performer. In addition, you may wish to call up the personnel directors of other employers in the area, and let them know who is available. If the cutbacks are largely regional, you may be able to make contact with firms in other areas, too. If the cutback is the result of a severe recession, there may be special agencies established for counseling jobseekers, to which you can refer the terminated employee.

In all, this is not a happy experience for entrepreneurs. The fact that almost everybody has to face it sooner or later may be some consolation.

A Note on the Personnel Function

In the small company the function of personnel management tends to be an orphan for quite a while. Just the management of employee records, withholding statements, preemployment medical exams, coordination of health insurance claims, etc., can be a substantial burden. If you're very lucky, you may find a secretary or accounting clerk whose inclinations tend in this direction. If so, give him the job, and fill in with other work. The person who handles time sheets and payroll may be a good choice for the responsibility, to prevent wide dispersion of salary or other personal data. Just be sure somebody is responsible for the whole job.

Fairly early in your growth, you should develop a personnel manual that deals with every phase of employment, including rules, policies, benefits, and patent policy. The easiest way to do a good job on this is to get somebody else's, and edit it to suit your needs.

Conventional Wisdom. Small companies have limited resources, so people expect to earn a little less.

Reality. Small companies have limited resources (and benefits) so people expect to earn a little more.

References

1. Black, J. M.: *How to Get Results from Interviewing*, McGraw-Hill Co., N.Y., 1970.

   This is a very practical guide to planning interview strategy. Covers specific cases such as hiring, promotion, discipline, and exit.

2. Hariton, Theodore: *Interview! The Executive's Guide to Selecting the Right Personnel*, Hastings House Publishing Co., N.Y., 1970.

   This is an excellent guide to hiring interviews. Very practical, incorporating suggested forms and interview formats. "Must" reading.

3. O'Neal, F. H.: *Expulsion or Oppression of Business Associates: "Squeeze-outs" in Small Enterprises*, Duke University, N.C., 1961.

   One of the few books on a delicate topic: How to be a successful squeezer, or avoid being a squeezee.

4. Peter, Lawrence J., and Hull, Raymond: *The Peter Principle*, Bantam Books, N.Y., Wm. More and Co., 1970.

   How to tell when you've reached your level of incompetence.

MARKETING IV

Chapter 18

SELLING

"Nothing happens until you get a purchase order."

. . . Anonymous

Selling is the central activity of the business enterprise. If you have this ability, you will always be able to find a useful product to sell; if you have only the ability to engineer or produce products, you may be a bankruptcy looking for someplace to happen. The value of selling is often driven home to manufacturers in a dismaying but forceful way: The firm selling its output through an independent sales organization (such as Sears, Roebuck; Radio Shack; J.C. Penney) usually at some point realizes that the selling organization is making much higher gross margins and net profits than the manufacturer. Is this unfair, or merely the marketplace placing a proper valuation on the function of selling?

Image versus Reality

In the very earliest phases of company growth, there will be a great divergence between the image you wish to project to the market and the actual substance to back it up. It is doubly important at this phase that your actions, statements, literature, and advertising do not bespeak an amateur, unprofessional or fly-by-night operation. We have addressed this issue in Chapter 5 with regard to the

149

preparation of initial literature. However, it applies to other phases of your selling efforts as well.

Most of your customers and prospective customers will never see more of your company than your salespeople, advertisements, documentation, and products. Most will not see your plant, your beautiful lobby and conference room, and your spiffy shop. This is fortunate. Remember, although the plant may be a source of great pride to you, it still looks pretty small-time to a visitor from IBM considering your product. Be sure that the things he *does* see are not small-time. You want him to have the impression of a solid, growing company that is going to be around to back up its products, to supply his future needs, and to be a source of pride for him if your product is included in his. Remember that the buyer feels his neck is out a mile if he's purchasing from you, rather than from your much larger competitor. Poor literature, clumsy presentation, and improvised product documentation only add to his inherent sense of uneasiness. Do these things *right* even if it costs a few dollars. They are as much a part of your product as the hardware itself.

Literature. Be sure that it looks at least as good as your best competitor's. List a variety of models, options, accessories, even if they aren't ready for delivery yet.

Find a designer to work with you, by looking at other firms' good literature and finding out who does it.

Stress user benefits, not specifications. Stress only the specifications that matter, that set you apart from the competition. Use only first-rate photography and be sure your diagrams and art say "professional." Use cutaway drawings to show unique function and consider cartoons to illustrate user benefits. Remember, color sells. Design your brochure with an integral, tearoff return card. Don't forget your phone number and leave room for dealers or reps to add their sticker. Finally, an "800" phone number is often a help in eliciting responses and can be obtained very inexpensively via answering services.

In addition to product literature, one of the things a small firm can do better than anyone is to write the bible for the industry. This can be anywhere from four to 100 pages long, and could describe the technology, the applications, the economics, the benefits, the alternative ways of using the product, the accessories—the unabridged story. The Digital Equipment Corporation Logic Handbook was for many years the chief exemplar of this type of sales aid. Once it exists, the bible can be the subject of press releases, free giveaway offers, trade-show handout, and training aid for schools and seminars. Consider, where would Christianity be without *its* main sales tool— The Bible?

Pricing and Price Lists. Try to stay within the conventions of the industry, at least initially. You should use the same methods of discounting, commercial terms, and so on that your customer is accustomed to. Don't try to innovate initially.

Advertising. If you can't justify the cost of competing at a respectable level with your competitors, consider deferring magazine advertising altogether. Or use the occasional big ad with less frequency, hitting the annual buyer's guide issues, etc. Try some innovation instead. Use some direct mailings, telephone solicitation, recorded cassette pitches, and demonstration van. Think of ways to make yourself appear more *innovative* than your competitor.

Promotion. This is the area in which you can shine, at reasonable cost. Create lots of press releases on new products, new developments, new building, new contracts, and new overseas agents. Write articles for the trade press and the popular press. Present papers at society meetings. Hold application seminars at strategic locations around the country, and invite the press as well as customers. You can come off looking much better than a less ambitious competitor.

Product Documentation. Be sure that your operation manuals, instruction sheets, and maintenance manuals are up to the standards of the industry. Nothing makes an expensive, engineered product look sillier than sending a blueprint of a circuit diagram instead of a professional looking manual. This documentation is *part* of your product. Treat it accordingly.

Advertising Agencies

It is probable that at the outset at least you do not need a regular ad agency. What you *do* need is, ideally, a part-time artist and layout person who has worked for an agency. You need good advice and good art in designing letterheads, logo, literature, and perhaps occasional ads. Your designer also can be helpful in the design of trade show exhibits and visual aids for speeches. Find the right person for this role and you will save yourself thousands of dollars and untold aggravation.

As your company progresses and an advertising agency appears justified, do some shopping. Some will want to take over your whole marketing effort. Others will want to push for big, commissionable magazine ad budgets. Some will want to give you a whole funky new image. What you want is a small, hard-working, cost-conscious and practical agency that will do what *you* want at a price you can afford. And even then, you will want to keep some of the work with your part-time person—especially literature, which requires some continuity of appearance.

Your agency may also wish to handle your public relations and publicity. This is seldom a good idea, because editors and reporters like to talk to the president. Moreover, product releases and stories written by you will be much easier to generate, cheaper, and better in quality. Just be sure it gets done.

Pricing

The pricing of your product offers opportunity for many commonly committed errors. Here are some of them:

1. Basing pricing on cost of manufacture, rather than on value to customer. Engineers are particularly prone to price new products on "cost-plus-overhead-plus-profit" formulas, neglecting the fact that the product may be worth far more to the user.

2. Basing pricing on present low overheads, rather than projecting into the future to see how the overheads will grow.

3. Failing to include allowance for warranty costs, future servicing, design amortization, application engineering, cost of capital, etc.

4. Assuming that because you are the newest firm in the field, you must of necessity have the lowest prices to get established. Your product strategy might, on the contrary, be to build the Cadillac of the industry, leaving the larger volume sales to other competitors.

5. Failure to even estimate the demand elasticity for the product. How much *would* sales volume increase if prices were lowered 10 or 20 percent? Is your product unique enough to command a premium over others if you increase the price? Finally, what is your *maximum profit* volume, given the price-volume curve?

6. Failure to employ some version of "market skimming"— starting off with a high price until demand is saturated, then lowering the price gradually. This way, in theory at least, each person gets a chance to pay his maximum price for the product.

High pricing has its perils for the new company, like any other prescriptive measure. For example, if your prices and profits are outrageously high, you may be inviting early competition that would not otherwise enter your market. Remember, too, that your latecomer competitor will have little of the market research, product development, and lost-motion cost that you incurred, so he will be in a position to cut your prices substantially.

This factor notwithstanding, the burden of proof is definitely on the low, rather than the high price in a new business venture. It's a lot easier to lower prices if you err on the high side than the other way around.

Continuous Market Research

In Chapter 4, we treated the development of a first-cut market research project which would have a specific result for fund-raising efforts. However, market research does not end there; it is a continuous process in which the president is subliminally engaged all the time. Observing needs that the company can fill; scanning the literature for new developments: pricing trends, competitor actions, and availability of customer funding; acquiring customers or competitors—these are all ways in which the company president must tune himself to signals from the marketplace. In addition, the company may be engaged in a series of more or less continuous formal market analyses for products you are contemplating introducing. Scanning *all* the relevant periodicals; travelling to visit customers; working with salesmen; attending trade shows and professional meetings, and trade fairs are the principal means of staying open to market intelligence. Do not permit your new sales manager to isolate you from contact with the customer, with salesmen, or reps. These are your communication lines with reality. Guard them jealously.

Building a Rep Organization

Independent sales representatives are the marketing backbone of many industries. For present purposes, let us also include in this category agents, discount dealers, jobbers, and others who sell your products without actually being on your payroll.

Unless reps are completely unsuitable or unavailable for your product, you will wish to consider using reps as your initial sales organization. The advantages and disadvantages of reps as opposed to direct salesmen are as follows:

Advantages

1. The rep requires no fixed cost. Reps get paid only when they make a sale. Dealers who stock your product pay in advance as a rule. Both effects greatly enhance the cash flow and minimize the capital requirements of the small company.

2. The rep has knowledge of territory and prospective customers.

3. A rep may have several reasons to visit a prospect (i.e., several product lines of interest). Thus his frequency of contact per customer may be higher than that of your own salesman.

4. He may have special capabilities to offer you or your customer, such as installation and repair services, application engineering, and stocking against special needs.

5. He may be conducting his own advertising and promotion efforts and be willing to share in the costs of advertising your product in his territory.

Disadvantages

1. Most reps have a lot of lines but devote most of their energies to selling one or two established, bread-and-butter lines.

2. A rep may not push even a successful line too hard, for fear that the company may decide to replace him with a direct salesman at lower total cost.

3. Many reps can function effectively only as finders, and require a great deal of factory personnel support to actually close a sale.

4. Reps are difficult to monitor, train, and motivate. The successful reps may lack the time, and the unsuccessful ones the inclination, to work intensively with you in building up your market.

Despite the disadvantages, however, reps give the young company a running start on the market. They represent the only way that many small firms can even consider establishing national marketing in the first year of operation.

Identifying and Recruiting Reps

There are several more or less orthodox ways to identify possible reps. The first is through searching in trade directories. Although these are often out of date, due to frequent changes of line (and identity) among reps, directories can tell you what reps are in a given area, what types of lines they handle, and what types of customers they service. You may be able to find the reps of your competitor or of a maker of complementary products. Identification can also proceed through associations of reps and dealers. These may be national (e.g., the Electronic Representatives Association) or local rep organizations. Chambers of commerce, at both city and state levels, often maintain lists of reps and agents as well. Also, if you can identify a friendly manufacturer of complementary products, you can simply call his sales manager and inquire whether they have a good rep in Dayton. He may welcome the chance to pool data with you.

Recruitment normally begins with a phone call or a letter, outlining your product, your company, your prospects in the rep's territory. If he's not interested, he can often tell you who else to talk to. If he is, your next step is a visit to his office. Ideally, this visit should include scheduling two or three actual sales calls to prospective customers in the territory. This gives you some opportunity to assess his contacts and his selling approach, while at the same time *he* can calibrate customers' interest in your product. Since you've gone to the trouble and expense of visiting the rep, don't leave without making the direct sales calls. If he seems reluctant, this may tell you something, too.

Before signing up a rep, you should both have some understanding as to the range of sales volume that you might realistically expect from the territory for the ensuing several quarters. He may be a much better judge of this than you are. You will also want a signed contract. These are normally quite informal; reps and other sales managers are a good source of samples. Finally, you should check him out with his other principals as well as with some of his local customers.

Succeeding with Reps

Recruiting a rep organization is one thing; making it a success is another. The initial blush of enthusiasm wanes quickly on both sides, as the hard digging of actually building sales begins in earnest. You both are destined for a number of disappointments. You may think he personally flubbed the biggest contract you've gone after yet. He may seem to be always and forever requesting some non-standard product modification, or unrealistic price concession. *He* may think *you're* an idiot because you wouldn't promise to deliver fast enough to get the order. He will probably consider your company unresponsive to market needs. In short, there are many more opportunities for the relationship to run awry than to run smoothly. The smart president will anticipate this and work hard to make the relationship work. Here are some things you can do:

1. Contact every rep once a week, by phone or in person, even if there's no pressing reason to do so. Ask what's going on, and how you can help.

2. Supply plenty of sales leads for him to follow. Don't oblige him to go sit in the lobby and talk cold to purchasing managers (most reps won't anyway). This is one important function of your advertising/promotion program.

3. Give him a decent sales manual. Don't force him to rely only on your data sheets and price lists. Include applications notes, competitive comparisons, glossy product photos, including "inside the box" shots. Give him sales arguments. List the possible objections and the counterarguments. Give him a list of happy users for cus-

tomer reference. Provide reprints of impressive journal articles. In short, give him all the ammunition you can think of—he's your man in the trenches and he needs it.

4. Try gimmicks to keep reps informed and keep their attention. A newsletter, describing new company developments, product of the month, *Rep* of the month, sales volumes, etc., can be inexpensive and effective. Send him copies of all the press release packages you send the press. Try sales contests, prizes, incentives, "this-month-only" discounts, or double commissions on specific products you want to push. Let them know you're alive. Remember, you're competing for his time with all his other principal companies.

5. Get someone out in the field to work with him. Be ready to jump on a plane when the call for help comes. Be prepared to close the first few orders yourself. Support him when he needs support. Take an occasional swing through the country and work with each rep. Get on a first-name basis with all his salespeople.

6. Follow up your sales leads. Keep your own lists, find out politely but firmly what he's done on each of them. Let him know you appreciate his follow-up, and are interested in the unsuccessful quotations as well as the hot ones.

7. Pay your commissions on time. Nothing throws cold water on a rep relationship faster than unpaid commissions. Some companies, when they get in a cash crunch, include commissions in the deferrable expense category. You could not make a bigger mistake. Loss of a key rep can cripple a company for many quarters. You'd be better off laying off a few plant personnel than risk the dissolution of your sales organization.

8. Have an annual sales meeting at the plant. Put on the dog a bit. Let the reps pay their transportation, but you pay hotels and meals. Let them meet all your people and see your plant. Have some sales sessions, some technical sessions, and some gripe sessions. Work on specific problems individually. In short. let them become a part of your team—this, basically, is what good reps *want* to do.

9. Deliver on your product promises. Nothing gets the rep in hot water faster than late delivery, improper operation, balky warranty service, or other forms of bungling by the factory. He *must believe* that the product he sells is going to be the answer to his customers' prayers. If he believes anything less, your chances of getting sales are seriously compromised. If, as is often the case in a small company, the rep has a very souring experience with you, you may want to get rid of him, even though he has not resigned. Once his confidence has been damaged, it may not be possible by ten successes to restore it.

Remember, he needs the long-term goodwill of those big firms in his territory a whole lot more than he needs you. When the chips are down, he'll be forced to side with his customer and find a better source for the product he wants.

10. Try to avoid "house" accounts. Nothing is more demoralizing to a rep, even if he initially agreed to it, than to see large shipments going into his territory without commission to him. Even if he understands it, he will never appreciate it—especially if it's a company he has to call on for other principals anyway. On your part, it may be tempting to exclude a fat customer you've already developed on your own from the first rep that comes along. A reasonable compromise may be to offer the rep the house account as soon as his volume from other customers passes an agreed-upon target, say $200,000. Then he has a great incentive, and you are not risking handing over a commission check each month to a do-nothing rep. Or, some would argue, you want ideally to *give* the rep enough volume at the outset to make your line one of his most important— another way to command a major portion of his energies.

Beyond Reps

It is commonly believed that the direct sales force is always the best way to sell. Salaried salespeople are, it is argued, easier to control and motivate, have no conflicting loyalties, are able to spend full time on your product and, when volume passes breakeven, are cheaper. These are persuasive arguments. However, there are many companies with the volume, cash flow, and profits to sustain direct sales forces who stay with reps exclusively, and there are many more who use a mixture of reps and salesmen. So the jury is still out on this question. Or, more accurately, there is a profit-maximizing mix in each case, depending upon the product, rep quality, market characteristics, and other variables. For this reason you should carefully assess the question of whether to replace all reps as soon as possible with direct people. It is just possible that that nice breakeven volume may follow your old rep to your competitor's organization.

A realistic intermediate step is the establishment of regional offices, each a one-man operation initially, charged with coordinating sales and service for a specified territory. The regional manager can then work directly with your reps in the territory, recruit and train his own reps or, perhaps, handle some of the territory on a direct sales basis himself. Through this route, your move toward national marketing is advanced one large step further without foreclosing *any* options. Finally, when and if the time comes for additional direct salespeople, you have the framework in existence for their deployment and supervision.

Your Job as Cheerleader

As Napoleon Bonaparte observed, an army marches on its stomach. In precisely the same sense, a sales organization marches on its heart (or transverse colon, or whatever other organ is used to store enthusiasm and morale). *You*—nobody else—are the sparkplug whom everyone is looking to for the zeal, the confidence, and the incentive to get out of bed in the morning and face some hostile customers, traffic jams, a lobbyful of competitors, and the various snarl-ups that enrich the salesman's day. You are permanent cheerleader, morale officer, and chaplain rolled up in one. You must be accessible to reps, salespeople, and regional managers. You must show them that *sales*—not engineering, not accounting, not manufacturing—comes first in your outfit.

You must be willing to put your hand in the fire occasionally to add conviction to your rhetoric. You're the one who has to whip up enthusiasm for the new product, the new lower prices, the new demonstrator van. You're the one who has to head off delivery trouble, take over negotiations with problem customers, and authorize special concessions to meet competition. Likewise, you are the one who must set the sales goals and enlist the commitment of all concerned with reaching those goals. You're the one responsible for seeing that the successful salesman or rep receives more than a paycheck or a commission check—that he also receives recognition from everyone in your organization. Or, if warranted, a cordial kick in the tailfeathers. Salesmen are supposed to be self-starters, but it is nevertheless incumbent on you to be sure that the ignition key gets turned.

Selling Can Be Learned

Even the entrepreneur who is not a great natural salesman can learn a good deal about the art of selling, without long costly trial-and-error education. Much is known about selling, since people have been doing it for so long. Regardless of the market you serve, it is likely that there exists some sales course, weekend workshop, or seminar related more or less directly to your situation. These may be run by colleges, by the SBA, by the American Marketing Association chapter, the local representatives' association, etc. It is not beneath your dignity to enroll in such a course, or even to insist that your salespeople or partners do also. It is almost certain that you will gain some different perspective, insight, or usable ideas from the experience, as well as getting a chance to meet other sales people with problems comparable to your own.

You can also learn a good deal by studying the marketing

methods of companies that have been successful, and from talking to their executives to gain some understanding of *why* they did what they did. The president of another growing firm, perhaps a stage or two ahead of your own, can be a good sounding board for marketing and other ideas.

Conventional Wisdom.   Sell, sell, sell.

Reality.   *Sell, sell, sell.*

References

1. Haas, K. B., and Ernest, J. W.: *Creative Salesmanship: Understanding Essentials*, Beverly Hills, Calif., The Glencoe Press, 1969.

   This is a practical, though academically respectable, treatment of the entire topic of selling. It gives a particularly good treatment of buyer psychology and closing techniques.

2. Kotler, Philip: *Marketing Management, Analysis, and Control*, Prentice-Hall, Englewood Cliffs, N.J., 1967.

   A very good basic marketing text covering each phase clearly and completely. Could be considered a reference work for the new president.

3. DeVoe, Merril: *How to Tailor Your Sales Organization to Your Markets*, Prentice-Hall, Englewood Cliffs, N.J., 1964.

   Very pragmatic, how-to-do-it information on organizing, recruiting, and motivating a sales team. Very good.

4. Steinkamp, W. H.: *How to Sell and Market Industrial Products*, Chilton Book Co., Philadelphia, Penn., 1970.

   Similar in level and competence to DeVoe's book, but focused on the industrial product

5. Levitt, Theodore: *The Marketing Note: Pathways to Corporate Growth*, McGraw-Hill Inc., N.Y., 1969.

   A long essay on marketing innovative products, by one of the most innovative marketing minds on the American scene.

6. Gissel, P.: *Launching the New Industrial Product*, American Management Association, N.Y., 1979

   This is brief and very practical, although directed more toward the established firm. It will tell you how you should do it if you had the people, money, and established market momentum.

7. Roth, C. B.: *Treasury of Sure-Fire Selling Tips*, Prentice-Hall, Englewood Cliffs, N.J., 1960.

   This is a typical specimen of the pep-rally, "Yes you can" school of literature for salesmen. May give you some ideas on training salesmen to plan sales calls, and follow them up for maximum effect.

8. Smyth, Richard C., and Murphy, Matthew J.: *Compensating and Motivating Salesmen*, American Management Association Inc., N.Y., 1969.

Very practical handbook for designing compensation packages, measurement, sales contests, and other motivators. Includes several excellent specimen agreements.

9. Krause, Wm. H.: *How to Hire and Motivate Manufacturers' Representatives*, AMACOM, N.Y., 1976.

Written by a sales rep, this is the best practical resource I have seen on the subject.

Chapter
19

THE CUSTOMER

*"It is naught, it is naught, saith the buyer: but when he is gone
his way, then he boasteth."*

. . . Proverbs 20:14

The customer is, by definition, someone who needs what you
can supply. He is the only reason for the existence of your business.
Your greatest challenge will be to identify him, analyze his needs,
and satisfy his requirements.

Identifying Customers

Before your Business Plan was even put to bed, you had a list
of prospective customers for your product. These were people
whom you had surveyed, people known to be buying similar products, and people surmised to require your product. Now, however,
you are in the marketplace, have rung all those doorbells, and
closed a few sales. What now? To build up a dynamic list of prospective, qualified customers is a big job. To keep it current and
keep the deadbeats off it is a bigger job yet. Among your tools will
be:

1. *Leads from advertising.* Readers' service ("bingo") card replies
require further qualification, via return mail or phone contact with
respondents. Direct letter replies and telephone contacts originating
from advertising are among your best leads. Returns from direct

mail campaigns are likely to be of higher quality, especially if the respondent must supply some data on his needs.

2. *Leads from Trade Shows.* These may be readily qualified on the spot by the employee who talked to the prospect. The prospect has also had the advantage, in most cases, of having seen actual hardware at the show, further qualifying himself.

3. *Leads from Trade Directories.* If your product is bought mainly by hospitals with intensive care units, for example, you can readily find most of your prospects in a directory. If it is bought by people who own sports cars, you probably can't. Between these extremes lie many classes of customers, who can often be reached and qualified by mail, through lists extracted from trade directories.

4. *Personal Knowledge of Reps and Employees.* This may be among your most valuable sources of prospects because it has already been prescreened.

5. *Self-Identification.* The Commerce Business Daily, advertisements soliciting proposals, form letters sent to suppliers, and government solicitations from firms on bidders' lists are some examples of this.

6. *Leads from "Data Bases."* This is similar to the directory approach, but may permit greater pinpointing starting from a bigger sample. For example, the Dun and Bradstreet tapes might permit you to do a direct mailing to every firm performing ferrous casting operations with over 50 employees, in the eastern half of the U.S.

As your list of prospects grows, it can become a mailing list for direct mailing pieces, company announcements, newsletters, new literature, and price lists. Try to reach your list on a regular (say monthly) basis, just as you try to contact each rep weekly. Make it a habit to let them hear from you. Be sure that the reps have all the names for their territory, so they can follow through. Try to keep the list in two sections: the mass list, and the "top hundred." Keep it current. Make its maintenance the special responsibility of one person in the company.

Analyzing Customer Needs

In some businesses (e.g., ball bearings) the customer's requirements are rather straightforward (he needs ball bearings). In other cases, however, it isn't so easy. In most capital equipment decisions, for example, there may be several equally feasible definitions of need. If a customer wishes, for example, to improve his accounting procedures, he may "need" a computer, or a time-sharing service, or a bookkeeping service bureau, or an accounting machine, or maybe he just needs a better accountant. If your firm sells computers, it is immediately incumbent upon you to determine whether your computer really *is* the way to solve his problem. If you think it might be, then your problem is to convince him that (a) he needs a computer, and (b) he needs *your* computer. In other words, you have three distinct chances to lose the sale. But note: The customer's *need* was for a solution. He may have had some preconception of the way to solve it; however, if you honestly disagree with him, it is best to state your belief, because if you sell him something that is mismatched in cost and capability to his actual needs, he will not be grateful.

During the course of introducing your product and analyzing customer needs, you may detect a substantial misfit. You may be selling a high-performance unit for $5,000, when in fact the market keeps asking for a minimal unit in the $2,000 range. You may have developed a technically advanced electronic actuator, when most needs could be satisfied by an inexpensive pneumatic unit. Or, perhaps you're marketing a nicely packaged laboratory instrument which, if stripped, could be sold on volume OEM basis to builders of larger laboratory systems. The point is that, regardless of how hard you tried to analyze the market before starting your sales effort, your analysis is probably, in the heat of battle, going to prove wrong in some respects. One of the great strengths of small companies is their ability to adapt and change direction quickly; don't permit yourself to get locked into a losing situation by your Business Plan. The feedback from customers should be the principal consideration.

In analyzing the specific needs of prospective customers, try to remain sensitive to their *other* needs as well. In selling chart recorders, for example, you may discover that there is a great need for chart paper that will not curl when humidity rises. This might be a profitable additional business opportunity for your firm, if suitable paper can be found and marketed through your organization. What else does this person buy, anyway? If he buys typewriters, can you also offer him adding machines? Desks? Dictating equipment? If he buys machine tools can you also sell him cutters? Measuring machines? Gages? If he buys pressure transducers, can you sell him a complete system with electronics? Your main cost in business for a long time is going to be that of reaching living, breathing customers. Make it your challenge to see how many of the needs of each one your firm can reasonably attempt to fill. Try not to freeze the definition of your business too early; the longer you can remain opportunistic, the better the chances you may uncover a much better opportunity than the one you set out to pursue.

Servicing the Relationship

A major customer, even a tough one, is a priceless asset. However, it is surprising how many entrepreneurs are prone to ignore their existing customers, in the thrill of the chase after new ones.

Yet, logically, the emphasis should be reversed. The existing customer requires much less effort and cost to sell additional volume; if you do a good job with him, he will become your staunch advocate, enabling you to sell other firms more easily. He will provide the cash flow upon which your further marketing will be based. Therefore, be sure that you have exhausted every opportunity to satisfy him, before turning your energies to the chase. This may mean:

1. Occasional personal contact, just to make sure everything's O.K. (and to find out what the competition is saying to him, what he thinks of your salesman and of your product).

2. Rapid field service when required. Follow-up procedures should be instituted to make sure the problem was actually solved. Don't take your technician's word for this.

3. Personal involvement in any negotiations involving substantial purchase quantities or deviation from normal specifications.

4. Occasional surveillance of the accounts receivable, to make sure that petty items, such as spare parts or service billbacks, are not creating irritation with the customer. Be prepared to bend (conspicuously) on these small matters.

5. Little Remembrances. While Christmas gifts, etc., are normally considered to be in poor taste, and are actively discouraged by most major firms, there are exceptional circumstances. If you feel that a particular customer relationship would be enhanced by a gift in good taste, and no rules dictate otherwise, it is probably O.K. Occasional entertainment for the customer may be better, however, since it creates an atmosphere of personal rapport without the possible nuances of a gift.

As a final note on the value of customer relationships, try asking yourself the following:

1. How much have we invested in direct negotiations, person-hours, phone bills, travel, and face-to-face contact with this customer?

2. How many prospects did we have to sift before finding him? What did that cost us?

3. How much did we spend in advertising, promotion, and prospecting before we even came up with that list of prospects?

If most firms performed this calculation honestly, they would be astounded at the amount of actual hard dollars they have invested in each customer relationship. Be sure that each relationship is secure and fully exploited before rushing forth to invest in further ones.

No matter how hard you try, sooner or later you're going to foul up. When it comes, it may be a real beauty. Picture this: You are two months late in delivering a machine to your customer. You've heard three times this week from his attorneys, but at last it's gone out the door. Next, the truck gets rerouted to Los Angeles instead of Minneapolis. Two weeks and several pints of blood later, the unit is delivered. Then you get a call at midnight from their president, informing you that the unit delivered was metric, and they ordered English.

What do you do now? Well, the first thing to do is face the fact that *you*, not your regional manager, your chief engineer, or your sales manager, had better handle this. When everything goes haywire, the customer expects to hear from the president—not from a hired hand. Trying to delegate at this point will make things worse. Depending upon the value of the customer and the possibility of some retaliatory action on his part, you may be well advised to propose a meeting at his plant, as opposed to trying to solve the problem over the phone. This has two advantages:

1. Offering to get on a plane the next morning underscores the great concern on the part of your company. It reveals how *extraordinary* this circumstance is (never reveal that it also happened last week to somebody else).

2. The time it takes for the meeting to occur gives everybody a chance to cool down and consider realistic solutions.

At this point, your skill as a negotiator will be put to the test. You must be willing to appear ready to make the situation right, even at the sacrifice of your firm. This proferred sacrifice may take the form of unbilled overtime to correct the problem; compensation for direct loss suffered by the customer; replacement or substitution of a loaner unit while his is being corrected; offering other compensatory considerations, such as extended payment terms, or discounts.

At this point, in reading the fine print on the back of your quotation form, you may discover some loophole or other, which may seem to absolve you of liability for costs resulting from this problem. *Invoke the fine print at your peril.* If the customer feels that he has been slickered, you can forget about ever selling him anything again. Your safest tactic at this point is to ask the customer what *he* thinks is fair. This, in effect, places the burden of fairness upon him, and his demands may turn out to be unexpectedly reasonable.

In resolving problems of this sort, it is necessary to take the long view of the short-run concessions you may be considering. What did it cost us in dollars and time to get this customer? What will it cost us to replace him? What will be the volume and profitability of sales with him over the next couple of years if we keep him? You may be much better off to relinquish the profit on this particular sale (or to take a loss) than to lose the customer. This negotiation is also a good opportunity to further solidify the loyalty of your customer, by your manifest integrity and desire to make the situation right.

The Problem Customer

Every company eventually acquires a few problem customers. It is often difficult to balance the benefits of their business against the time, aggravation and petty costs of doing business with them. These customers may fall into the following classes:

1. The slow payer. Slow payment may be his business policy, and will likely be justified by a sequence of "lost" invoices, product "deficiencies," etc. He may tell you that, prior to the sale, he told *your* salesman that he would pay when his customer pays *him*.

2. The specs changer. This customer either feels that his needs are so unique that he *must* have a special version of your product (at the price of the standard unit), or feels that, until delivery, he has the right to keep on making changes in the specifications at no cost.

3. The backroom lawyer. This fellow prides himself on his completion of a commercial law course somewhere along the line and misses no opportunity to show his skill in outflanking his suppliers. He will find loopholes in your contract justifying eternal free service, exclusivity with his firm, product return privileges, etc.

4. The wheeler-dealer. This is the customer who lets you know, none too subtly, that he's found another supplier willing to supply the same product as you for about 60 percent of your price. He will change suppliers for such marginal advantages that the changeover costs negate them, but he prides himself on being a tough negotiator. Anyway, his boss only hears about the savings he's made—not the costs of obtaining them.

These and other problem customers can absorb a very large portion of your time and energy in maintaining their business and heading off additional problems. When such a customer has identified himself, weigh realistically the benefits and costs of keeping him—then, if you must cut him off, have no compunctions. It is simply impossible to work with certain types of firms, and your decision connotes no failure on your part.

It is especially easy for new firms to acquire problem customers for several reasons:

1. The customer may have already been rejected by all the existing suppliers in the industry, and come to you as a new victim.

2. The new firm often has inadequate or nonexistent credit check procedures, or other sources of market intelligence.

3. The salesman for the new firm will exert great pressure or temptation to take on what is perhaps a visibly marginal account.

4. The new venture may seem like a softer touch to the problem customer than his bigger, older suppliers. When the heat is on, he will pay them first and let you wait.

The entrepreneur who intends to survive should be aware of these perils and be sure that some mechanism exists for a suitable degree of screening of new prospective customers. It's much better, for all concerned, to request payment in advance "until credit is established," even at the risk of affronting a customer, than to spend the next two years trying to collect.

Enforcing Contracts

It often develops that a business contract undertaken in good faith by buyer and seller becomes inappropriate to the emerging situation. For example, a customer may contract to purchase 1000 of your units, but discover that he can only use 200; completing the contract may be very poor business for him—in fact it may put him out of business. Another firm may buy your equipment, only to discover that the job intended cannot be done on your equipment—despite the fact that the specifications of your equipment were clearly stated in your quotation, and regardless of the fact that you do not warrant "fitness for purpose."

You have a contract. The question is, to what extent do you enforce it? This is a business decision, not a legal one. If you succeed in pushing your contractual demands down the customer's throat, he is no longer a customer. In fact, he may become a very costly adversary in a courtroom. In selecting a route of action, you must again take the long view: What was the cost to obtain this customer? What is his future value to us? What will be the cost of enforcing our contract? What will be the *net* dollar gain on this contract from so doing? Will our willingness to negotiate simply be interpreted as softness, encouraging future transgressions? These are hard questions, but they should be asked *before* calling in the lawyers. A court action usually benefits nobody; it is, rather, evidence of failure and ineptitude on the part of both parties, in solving their mutual problems to their better advantage. Above all, try to avoid involving your ego and emotions in a situation where, objectively speaking, you've been had. So doing merely diminishes the possibility of achieving any sort of rational decision, and robs your energies from more creative enterprises.

Conventional Wisdom. You can delegate responsibility for customer relations to your marketing department while you attend to more important matters.

Reality. You isolate yourself from your customer and his problems at your peril. You don't *have* anything more important to do.

References

1. Bender, Paul S.: *Design and Operation of Customer Service Systems,* New York, AMACOM, 1976.

   This short book explores the entire spectrum of the company's relationship to its customers, covering not just product service but all forms of support, including the setting of internal standards. Excellent.

2. Gannon, Thomas A, (ed.): *Product Service Management,* New York, AMACOM, 1972.

   Seven sections by various authors on organizing, delivering, training, and administering all phases of product service. Short and sweet.

3. Redding, Harold T., and Knight G. H., III: *The Dun and Bradstreet Handbook of Credits and Collections,* New York, Crowell, 1974.

   This highly indexed manual offers you or your controller extensive and useful advice on how and when to extend credit, where to look for credit information on your customer, and how to manage the collection process. The whole ballgame is lost if you can't collect your money, so here's how to do it.

Chapter 20

COMPETITORS AND WHAT TO DO ABOUT THEM

"He that wrestles with us strengthens our nerves and sharpens our skill. Our antagonist is our helper."

. . . Edmund Burke

Who is a Competitor?

Your very earliest efforts to assess the market for your proposed product included an initial look at the competition. Once you are in business, however, it will become apparent that your initial definition of competitor may have been rather narrow. Most entrepreneurs tend to think of the competitor as the firm which has very nearly the same product for the same markets as their own. However, some reflection will reveal that the term *competition* is in fact much harder to define.

Conceptually, the competition is any other entity which is competing for the same funds that we are competing for. This means that the cinema operator is not just competing with other cinemas in his area; he is competing with all other entertainment media (e.g., sporting events and stage shows). The builder of hydraulic motors is not just in competition with other hydraulic motor firms—he is in competition with electric and pneumatic motors, too. The vendor of consulting services is in competition with other consultants, but also with in-house experts within the client's firm. In determining *what* sales appeal will be most successful, you must first place yourself in your customer's shoes and imagine what his real alternatives are. Then, and only then, can you compile a convincing case, contrasting your solution to the others.

Competitors as an Idea Source

Enlightened imitation is among the surest roads to business success. It is beneath the dignity of no businessman to imitate, adapt, and improve upon the innovations of other companies. The incredible trajectory of the Japanese economy has been, until very recently, the result of intelligent adaptation and improvement of nonoriginal ideas. On the other hand, England, long a pioneer in the inventive technologies, has been far less successful in innovation and adaptation of existing ideas for commercial uses. The enormous advantage that the imitator has over the innovator is that the imitator does not have the development costs, the market testing, the unsuccessful false starts, and the tremendous lead times that plague the true innovator. Remember, the pioneer is the guy that gets an arrow in his back.

None of which is to say that your imitation must be blatant or unimaginative. Skillful adaption implies learning from the mistakes of the innovator, as well as his successes. Very often, the second, third, or fourth imitator is the one who really rings the commercial bell, through benefit of observing the mistakes and weaknesses of several other competitors. After all, IBM did not invent the computer, nor were they the first to market it. Moreover, they did not introduce Xerography, although their entry into office copying incorporated a number of improvements.

It is also constructive to observe, where possible, some of the failures as well as the successes of your competitors. What products have they introduced with fanfare, but silently deleted from their last catalog? We all have our little Edsel, after all. Just be sure that your fantastic new design is not already somebody *else's* Edsel.

Competitors as a Basis for Comparison

In addition to such obvious comparisons as price, specifications, and market share, some other comparisons may prove instructive to the extent that they can be made. These include:

1. Gross margins

2. Overall profitability

3. Allocation of sales dollars to labor, material, R&D, advertising, etc.

4. Marketing setup, salesman incentives, dealer policy

5. Areas of product development

6. Current market research in progress

7. Quantity and costs of materials purchases

8. Current production and shipping rates

9. Identity of major customers

10. Pricing policies, formulas

Depending upon your situation, there may be a number of other things you ought to know about your competitor, as well. This knowledge is almost essential for intelligent development of offensive strategy and defensive tactics. It is especially critical for the new enterprise, because:

1. New ventures are very often established because of a market gap, an oversight, or a quirk in the competitive structure. If this is about to change without your knowledge, the game may already be over.

2. The established company, including competitors, can afford a few mistakes; one major mistake will probably kill the new venture. The easiest way to make it is by misreading the competition, both as to its plans and as to its probable reaction to your own planned actions.

Finding Out About Competitors

Short of calling in the CIA, there are ways in which one can learn as much as necessary about competitors. The following list is only suggestive; the imaginative entrepreneur will be able to come up with others as the occasion demands.

1. *Financial Sources.* In addition to annual and interim reports, public companies must file various other classes of financial data and other information with government bodies. These include NYSE listing applications, SEC Form 10-K, offering circulars for new security issues, and, in some states, annual statements of condition. In addition, you can obtain Dun and Bradstreet or NCO reports. You can check with City Hall to find out whether financing statements have been filed pledging collateral. You may also be able to unearth a financial analyst who has recently studied the company who can give you some insights without disclosing sensitive information.

2. *Former Employees.* One can often learn a good deal about a firm from its former employees—especially disgruntled ones. Even present employees are often a good source of intelligence when, for example, they are interviewed in response to a job opening you have advertised.

3. *Dealers, reps, distributors.* These people are usually anxious to fill a sympathetic ear with their grievances against your competitor, whom they represent. You will learn about late deliveries, quality problems, design deficiencies, late commissions (cash problems), and field service problems to a degree that may astound you. Everybody has problems—even your smooth-looking competitor.

4. *Suppliers.* A classical example occurred a few years ago, wherein a firm making motors had always carefully guarded its volume data. Its competitor, however, discovered the source for one of the key purchased components in the motors, which *in turn* had one key purchased component. The level two vendor unconsciously gave away the monthly shipping volume of his customer's customer without ever having heard of the motor manufacturer. There are several ways to approach your competitor's supplier. The best way is as a potential customer. You'd like to see the shop; you'd like to see what sort of work he's doing for others in the industry; you'd like to get some idea of how much he could ship you when volume is required. In short, give him as many opportunities as you can to tell you what a great job he's doing for your competitor.

5. *Professional meetings.* Pay attention to what the competitor's scientist is saying about his work. His president might be quite chagrined at the amount of competitive information being disclosed in the interest of scientific progress. Observe also what they are writing in the professional journals.

6. *Other companies' salespeople.* While Competitor A's salespeople will probably be quite close mouthed about their company's activities, they may be quite effusive (and knowledgeable) about the activities of your mutual Competitor B. What-are-those-bastards-up-to-now is your favorite game played in hotel bars across the nation every night. Likewise, the salespeople for their suppliers can be a source of some occasional insight.

7. *Unethical sources.* While there is in reality a continuum of ethicalness from pure white to pure black, most of us think we know about where the line is. Methods such as the Watergate plumbing, espionage techniques, bribery, employee "plants," etc., are not unknown in business. Ethical questions aside, however, such questionable methods seldom justify the cost of possible exposure and are likely to backfire. Once your own integrity is called into question, there is no real way to repair the damage.

Competitive Structure

There are, roughly speaking, three distinct types of competitive structures:

Type A: The market dominated by one large competitor. IBM is the classic example in the computer industry.

Type B: The market shared by five to 20 fairly comparable firms. The semiconductor industry might be cited as an example.

Type C: The fragmented market, shared by dozens of small competitors. Film processing is an industry of this type.

In picking new markets for your firm, you are probably better off with either Type A or Type C competition than Type B. In Type A, you will not be as likely to encounter immediate retaliatory action, and your pricing may be supported under the large company's pricing umbrella. Granted, you may be very weak when at last he retaliates in some way, but usually you can find some job he isn't doing too well, and prosper at filling the gap. Also, he risks antitrust action in moving to limit your competition.

A Type C market permits a vigorous firm to establish market dominance rather quickly, by outselling, or buying out the small competitors. If you can become the dominant force in this market, then *you* will be establishing the pricing, the standards, and the rate-of-change for the industry.

Type B markets, in contrast to the others, are tough to enter because they have strong incentive to retaliate quickly to additional competitive pressures; because market dominance will be difficult if not impossible to achieve; and because existing competition among coequals probably has eliminated any comfortable price umbrella, allowing you no temporary period of extraordinary profits to offset startup costs.

Hiring Competitors' Personnel

The hiring of competitors' personnel is as much a part of the American competitive tradition as the spitball. The rate of success of new ventures, it could be argued, would be greatly diminished were it not for the ready availability of experienced (i.e., competitors') personnel. One of the reasons, in fact, why it is much easier to start a company in America than in many other countries is the lack of any excessive employee loyalty, and the general absence of ethical sanctions against job-hoppers. In the U.S., the job is considered to be something you do until something better comes along. In more traditional societies, such as Japan and Germany, on the other hand, your employer is a sort of alter-father to whom you owe loyalty, in return for security.

Often, there is simply no alternative to hiring competitor's personnel. If there is a scarcity of skills, you and your local competitor are almost automatically bidding up the price for those skills. However, even in cases where there *is* a choice, many firms believe they are better off hiring the competitor's employee, rather than recruiting from outside the industry. The reasons are pretty obvious:

1. They help themselves *and* handicap the competitor in a single act.

2. The employee likely will require minimal training and break-in time since he already knows your business.

3. They may be able to elicit important information from him regarding the competitor's operations and customers.

However, the advantages can be short lived, since two can play the game. Moreover, the job-hopper doesn't become a loyal employee just because he comes to work for you; he may be working for another competitor (or maybe the original one) in another year with *your* business plan in his file.

Economists have argued that, on the whole, job hopping may benefit the economy by promoting competition; information flows so freely between companies that nobody can keep a secret for very long. This is slight comfort to the entrepreneur interested in survival, however. Perfect competition is exactly what he *doesn't* need. Employee swapping, like price cutting, is one of those things most business people would like to see go away; however, until human nature changes significantly, it is with us to stay. The pragmatic entrepreneur must resign himself to playing the game, initially at least, by whatever rules his particular industry dictates.

Conventional Wisdom.   Free competition is what makes America great.

Reality.   Free competition is what makes entrepreneurs grate.

Reference

1. Greene, Richard M., Jr. (ed).: *Business Intelligence and Espionage.* Dow Jones Irwin, Homewood, Ill., 1966.

   This book of readings will tell you more than you want to know about this subject. And, if you choose not to employ the methods discussed, at least you'll know how your competitor is finding out about you. Suggests many sources available in any good library.

RUNNING THE SHOW

V

A RACE WITH THE CLOCK

"Even if you're on the right track, you'll get run over if you just sit there."

. . . Will Rogers

The day that your round one financing is complete, the document signed, and the cash in the bank is the day you begin a contest—perhaps the toughest of your life. It is a race with the clock, or, more accurately, with the calendar. You have succeeded in convincing investors of your merit of your deal. They have delivered. Now it's your turn. In your business plan you yourself wrote the rules and time limits in which the game was to be played. Those dates that once seemed like soft targets to you now take on the character of grim deadlines. Your cash-flow projections tell you when you will run out of cash; whether you can get more at that point depends upon how well you've met your other objectives. If you go through the money and the results aren't visible, it doesn't matter whose fault it is—the game is over.

The Importance of Meeting Targets

In the early phases of operation it is very often tempting to move the targets around, rather than making a genuine effort to hit them. It is nearly always true, for example, that engineers will want a couple of more months to polish the product design before it is

released for promotion. Or maybe now that you've got money in the bank, this is the time to find some nicer quarters, instead of putting the money and energy into the marketing setup as planned. Nothing is more upsetting to the initial operations of the company than an immediate abandoning of the plan. And needless to add, this makes your investors not a little uncomfortable. Get into the habit of holding your own dates as earnestly as you hold your customer delivery dates. Get into the habit of meeting targets.

Entrepreneurs versus Custodians

Very early in the game of operating a new company, you may come to recognize that your own activities fall more or less into two categories: the entrepreneurial and the custodial. Roughly defined, the entrepreneurial tasks involve the *setting up, planning,* and *motivational* activities of the firm. They would include such things as initiating market research, recruiting a banker, an accountant, an ad agency, finding a building, setting budgets, and so on. The custodial tasks, by contrast, are such things as tracking budgets, developing financial reports, purchasing materials, supervising production, refereeing disputes between production and marketing. Entrepreneurial tasks are much less delegable as a rule than are custodial tasks.

Also, among managers there is a spectrum ranging from pure entrepreneur to pure custodian, along which everyone falls. Although you will be obliged for some period to handle *both* the entrepreneurial and custodial tasks of your company, it is well to decide, based on your perception of yourself in the spectrum, which tasks you should get rid of by delegation, and which you should keep to yourself. You might be successful at delegating certain entrepreneurial tasks (e.g., advertising responsibility) while hanging on to certain custodial tasks where you felt a strong interest (e.g., accounts receivable management). Yet, in general the more of the custodial tasks you can get rid of without losing control, the better job you're probably going to do as an entrepreneur. However, as the company matures and its operations require skilled custodians, you may find that you must move aside or move out. It is generally recognized that entrepreneurs often make lousy managers.

The Principle of Enlightened Mediocrity

The author is indebted to Nick De Wolf, founder of Teradyne Corporation, for the pungent phrase "the principle of enlightened mediocrity," which captures so beautifully the essence of what every successful entrepreneur learns sooner or later. Basically, it is this: There is very little hope for a perfectionist trying to run a growing

new enterprise. There are *so* many things to be done, *so* many problems to solve that weren't in the business plan, and *so* little time to do it in, that a first-rate job is not only impossible for each—it may be undesirable. It has been asserted, with some truth, that we accomplish about 80 percent of any given project with the first 20 percent of the effort. Which says, mathematically at least, that one should be able to do about five 80 percent-quality jobs with the time and energy required to do a *single* 100% A+ job on any of them. The entrepreneur who shoots for 80 percent quality will not go far wrong. There are, nevertheless, some areas which you will wish to single out for 100 percent quality treatment. It may be product quality control, customer service, or some one or two other key areas which drastically affect the company's position in the marketplace. In these areas, you must ruthlessly demand perfection; in the others, you should learn to settle for less without getting ulcers. To illustrate a bit further, a certain sort of manager may spend a month working out the details of a computerized production control system for the shop, when in fact, about the same result might be obtained with a couple of wall charts in the foreman's office. In fact, the result may be better if the foreman thought of it himself. In learning to settle for 80 percent in most areas, you at least have a fighting chance in your race with the clock.

Cash Balance

Among the hardest things for the starting entrepreneur to get onto is the function of cash in the enterprise. It seems incredible to many that a company with growing sales and good profits could go bankrupt, but it happens. It happens because the very condition of growth can create overextension of existing working capital and cash. When and if the company's bank debt is called and cannot be renewed (as in the cash crunch of 1970), good companies as well as bad go down the tube. A major customer's failure, a serious collection problem, or a supplier problem can have the same effect.

The existence of a good-sized lump of cash in the bank following financing tends to defocus the crucial significance of the cash balance as the company's blood supply. Then, one cold morning, it is gone; it has been devoured by the business operations: equipment, materials, salaries, work-in-process, development. At this point it dawns on many managers for the first time what that cash-flow projection really is: a survival weapon.

A manager who cannot predict a cash shortage in his business is not running the company—the company is running *him*. An unexpected cash crisis can cause much embarrassment and in some cases permanent damage (e.g., bankruptcy) to the company. It may make it impossible to meet such "no fail" commitments as loan interest, the payroll, or (God forbid) withholding tax payment. To say that these events reduce the confidence of the bank, the staff, or the government, is to somewhat understate the case. It is extremely serious. Other forms of awkwardness can include missed shipping dates, due to materials withheld by suppliers; panic calls to your investors from suppliers; emergency calls to one's investors to help meet the Friday payroll; major price concessions to customers to obtain early payment.

The best and only way to avoid this is to *plan* your cash flow, and guard it jealously. Work out a format appropriate to *your* needs with your accountant. Schedule your accounts receivable into it *by major customer* so that you can pinpoint collection problems one by one. Schedule major cash payments *by major supplier* or so that aggregation does not hide reality. Try to plan about six months ahead; review and update weekly. If you see a cash shortage developing two months out, *now* is the time to do something about it. Go see your banker, go over your cash-flow statement with him, show him when and why the shortage will develop, plus when and how the desired loan will be liquidated. He will be far more disposed to cooperate now than 60 days hence when your checks unexpectedly started bouncing. So, even if there is no cash shortage now, start operating as though there were. Sooner or later there will be. You may be growing faster than expected, or another cash crunch may cause your customers to start delaying payment, or something may go wrong with a major shipment, causing delayed payment. Get control of your cash today. Your race with the clock can be equated with a race to reverse the direction of the flow from negative to positive before crossing zero—not unlike pulling an aircraft out of a dive.

Maintaining Investor Rapport

You can make no greater mistake than shutting your investors off from the progress of the company or, worse, permitting an attitude of suspicion or hostility to develop between you. One of the functions of directors meetings is, theoretically, to keep the investors informed. Unless the investors insist on them, however, most entrepreneurs can find better things to do with their time than holding a directors meeting. This, however, in no way absolves you of the need to keep your investors informed. A monthly memorandum to the investors, detailing large pending orders, various nonfinancial milestones attained, significant research results, and developments in the marketplace will be very valuable. Attach recent press clippings, literature, etc. The purpose of such communication includes:

1. Offsetting the impact of the (probably bad) news in the monthly financial statements.

2. Giving investors some interesting information on their deal.

3. Letting them know you care what they think, creating vicarious participation.

4. Establishing a fund of goodwill upon which you can draw when the company is in a cash crisis, or when you are raising large amounts of additional capital and require their votes for approval.

The stockholder who is ignored until there is a problem, or until his vote is needed for some deal that has sprung on the scene is going to be understandably difficult to deal with. Make the effort to keep him on your side as a partner in the venture.

The Entrepreneur's Credibility

As noted earlier, the importance of hitting your early targets can't be overemphasized. This is the honeymoon with the investors, with suppliers, with the bank, with the customers. Your performance will never again be under such intense scrutiny, because these people are still nervous about you, your integrity, your ability to perform.

If all goes along nicely and according to schedule, you have nothing to worry about. Just be sure they all know what a lot of effort it took to do it. If, however, things do not go exactly right, your credibility can still be salvaged. When serious problems arise, you will be very foolish indeed to try to hide them to make yourself look good. Most business problems get worse with time (e.g., quality problems, collection problems, employee dishonesty) and by the time you *have* to acknowledge them, the situation can be very bad, indeed. You can have investor support with your problems if you acknowledge the problem and if necessary, ask for help.

Naturally, the same principle applies to your customers and suppliers as well. If you discover that a shipping deadline is going to be blown, it is far better that the customer learn about it—immediately—from the president than from your shipper on the scheduled delivery day. If you're going to be late in paying a large invoice, have the courage to call your supplier personally and explain; give him a chance to plan *his* cash requirements around your problem. Tell him when you *will* pay and make it happen. These may all seem to be rather obvious, common-sense actions but when things get rough you're going to need these people. If they doubt your integrity, they won't be there.

Planning Your Time

Most entrepreneurs do a much better job at planning the year's activities for the entire company than they do planning their own day. Consequently, they end up taking 14 hours to accomplish in a day what should be done in 10 (hence the legendary 84-hour week).

However, despite a certain heroic aura borne by the 84-hour week, it is really dysfunctional and can almost always be shown to be due to poor planning, rather than heroic devotion. It is dysfunctional for the company because:

1. After about 10 hours of work, anybody's efficiency tapers off enormously; you will accomplish little more during the next four hours than you would in one hour when you're fresh.

2. It creates an atmosphere of tacit disapproval toward other employees who can't or won't work your hours. This can strain the relations between you and key people.

3. The long hours are naturally necessary when the big push is on. As a steady diet, however, they merely exhaust you and rob you of the vitality necessary to get customers excited about your product, or to inspire your own employees.

The better answer is to try planning your day better. A few tips:

1. Identify your own "creativity cycle" during the day, and be sure that those hours are reserved for your really creative work.

2. Try scheduling the entire day—not just appointments—scheduling yourself as though you were an expensive production machine (you are). Have *specific* attainable goals or milestones to be accomplished in each interval of time.

3. Ignore the telephone. Save one hour at the less creative part of your day to return all calls. Do not become the slave of this instrument. Use your secretary to filter off (politely) all but the most vital callers.

4. Work outside the office. If you have a major report, five-year plan, technical paper or speech to prepare, go work someplace else (not at home). A library is often the best place to get things done.

5. Try batching, rather than real-time operation. Set up a few regular weekly, biweekly, or monthly meetings to keep abreast of progress in specific areas, rather than constantly interrupting your employees' work, or letting them interrupt yours.

6. Batch your travel. This is often less costly in out-of-pocket terms, as well as being efficient. If you plan to be gone two solid weeks next March, everyone knows you'll be away and can plan around you.

7. Batch your correspondence. Get used to using a dictating machine instead of dictating to your secretary (you'll get a better person for the same money if you don't require shorthand), so you don't keep interrupting her work. Batching your correspondence

permits you to get all files, orders, etc., in order and get it all done quickly.

8. Use the telex instead of committing yourself to long telephone conversations. It is cheaper, just as fast, and gives a written record. Try using it also instead of writing letters. People will forgive you if you're terse, and remember, the average business letter costs over $6.00 to dictate, type, and send.

9. Set aside some time for thinking—even if it's only a half-hour in the shower each morning. Nothing is more inimical to good management than a constant rat race with every minute jammed full.

10. Don't overdo priorities. Some things are important—others are merely urgent in a time sense. Some require large blocks of uninterrupted concentration, while others are short and can be fitted between more important or nonschedulable events. Don't get yourself tied up in a system that tackles everything in order of "importance" or "priority."

11. Get some regular exercise. There is no better defense against the physical and emotional depreciation of the entrepreneur than some daily vigorous exercise. It helps you wake up, metabolize your food better, and maintain a higher general level of vitality.

12. Get out of the office. Whether to work on a major project, or have lunch with your banker, or make some sales calls with the local rep, make it a point to get out of the office and frequently expose yourself to new people and fresh ideas. This helps to revitalize both you and your staff.

13. Employ the principle of enlightened procrastination. It is truly amazing the number of problems which, if ignored, simply disappear. Someone else solves them, or a deadline passes, or the need for their performance disappears, or somebody discovers it really wasn't needed after all. In sorting out your In Box, you will discover that about 70 percent of its contents can be put in the circular file, 20 percent in a bushel box marked "pending," and the 10 percent remaining earmarked for action sometime this week.

Helping Others Plan Their Time

No matter how efficiently you use your time, the ability of the company to meet deadlines depends on your employees' ability to plan theirs. As president, it is up to you to instill a sense of day-to-day urgency to show people why it is essential to get their tasks done on time, and to enlist their commitment and pride in making sure it happens.

Time-driven behavior is not natural to many people, especially if they have come from staff jobs in much larger organizations. You must make it clear that here in your small company environment, people are judged on *output* (tasks completed on time), not *input* (eight hours put in today). They are expected to finish on schedule, even if it means an occasional evening or weekend invested. Here are some tips to help your people meet their goals:

1. Each professional should have a written schedule, showing when jobs are to be started and completed. The classical Gantt charts and bar graphs are good visual formats. Progress should be reviewed weekly by supervisor.

2. Flextime should be employed. When deadlines impend, let people work at home, or in the office at hours of their own choice.

3. If a critical deadline (e.g., a major proposal) is due Monday, work the weekend and give the people two other days off.

4. Encourage people to take work along on trips. The long hours in airports and hotels afford excellent, uninterrupted intervals for creative work.

5. Pay bonuses for specific, extraordinary tasks accomplished. Consider prizes that will be used by the spouse (e.g., a Cuisinart or microwave oven), if you want double mileage. After all, the spouse is the one who suffers most when the company demands that leisure be rescheduled or foregone.

Conventional Wisdom.   The entrepreneur's shortest commodity is time.

Reality.   The shortest commodity is not time, but energy and organization in its use.

References

1. Webber, Ross A.: *Time and Management.* Van Nostrand Reinhold Co., N.Y., 1972.

A 160-page essay on time, how it gets lost, and concrete measures for its management, as a corporate resource. This book, although intended for the manager of the established firm, has many important insights for the entrepreneur.

2. Naumes, William. The Entrepreneurial Manager in the Small Business. Addison Wesley, Reading, Mass., 1978.

Readings and original text on what managers really do.

Chapter 22

MORE ON NEGOTIATION

"Let us never negotiate out of fear, but let us never fear to negotiate."

. . . John F. Kennedy

Many successful business executives would, if pressed, acknowledge that negotiating skill, more than specific business knowledge, administrative technique, or other management skills has influenced their ability to achieve. Negotiation is the common, central element in *all* of business—whether between two camel traders in the bazaar, or between a giant corporation and a tough labor union. Skill in negotiation appears to be one constant factor in nearly any successful enterprise. It is extraordinary, therefore, that it is seldom if ever treated explicitly in business schools or other management development programs.

Negotiation impinges on nearly every activity in business life, regardless of the size of the enterprise. It is especially significant, however, in the early operations of a new company. An established firm has the substance, the ongoing sales, the reputation for delivery and payment, and a huge vested interest to protect. They have much to offer as well as to gain from their opposing negotiators. Contrast this, then, to the situation of the new company: It has no record and no significant substance or proven ability to deliver on its promises. Worse yet, the opposing negotiator may have had some unfavorable experience with very small companies. Nonetheless, the only way that substance, track record, and reputation *can* be built by the new firm is through negotiation.

You will at the outset be negotiating lines of credit with suppliers and banks; compensation packages with employees and prospective employees; complex, multidimensional contracts with customers. You may find yourself also negotiating with people who are supposed to be your paid helpers. For example, you may become engaged in a negotiation with your auditor over proper treatment of inventories. You will be negotiating schedules and budgets with each department head. You'll be negotiating vacation schedules with your wife. You will be negotiating with *everyone*.

Your Opponent is Usually at a Gross Advantage

In Chapter 11, we observed that the financier with whom you are negotiating for capital is invariably at a great advantage over you, the entrepreneur. This is also true to some significant degree of nearly every other outside entity with whom you may be negotiating in the early stages of growth. Your opposer is negotiating similar deals with other companies every day of the year. He has heard all your arguments before and knows how to counter them; he has seen three better deals than yours already this week; moreover, he probably understands the strengths and weaknesses of your position better than you do yourself. Finally, he probably needs your patronage a great deal less than you need his—and he knows it.

In short, the entrepreneur is attempting to negotiate a place in the world for his company at the very time when his inexperience, coupled with the firm's lack of substance, least qualify him for success. Therefore, he should take whatever steps are possible toward improving the probable outcome by:

a. Improving his negotiating skills, and

b. Enlisting the skills of experienced negotiators.

The Negotiating Process[1]

Inexperienced negotiators are often handicapped by their very concept of what a negotiation is supposed to be. They tend to view the process as a form of combat, in which there will be a winner and a loser. Tactics and strategies will be used, if at all, to drive the other guy to the wall. To back this up, logically, they would tend to believe that the threat of force (play it my way or else) will elicit the desired concessions from one's opposer.

A little reflection will reveal how invalid this view of negotia-

---

[1]The author is much indebted to Gerard I. Nierenberg for several of the key ideas in this section (see References).

tion actually is. First, there would be no negotiation at all if both parties did not perceive some potential benefit from it. In fact, the purpose of negotiation is precisely to establish how the *joint* benefits of a new situation can be made to exceed the benefits of the old situation. To put it in economists' terms, you both should be striving toward a *higher* tradeoff curve—not merely forcing one another up and down the same curve you both started from. Second, it is an experience of everyday life that "agreements" struck under duress tend only to last until the weaker party feels he has the strength to tear them up. If your opposing party *feels* he has been driven to the wall (whether or not it really *is* a bad deal for him), his prime energies from that point forward will be directed toward evening the score with you. The fact that he may be violating a contract to accomplish this merely ensures that your lawyer will be able to meet his yacht payments for another couple of years.

Another handicap with which inexperienced people enter a negotiating session, is that of a prematurely frozen position (here's our deal, take it or leave it). There is almost no way you could better guarantee that you will not get *anything* you want from a negotiation, than by presenting an ultimatum demanding everything. Even if you feel that what you desire is reasonable, attainable, and beneficial to some degree to the opposing party, you must *still* let him prove all this to himself. He must take the intervening steps himself. Along the way it is possible that he will come up with alternative formulations that you haven't even considered which may be more beneficial for both parties (e.g., a method of structuring the purchase of a company to minimize the taxes for both sides).

Knowing Your Opposer

The better understanding you have of the individual you will be facing in a major negotiation, the better will be your chances of working successfully with him. Some basic facts on his education, business background, tax status, and general personality can be truly invaluable. What personal needs is he going to satisfy by entering this negotiation? Sometimes it is difficult to find out much in advance along these lines, especially if the organization with which you are negotiating elects to put in a new person to run the negotiation. However, rather than going at it cold, you may be able to use some tactic, such as a "fact-finding meeting" or other occasion to meet with the individual prior to the actual negotiation. You may also be able to identify someone who has recently dealt with the person in a similar context.

It is also desirable to know a good deal about the organization he represents. What are their unannounced motives? What are their legal constraints? How far have they gone with firms similar to yours? What is general practice in their industry? What special circumstances might cause them to bend their policies slightly in your case?

For a concrete example let us assume you are applying for a line of credit from a local bank. Their motivation for dealing with you may be a good deal more complex than simply a lender finding another borrower. They may have some *motivation* to deal with you because:

1. Your firm is local, only a few blocks from their office.

2. Your account, though small, has the possibility of growing very large.

3. Your firm's presence will attract the private accounts of your employees to their bank.

4. They may need to create an image of public servant, friend of small business, or supporter of the prevailing minority in the neighborhood.

However, on some investigation you may find that they have definite *limits* imposed by regulatory agencies and character, such as:

1. Requiring signature of the principal on unsecured notes.

2. Balance sheet tests (e.g., debt-equity ratio).

3. Avoiding long-term debt, as opposed to seasonal or self-liquidating loans.

4. Charging higher rates for riskier loans.

In addition, they may have operating *policies* which, in times of tight cash, funnel money to their older customers, instead of shaky new accounts. They may or may not prefer the pledging of assets (e.g., receivables). All of these are facts which, if known in advance, would greatly simplify the entrepreneur's negotiating process. It might, in fact, convince him that no negotiation was even warranted. The point is, the more you can learn in advance about your opposer and his organization, the better.

Strategies and Tactics

Negotiation is an art upon which substantial study has been expended, especially in the application area of labor relations. It is not the purpose of this book to advance the frontiers of this literature, but merely to catalog a few of the approaches which the entrepreneur may find useful and also which he should anticipate having used against him in negotiation. Nierenberg offers the following:

1. *Forbearance.* Hold off answering, call a recess, suspend discussions, call a "cooling off period." This will sometimes give the op-

position a chance to see the merit of your position, to break the momentum of a negotiation that is going poorly, or just to show that *you* are under no time pressure to reach agreement.

2. *Surprise.* Often a skilled negotiator may elect to become totally unreasonable during a negotiation, to take his opposer off balance. Surprise can also take the form of totally altered demands, a whole new set of facts injected, a relaxation of some "nonnegotiable" demand, etc.

3. *Fait Accompli.* Make your move, then let the other side react as they will. For example, if a final written contract is unsatisfactory, cross out those portions you dislike, initial each correction and sign the document. Or, if there is disagreement on a price, simply write the check for the amount you think it should be and let *them* decide if the difference is worth the cost of collecting it.

4. *Bland Withdrawal.* (Who, me?) Sometimes it's better to violate someone's presumed rights for awhile than trying to negotiate initially. For example, you might elect to violate a known patent for awhile to get established in a market, calculating that it either won't get enforced, or that it will be worth your while to pay whatever the possible penalty would be.

5. *Apparent Withdrawal.* This can often be combined with surprise for the desired dramatic effect. Stomping indignantly out of a meeting can be risky but is used effectively by some negotiators. The threat of withdrawal can be equally effective, if the demands of the opposer seem unrealistic.

6. *Reversal.* In one form, this can mean the exacting of symmetric concessions from the opposing side. For example, if the union feels wages should go up because profits went up, oblige them to agree to wage cuts in case profits go down. In another form, reversal could cause you to increase your bargaining demands, rather than lowering them in exchange for other concessions. For example, after a recess from financial negotiations in Boston, you could conspicuously "disappear" to New York for a few days, later reopening negotiations with a much higher price-per-share demand. Let your opposer wonder who you saw in New York.

7. *Time Limits.* The press of the calendar often provides the best impetus to a speedy conclusion. If your position will be served by time pressure, schedule your meeting a few days before Christmas, or before the opposer's plant shutdown. Look how many negotiations are settled in Congress just before recess. Other limitations are useful as well. For example, in raising capital, if your opposer knows your company will be out of cash shortly, he has a very real limit working in his favor.

8. *Feinting.* Yield the concessions you make reluctantly. Make

the opposition work for them. Bury the opposer in facts to conceal the weaknesses in your proposition. Make sure they know there is someone else very eager for a piece of your proposition. Let them feel at the end that they should be glad they got as good a deal as they did.

9. *Participation.* Explain *why* the proposed package is unacceptable and ask the opposer's help in showing how your problems with it can be answered. Enlist his ideas in a sincere, nonmanipulative way. This may result in a solution, or in his recognition and acknowledgement that his position is unrealistic.

10. *Dissociation.* Make sure he understands why your firm is totally different from those other new ventures in which he lost all that money. Be sure your customer is able to differentiate between your product and all its inferior imitators.

11. *Crossroads.* Be prepared to meet any unreasonable new demand with an equally unreasonable counterdemand, until the initial demand is withdrawn. If labor wants a shorter workweek, you agree, provided they give up several paid holidays.

12. *Blanketing.* Inundate the opposer with data, with detailed questions, with prearranged meeting agendas, etc., to take away their initiative.

13. *Randomizing.* This can involve nonnegotiating tactics, such as splitting the difference, flipping a coin, etc., all invoking irrational chance to break deadlocks.

14. *Nonrandom Sample.* As evidence, you introduce verbatim interview recordings with 10 engineers who like your product. Of course, you don't tell them about the other 50 who hate your stuff.

15. *Salami.* Try for small concessions, a slice at a time. Get them in the habit of saying yes. Tell the customer you only want to give him a sample of your product at an introductory price, etc. Get rid of that manager by first giving him a Chevy instead of a Cadillac, then an incompetent secretary, then no secretary at all, etc. This is especially common as a tactic in large corporations.

16. *Shifting Levels.* If your opposer keeps pleading that he hasn't the authority to grant that concession, then go over his head. You may then be talking to a higher person with broader understanding, as well as authority. Or, make a supplier justify his price in terms of his costs instead of benefits to you. Or shift time horizons. Try negotiating for a whole year's supply, rather than simply for the next price-break quantity.

This list of negotiating tactics can be greatly expanded by your own experience, as you discover what works well for you.

Some advance preparation for any negotiation will serve you well. In addition to scouting the opposer fairly well, you should be sure that you have done your homework in other areas, too. Try to anticipate which way the negotiation will go, and be prepared with countertactics. Try to anticipate objections to your position and have the counterarguments and facts available to back you up. Some people find play acting a useful preparation. Cite chapter and verse. Be prepared to justify all demands (even your arbitrary ones) in terms of rational considerations which the other side can accept. For example: "We cannot consider owning less than 52 percent of your stock, because otherwise we cannot file a consolidated earnings statement with the IRS." Or, "I cannot meet your price demand because I would be in violation of the Sherman Anti-trust Act." Let them know you would happily concede the point, if only you had a choice.

Try to maintain control of the place of the meeting, as well as of the agenda. The order, as well as the content, of the agenda can be very important—for example, if there is a time limit, reserve your weakest areas for last, so that they may get cut out altogether. Try to keep the initiative.

Be sure that you get an attorney who is a skilled and experienced negotiator, and that you have him present as a team member in any significant negotiation. There is no better protection against your own inexperience.

If there are others who must ratify the agreement reached by negotiation (e.g., key stockholders or partners) try to have them present at the negotiation, or at least keep them fully informed of progress so that they will know not only where you are, but also how you got there. This will make it far easier to enlist their cooperation at the final stage. Try to remember that, to succeed, the final agreement has to be good for everybody. If any principal feels he's being coerced or short changed, the agreement will probably be in litigation next year.

Conventional Wisdom   My gain is your loss.

Reality.   In a professional negotiation, both sides should win.

References

1. Nierenberg, G. I.: *Creative Business Negotiating.* Hawthorne Books, Inc., N.Y., 1971.

2. Nierenberg, G. I.: *The Art of Negotiating.* Cornerstone Library, N.Y., 1968.

References #1 and #2 are about the best books available on the area of negotiation. Both discuss Nierenberg's needs theory.

3. Strager, M.: *Acquisition and Merger Negotiating Strategy.* Presidents Publishing House, N.Y., 1971.

This is a very useful work on negotiating strategy from the viewpoint of the acquiring firm.

Chapter 23

LAWYERS AND THEIR USES

"It's impossible to tell where what is legal ends and where justice begins."

. . . Anonymous

A lawyer can do a good deal more for the business person than advise as to whether or not a proposed course of action is legal. That, in fact, is probably the least creative of the many services which the right lawyer can render. Besides being a legal advisor, he functions as a business advisor, a negotiator, an interface with the financial community, as a sounding board for ideas and, of course, as a defender, should the occasion demand. A top attorney, rather than being a mechanic, is an artist. He will be able to envision creative solutions to problems of organization, taxation, and finance that would probably never occur to you. He will also be able to look ahead and anticipate problems and take whatever measures are appropriate to minimize them. He can deploy a wide range of knowledge, experience, and contacts to help you to solve your problems.

Lawyers as Legal Advisors

In the mechanical aspects of incorporation, qualifying you to operate in various states, electing officers, directors, etc., you do not need the top man in the corporate law field. However, if, at the outset, there are serious questions regarding employment contracts with your previous employer, or questions of nondisclosure, non-competition, or patent agreements, then you'd better have a pretty good man. The earlier in your corporate life you find your permanent attorney, the better will be the quality of important decisions you'll be making from now on.

Rather early on there will be questions as to the distribution of equity to employees, and you will need help and advice in drafting a stock purchase or stock option plan. There will be employment agreements, or at least invention disclosure agreements for your key people. There will be commercial terms and conditions to be worked out. At the appropriate stage, there will be the need for some legal assistance in the preparation of a business plan for the raising of seed and later, round one money. These are all activities in which legal and business advice blend to some extent, and you will want the best possible advice in their pursuit.

Lawyers as Business Advisors

In addition to the component of business advice inherent in the drafting of the contracts of the company, there are other areas in which it makes sense to enlist the ideas of your attorney. If his corporate law practice is an active one, he has come across many successful and not-so-successful businessmen and business ideas. This experience is at your disposal. He can be useful, for example, in suggesting tactics for collection of difficult accounts receivable; in proposing ways to deal with a partner who's gone sour; in dealing with the angry customer; in structuring stock offerings, purchase and sale agreements, etc., to take maximum advantage of tax laws. This list is only suggestive, but indicative that your attorney is in a position to have seen every conceivable sort of business problem, and is the best person to help you work around them or work out of them. Finally, though, be sure that you weigh your attorney's business advice, but make your own decisions. Attorneys are much better at identifying alternative courses of action and potential pitfalls than they are at evaluating the business risks and probabilities. That's *your* job.

Lawyers as Negotiators

In a complex negotiation (e.g., a major contract with a customer, a stock underwriting agreement with an investment banker, or a sellout agreement with another firm) an attorney skilled in negotiation will probably save you many times his fee (which itself may be quite sizable). The training and experience of attorneys in the adversary process, in the skilled researching of statute and precedent, and in the relativistic defense of the guilty as well as the innocent, all equip the attorney admirably to help you negotiate against other skilled negotiators. He can help you to sharpen up the objectives of the negotiation, to develop a negotiating strategy, and to help you counter the unexpected turn in discussions (see Chapter 22). In short, he can be a most formidable ally when you most need one.

Lawyers as Investor Interface

When you are raising funds for your venture, your lawyer is a most logical place to ask for suggestions as to possible investors. After all, he has a lot of money and a lot of affluent friends; moreover, he has some affluent clients, some of whom might be interested in exactly your kind of deal. He will, after having helped you draft your business plan, or offering memorandum, have a double incentive to help you pull off the financing; he knows his chances of getting paid will be a whole lot better if you have money. And, after having helped draft or review the document, he will have a detailed knowledge of your deal which will greatly help him in discussing it with other potential investors.

As a result of having handled private placements and public offerings in the past, your attorney should have some acquaintances in the investment banking community who can prove helpful, as well. Finally, he may be helpful in identifying and introducing you to your future banker.

Lawyers as Defenders

A hoary cliche has it, "When you're playing the game hard, you're going to get called offside once in a while." The penalty may come in the form of a lawsuit by an angry customer or employee; it may be an action brought against you by your stockholders; it may even be a petition for involuntary bankruptcy brought by panicked creditors. In any of the above, you're going to need a lot more from your attorney than friendly legal advice. You're going to need some decisive, intelligent action. This is where experience, skill, and prestige often hold the balance. In the words of no less an authority than ex-Attorney General John P. Mitchell: "When the going gets tough the tough get going."

Picking a Lawyer

In the selection of an attorney, unlike the selection of an auditor, the man is everything. He may be working in a large, prestigious firm, or in a smaller firm, depending upon his inclinations. He may even work independently. There are those who believe that, other things being equal, you're better off with a good man in a big firm than a good man in a small firm. The arguments are (predictably):

1. The large firm has a better known name, which may in some circumstances be of value; at least it won't handicap you.

2. The larger firm has a range of specialists in such matters as taxation, real estate, securities regulation, etc., who may from time to time be useful to you.

3. The large firm has more people to draw from, since your own lawyer may occasionally not be available.

In behalf of the small firm, you can probably expect more attention from the senior partners, you may find that people are more informal and accessible, and you may discover, too, that as an entrepreneur himself, your attorney has a generally better gut feel for your situation. It is the author's overall view that the new entrepreneur may be better off with the smaller firm in many cases. However, large versus small firm is not an issue of paramount importance. Selection of a good man is the key issue.

Your best source of leads for good lawyers is other entrepreneurs. Who are they using? Who have they dropped? What (if any) difficult situations have they confronted with this attorney and how did it go? What sorts of fees have they experienced? Did the man ask for stock or finders' fees in connection with financing (both considered mildly unethical)? Does the man seem to have plenty of good connections in the business and financial worlds? How has he been as an informal business advisor? How are his negotiating skills? These and other questions should be used to probe for actual information. Don't settle for an offhand, "Oh, our lawyer's a great guy—you'll really like him."

Recommendations from bankers, owners of large businesses, and other nonentrepreneurial types are likely to be slightly suspect because the recommender is suggesting somebody *he* would wish to have represent him—but his business problems are radically different from your own. As far as the local bar association is concerned, forget it. You might as well be looking in the Yellow Pages.

In interviewing the prospective lawyer, take along your first-cut business plan. Have a list of questions thought out ahead of time. Take up the same issues you raised with the other entrepreneurs. Who are some of his other corporate clients? Is there a present or downstream conflict? How much time is he going to be able to spend with you? With whom will you work when he's not available? How about fees? (Anywhere from $30 to $150 per hour may be justifiable.) Will he take some collection cases on a contingency basis? (Probably he won't if he's a top man.) How about his experience in financing and in public offerings and SEC registrations in particular? Your list will grow rather long, as you begin to consider all the things you'd like to know about your future lawyer.

In evaluating him, don't rely on analytical considerations alone; listen to your intuition. Do you like the guy? Do you think you could work together creatively as a team in strategy or negotiating sessions? Is he as tough as you'd like? How is he going to come across to the types of people you'll be dealing with? Do you get the feeling that he'll take a genuine interest in your company?

Try to interview the top three or four candidates, even though you may be perfectly happy with the very first guy. It's desirable, if only to see some of the range of types available. Additional acquaintances will never hurt you, either.

Patent Lawyers

Patent law is such a specialized field that even large firms do not ordinarily presume to practice it. When the time comes for a patent lawyer (or if you've come to doubt the abilities of your old one), your attorney can probably supply some valuable leads. Now you will be dealing with an area in which analytical considerations count for much, subjective impressions very little. Here, as in selecting your corporate attorney, however, anything but the best may prove very costly in the long run.

You will be particularly lucky if you can find a top man who is already working in or familiar with your particular field. This can save some substantial startup time and cost. One way of finding such a person is by examining the key patents in your field and contacting the attorneys who wrote them. An out-of-town patent attorney is probably O.K., since you will not have extensive day-to-day dealings with him, and the dealings you do have can be largely conducted by mail.

In general, just keep in mind: *There's absolutely nothing so expensive as a second-rate lawyer.*

Conventional Wisdom. The lawyer's the guy you call when you're in trouble.

Reality. The lawyer's the guy you call *before* you're in trouble.

Reference

1. Vorhees, Theodore: "Selecting a Lawyer for your Business," *Management Aids for Small Manufacturers, Annual No. 8,* Small Business Administration, Washington, D.C., 1962.

Practical advice and checklists for any startup firm.

Chapter 24

CUSTODIAL OPERATIONS AND HOW TO AVOID THEM

> *"We trained hard . . . but it seemed that every time we were beginning to form up into teams we would be reorganized. I was to learn later in life that we tend to meet any new situation by reorganizing; and a wonderful method it can be for creating the illusion of progress while producing confusion, inefficiency, and demoralization."*
>
> . . . Petronius Arbiter, 210 B.C.

In applying the principle of enlightened mediocrity to the day-to-day operations of the company, you must be prepared to strike a reasonable balance between custodial and entrepreneurial duties; then let loose of the rest of the custodial chores. This can be a lot harder than it sounds.

At the outset, you were president, operations manager, plant manager, and a lot of other things all rolled up together. The distinction between these duties was probably not clear, because you alone were doing them all at once. As the company evolves, you *must* get rid of many, if not most of these duties, even if you're convinced the people to whom you must delegate them can only do a 70 percent job. Your primary energies must be focussed on the *growing edge* of the company—not on the day-to-day struggles. You must be free to press market development, and to search for new markets and new products. You must have energy and time for working with new customer prospects, with your financial sources, with government agencies, with possible overseas business contacts. You will need to be looking for possible candidates for acquisition and for key staff members. You must, more than anyone else in your firm, assert to the world your firm's leadership. This involves speaking before technical and business groups, membership on industry and government panels, giving interviews to key publications in your industry, arranging press conferences for new product introduction. You, in short, must be the key, visible interface between your company and the outside world.

The fact that your time is largely allocated to these presidential duties does not mean that you are any less responsible for the ongoing operation of the firm. It simply means that you must establish the means for *delegation, communication of objectives,* and *feedback on performance*—all very elementary Management 101 stuff, you say. However, Management 101 does not tell you how to accomplish this in a tiny company, with rapidly changing problems. Moreover, you may have to redefine the jobs, juggle manpower, and rethink your system about every six months for the first couple of years. Things just don't stay neatly in place in the dynamic, sometimes chaotic, atmosphere of the new enterprise.

Your Organization Plan

Your delegation (organization) plan should be such that only three or four managers report directly to you. Who they are depends on what business you're in. In general, however, they ought to be:

1. Financial Manager (chief accountant, controller, treasurer)

2. Operations Manager (or plant manager, office manager, general manager, etc.)

3. Marketing Manager (or sales manager)

4. Chief Engineer (or VP, Engineering, or Technical Director, etc.)

If you have more than about four line managers reporting to you, you are going to get too involved in custodial management. Some presidents like to have reporting direct such people as Materials Manager (purchasing, inventory control, incoming inspection, etc.), or Quality Assurance Manager (Q.C., inspection, final test, standards, etc.), Personnel Manager, and so on. Important though these functions are, to the extent that you become enmeshed in them you will be unable to do your own job.

Following are some general comments on delegating jobs, communicating orders and eliciting feedback:

Financial Manager

Do not permit this individual to report to anyone but you. The finances of the company are its lifeblood, and you must keep your finger on the pulse. Your financial manager will have a great deal to do, much of which will not require your direct surveillance, once the systems are set up to your satisfaction. He will probably function very well with one clerk initially, perhaps adding one more for each additional million dollars' volume. The key areas in which you will wish to involve yourself will be:

1. Weekly review of cash flow projections and accounts receivable. A regular one-hour meeting every week will be sufficient except in times of crisis. This regular schedule will permit your accountant to get his data together and be prepared.

2. Preparation of budgets. This will occur at least every six months, under the general supervision of your financial manager. You will be spending substantial energy at budget time, working out all the compromises between programs desired by the operating groups and those permitted by resources available, and resulting with the inevitable conflicts.

3. Monthly review of operations, comparing budgeted to actual P&L. This would typically involve your entire team, including key third-level members with budgetary responsibility. These meetings should occur just as soon after monthly closing as humanly possible—ideally not more than ten day into the next month. Otherwise, in the general march of events, people tend to forget what went on, and the conditions causing those overruns will still be uncorrected.

Even if you lack an accounting background, make it a point to look over the general ledger, the cash journal, and accounts payable from time to time—unannounced. This will give you an opportunity to spot certain classes of problems, such as late or incorrect posting, jam-ups in certain accounting areas, impending payable and receivable problems, incorrectly computed rep commissions, and improper product price entries. More important, it will help to keep your financial manager on his toes. Ask plenty of questions—even though some may be naïve.

Operations Manager

You should meet at least weekly with this person, for a couple of hours. He will be responsible for many of the major classes of expenditure in the organization, including plant operation, personnel, purchasing, and maybe substantial subcontracting. He will also be responsible for the development and holding of shipping schedules, and the production schedules to back them up. He may also be responsible for the efficient operation of the office, which can be a hard problem in the growing company. In short, he may have more different things to worry about than anybody else in the company.

Your operations manager should be given rather great latitude in the way he does his job. He should be the one to originate requests for labor-saving equipment, design changes to simplify production or procurement, and various cost-reduction plans. At the same time, the heat is constantly on him for on-time delivery, acceptable quality, and on-target production costs. He will bear the brunt of many personnel problems, and will spend substantial time hiring and training people.

To understand what's happening in his bailiwick, you should try to attend most of his weekly staff meetings (he may call them production status meetings, or schedule reviews). This is where the real clashes occur, where tough decisions get made, where incipient ulcers get their start. His meeting is where you find out *why* certain jobs are in trouble, *why* there is a bottleneck in Test. You should not intervene in this sort of meeting, but neither should you isolate yourself from it.

In addition to your weekly meeting with the operations manager, it would be well to spot check, on a nonscheduled basis, the large-dollar areas under his purview. In many manufacturing companies, for example, purchases account for 50 to 75 percent of all expenditures. It is therefore one of the areas you should probe. Is the buyer doing his whole job, or just struggling to prevent unanticipated parts shortages? Is he getting multiple quotations? Is he maintaining decent vendor records of cost, quality, delivery? Is he actively seeking functional equivalents for high-cost items? Are your engineers getting suggestions and questions from him? Is he the first to raise make-or-buy questions? Is he approaching makers of major purchased items to negotiate annual buys? Is he, in short, initiating action, or just reacting to the press of events? Inventory and stock control are both critical areas in some kinds of operations. Be sure that you look at the inventories and test the methods used to control it from time to time.

Have a look at the phone bills and the Xerox invoices occasionally. Remember, you're not being nosey—just interested.

Marketing Manager

You'll have plenty of day-to-day contact with this man, in pursuit of specific major orders. However, he should meet with you monthly and review last month's bookings and the updated forecast for the next quarter. Who are the customers, what are they going to buy, and when? When can we plan to ship? Do this by territory, to give yourself some fix on the effectiveness of each rep or salesman. Who is making his quota? How did last month's bookings shape up against forecast? Review the problem areas: contracts lost, customer disputes, salesman problems. What changes in the product are needed? What additional literature? Advertising? Promotion?

The marketing manager must learn sooner or later to accept responsibility for the fact that his forecasts are the basis for all planning for the company. If he is consistently unable to meet reasonable forecasts developed by himself, you may have the wrong man in the job. You must not under any circumstances allow him to isolate you from contact with the customers or the salesmen. You should make it a point to spend at least a quarter of your time with customers and salesmen. If you lose the feel of your market, you've lost touch with the whole business.

Chief Engineer

If yours is a technology company, the chief engineer should report directly to you. If the emphasis is more on manufacturing and marketing it may be O.K. for him to report to the Operations Manager. In either case, it is incumbent upon you to stay abreast of what's going on in the engineering department. You will want not only a roster of its projects and progress, but also some reading on the department's productivity. Engineers are fond of saying "You can't schedule invention." However true this may be, it is also true that most of what goes on in engineering departments is not invention. It is straightforward application of well-known principles to modify or redesign existing products. You can schedule *and* budget this work, and the chief engineer has the same sort of managerial responsibility as anybody else on the team for meeting schedule and budget.

In the more creative side of his work, is he originating ideas for new products, significant improvements in old ones? Is he a positive force for keeping the company abreast of the state of the art, or is he merely implementing modifications as demanded by the marketing department? Does he provide any ideas for the production and test people? What little R&D projects is he "bootlegging" because he personally believes in them? Does he make it a point to go out and talk to customers once in a while?

Unless your company is heavily involved in innovation, you may not need a scheduled weekly meeting with the chief engineer. However, you should be a presence in the department from time to time, to nose around and get a feel for what is (or what is not) happening. And once a month, your chief engineer must be accountable for milestones and budgets, along with everyone else.

Too Much Information

203
*Custodial
Operations and
How to Avoid
Them*

A basic principle of operation which requires some time for most new presidents to grasp is this: *You should try to learn what the minimum level of information is for you to run the company satisfactorily.* It may be a great deal less than you think. It is literally possible to run certain kinds of companies knowing only the daily cash balance, or the day's shipments. The less operational information you personally must process and act on, the better.

There may be certain cases in which you will wish to immerse yourself temporarily in a problem, which will require a good deal more information than normal. However, resist the temptation of making the person responsible generate a new report on the problem every month from now on. You won't read them. Handle short-term problems on an *ad hoc* basis, in sufficient depth so that you can actually assist in the solution. Then let your manager see that the agreed-upon solution is implemented, and move on to a different problem. If you try to monitor everything all the time, you will have time to do no presidential work, and you will not contribute very much to the operations either.

It makes us all feel very important to have lots of staff reports, operating statistics, and computer printouts passing over our desks. However, this stuff all costs money to generate, and you should ask in every case: (a) Does this really need my attention, or could somebody else handle it? and, (b) Was there any reason for this report at all? What would happen if we eliminated it altogether?

Reports and memos are the basic tools of the empire builders in big companies. In the small company, they can quickly be carried to excess, simply because everybody has so much to do anyway. The net cost of being underinformed is probably much less than being overinformed.

Conventional Wisdom. You can't know too much about your operation.

Reality. Right.

References

1. Kelly, P., Lawyer, K., and Baumback, C.: *How to Organize and Operate a Small Business*, 4th ed., Prentice-Hall, Inc., Englewood Cliffs, N.J., 1968.

   If you're going to run your company by the book, here's the book to run it by. Covers every phase of small business management, including manufacturing, marketing, accounting, and control.

2. Thurston, D.B.: *Manual for the President of a Growing Company*, Prentice-Hall, Inc., Englewood Cliffs, N.J., 1962.

This is a big book of practical guidance in a nonexhaustive form. Good treatment of many administrative functions.

3. Easton, Allen: *Managing for Negative Growth,* Reston Publishing, Reston, Virginia, 1976.

   Provides many useful ideas for coping with difficult small-company problems. Deals with cutbacks, illiquidity and other gut topics. Excellent.

4. Buskirk, Richard H., and Vaughn, Percy J.: *Managing New Enterprises,* West Publishing Co., St. Paul, Minn., 1976.

   A hybrid but very useful book.

5. Eisenberg, Joseph: *Turnaround Management,* McGraw-Hill Book Co., N.Y., 1972.

   This is an excellent, hard-nosed treatment of many types of business problems, written from a survival point of view. Recommended reading.

6. Lasser, J. K.: *How to Run a Small Business,* 3rd ed., McGraw-Hill Inc., N.Y., 1963.

MILLSTONES AND OTHER FIXED ASSETS

"Beware of all enterprises that require new clothes."

. . . Henry David Thoreau

There is something uniquely and tangibly gratifying about having a beautiful plant, modern gleaming equipment, and a fully integrated operation. It is, in a way, a monument to the entrepreneur—a solid testament that *here* is a person who does things first class.

Regrettably, it is often the case that the monument becomes the tombstone of the enterprise. In a study of 95 small midwest manufacturing firms, Hoad and Rosko[1] observed that only nine were successes. Of the remainder, fully 45 percent of the entrepreneurs felt that unwise investment in capital equipment had been responsible for their failure. Indeed, it is hard to think of a worse use for venture capital than tying it up in bricks, mortar, and machinery. The reasons for this, while obvious, seem to elude a great many entrepreneurs:

1. Except in mature firms, the profit usually arises from sources other than skill in manufacturing. It may be from ingenious product design, proprietary technology, innovative marketing, or

---

[1]Hoad, William M., and Rosko, Peter, *Management Factors Contributing to Success or Failure of New Small Manufacturers*. Ann Arbor, Mich.: Bureau of Business Research, University of Michigan, 1964.

just tremendous demand. Very rarely does it arise because you can make things a lot cheaper than anybody else.

2. Tying up capital in machinery means there is that much less for product promotion, inventories, accounts receivable, product development, or the other creative or necessary costs of a growing company.

3. Committing funds to specialized equipment may be greatly increasing the total risk of your company. If the product folds, if a better production process is found, or if it's just plain cheaper to buy it elsewhere, you're stuck. To raise cash, you may be obliged to dump the machinery at a fraction of its value. If it ties up cash that could otherwise pay creditors, it may be the factor that topples you into bankruptcy.

4. Apparent cost savings due to improved machinery have a way of being very illusory. They are usually computed on a model of full utilization, long runs, minimal downtime, and other factors which are extremely difficult to guarantee in the fluid environment of a new company, or a developing market.

5. An elaborate plant usually entails costs that are hidden altogether or are hard to evaluate *ex ante*. These include maintenance, power, materials, production scheduling, and management time and effort.

Therefore, before committing large amounts of your capital to plant and equipment, weigh carefully the following alternatives:

1. *Buy the product completely made.* Give somebody else the manufacturing headaches and profit, if any. Contrary to intuition, his price may be substantially lower than your true cost to manufacture, simply because he is taking on the work to make a contribution to his existing plant overheads. He may wish to keep workers employed, to keep machines loaded, or to maintain volume with his vendors. For any number of reasons, it often costs *less* to have it made outside. And even if it doesn't, ask yourself if the premium paid isn't worth the extra aggravation and risk of being in manufacturing.

2. *Buy premade components, and simply assemble.* The same arguments apply as in (1), except that you may be less dependent upon a single source. You will be adding some value; however, it is likely that you will also be adding to working capital requirements, due to additional inventories of parts and work in process.

3. *Rent time in someone else's plant.* If your product requires operations on costly machines (e.g., large drop-forgings, large injection molded parts, centrifugal castings, etc.), you may be able to find a plant with the requisite machinery willing to sell you machine time,

possibly at their marginal cost. Other operations can then be done in your own plant. Computers, circuit testers, and environmental test equipment can also fit this pattern.

4. *Lease equipment instead of buying it.* This is the final step, short of outright ownership. You may find that the terms of the lease limit your flexibility to a degree, but at least your money is not totally frozen in company-owned plant equipment.

5. *Consider used or self-constructed equipment.* Depending upon your industry, if a plant seems inevitable you may be able to find used equipment which will serve the desired purpose for several years, at a fraction of new equipment cost. If you're looking for machine tools, presses, and other equipment of this sort, there are national listing services to help you locate the desired piece. If it's electronic production or test equipment, computers, simulators, environmental chambers, laboratory equipment, etc., there are innumerable sources for used equipment of this type. Auctions and bankruptcy sales are among the best places to pick up equipment bargains. If the machine is special purpose, consider the possibility of making it. You may surprise yourself. Give your plant manager a little applause when he *saves* the company $10,000 cash by a little innovation. Or, pay him a $1,000 bonus.

6. *Use low-cost production space.* If you must manufacture, consider separating your production operation from your front-office functions, such as sales. Then seek out older industrial space, mill buildings, empty school structures, vacant garages, or any other low-cost space that can be cleaned up, painted, and made into efficient, attractive production space. Consider manufacturing in high-unemployment areas, especially innercity locations, where substantial grants for plant, equipment, employee-training and property tax relief may be available, as well as a better pool of labor.

All of these routes should receive consideration before investing the company's future in more plant and equipment.

Make-or-Buy Analysis

The usual industrial engineering approach to make-or-buy analysis, while appropriate to large enterprises, may be quite misleading in the small company context. It focuses, predictably, upon the engineering aspects of unit cost. It does not take explicitly into account the overall corporate questions, concerning additional financial risk, liquidity, alternate use of capital, and risks of dependence on outside sources. These are likely to be much more significant questions than mere unit cost, but they cannot be properly weighed by your purchasing agent alone. They are decisions in which you yourself must participate. Similarly, decisions on optimal purchase quantities of materials are often made without adequate attention to the risks of obsolescence, illiquidity, and alternate uses of capital. Long-term supply commitments of any magnitude should involve top management, not just the purchasing agent. The apparent savings of volume buying may be dearly bought.

The Plant-Building Instinct

There are a number of reasons in addition to entrepreneurial ego why companies invest unwisely in plant and equipment. Among these are:

1. Relative to non-balance-sheet investments (e.g., market development, advertising, which are expensed), plant investment seems somehow "prudent"—after all, it's only changing one asset (money) for another (machinery). The apparent net worth of the company is unaffected.

2. The plant-building instinct is strong. Your plant manager tends to measure his own worth by the amount of resources he can divert into an ever bigger and better plant. Your production engineer will be quick to point out the "savings" and profit improvement that a more efficient plant would produce. Your workers will be quick to take up the cry for better conditions, if it seems to be in the air. Finally, even your financial backers may seem to give tacit blessing to a big new plant. After all, it's a lot more tangible than all that expensed R&D.

3. There is often a belief, sometimes justifiable, that customers will be impressed by a classy plant, and will therefore be influenced to give you the contract. There is no denying that in some cases this is the decisive factor—especially when dealing with the large company or the government.

4. Government programs to promote capital investment and "jobs creation" such as the investment tax credit and accelerated depreciation, as well as painless equipment financing offered by manufacturers, can create the illusion that enormous savings will somehow accrue, thus presenting further temptations to the instinctive plant-builder.

For all these reasons, you may find yourself besieged with demands that new plant and equipment be purchased. However, you may be the only person in the company who is in a position to perceive the total effect that this will have on the future of the enterprise as a whole. When you have weighed all benefits, costs, and risks, have the conviction to stick by your decision.

Remember, you will have plenty of other chances to play "You bet your company." Fancy plant equipment certainly is not a high enough pot for that sort of bet.

Parting Shot: If you've got $500,000 in the bank, do everything you can to keep it there. The cash you save by deferring plant outlays may just be the cash that keeps the company alive next year.

Conventional Wisdom. The prudent entrepreneur seeks to minimize unit product costs, thus maximizing profit.

Reality. The prudent entrepreneur keeps all costs variable, thus maximizing the amount of his cash in the bank.

References

1. Buskirk, Richard H., and Vaughn, Percy J.: *Managing New Enterprises,* West Publishing Co., St. Paul, Minn., 1976.

   See especially Chapter 19, "Acquiring Production Capabilities." Focused on results, not efficiency, used equipment, subcontractors, etc.
2. Gross, Harry: *Make or Buy.* Prentice-Hall Inc., Englewood Cliffs, N.J., 1966.

   This is a solid treatment of the industrial-engineering viewpoint on make-or-buy decisions.

Chapter 26

MANAGING THE R&D FUNCTION

"If it Works, it's Obsolete" . . . *Anonymous*

It has been the unintended but irresistible tendency of this book to talk in terms of technology-based companies, engaged in the design, manufacture, and marketing of some new product. Such companies, though far from a major portion of startups in any given year, are most often those marked for national markets, for significant growth, for venture capital eligibility, and ultimately, for public offerings. To the extent then, that technology companies are dependent on the talents of technologists, let us explore some aspects of living with them.

Engineers as a Species

As a group, engineers probably create more value than any other segment of our economy. It is that engineer, not the scientist, the banker, the businessman, the salesman, or the stockbroker, who creates the new products, the new chemistries, the new materials, machines, computers, satellites, ICBMs, heart lung machines, and nearly everything else that makes our industrial society run. His profession is demanding, in terms of native intelligence, educational duration, personal stamina, and professional standards. And unlike most of us, his performance is judged by the most stringent of yardsticks: His product has to work! No wonder good ones are so hard to find. Yet find them we must in a technology-based company.

What Engineers Do in Startups

The image of engineers sitting around all day, creating new products is just a bit misleading. In fact, in the typical small firm most engineering hours are absorbed by tasks that are anything but creative: Pouring over catalogs looking for parts and components to purchase, so that they need not be reinvented and retooled; prototyping and testing designs that were created months ago, possibly by others; writing specifications, test procedures, operator's manuals, production standards, and myriads of other documents; supervising or performing the drafting of engineering drawings; attending review meetings, vendor meetings, status meetings, technical conferences and a dozen others; testing the early production units; and so on, *ad nauseum*. The remarkable thing is that there is any time left to do engineering.

Although most of these functions are not "creative" in the strictest sense, all are essential to the success of your fledgling venture. And, given the usual financial constraints, there's no one to delegate them to, so the engineers do them all. While this may be inescapable for a period of time, the sooner you get out of this mode, the better.

As your venture matures, it should be possible to gradually improve the "creativity" component of each engineer's time, by supporting him with drafting, clerical help, technicians, and proper manufacturing support.

The engineering function in a startup is generally characterized by one other set of constraints: a very narrow time-focus. The initial product must get done at all cost, must work, and must be within budget. There is little time or energy to expend on future products, novel features, new application, or new technologies. This constraint makes it much more difficult for the typical engineer to function in a fast-track startup. An unusual combination of talent and single-mindedness is demanded.

Again, as growth permits, the time-horizons of the engineering department will expand so that different people can be concerned with different parts of the future. Thus, a current array of tasks might ultimately look like this:

Immediate (0–6 Mos.)	*Intermediate* (6–12 Mos.)	*Long Range* (12–36 Mos.)
• Get Prototype Working • Finish Production Documentation • Develop Test Fixtures • Write User's Manuals	• New Customer Applications • Cost Reduction Program • New Options and Features • New Software • Fix Field Problems	• New Technical Approach • Super Performance Version • Ultra Cheap Version • New Market Requirements

Product Engineering: Some Trends

In the 1980s, management will have to cope with several trends which will have a significant impact on the nature of the engineering function and the innovative process itself. Among these trends are:

Shortened Product Life-Cycles

The onrush of technology has created something of a Frankenstein for technologists themselves: Products may be obsolescent before they are ever shipped. This is not merely true of your company's products—it is also true of the products of your suppliers. Thus, if, for example, you design in a semiconductor component that is in full production today, you are almost assured that it will have been replaced by the time your product is in production. Obviously, then, making the correct guesses about the speed and direction of your vendors' development progress is as essential as appraising your competition's.

Greater Demand for Customization

Neither the commercial customer nor the private consumer is disposed to accept whatever he's offered any longer. If he buys a car, he expects a wide range of options, finishes, and accessories. If he buys a printing press, a computer, a chemical plant, or a jetliner, his attitude is the same: Give me what *I* want. The engineer will still be designing standard products, to be sure, but he must design products which can adapt, chameleonlike, to the needs of the individual customer in a routine way, without upsetting the engineering or manufacturing functions. This is a major engineering challenge in the '80s.

Black-Box Integration

What goes on in engineering departments will be greatly affected by this continuing trend. In 1900, an engineer designing a locomotive expected to design the boiler, the valves, the drive linkages, the wheels, the suspension, the operator controls, and all other parts of the system. Today, not only would there be a specialist for each part—the specialist would be working for other (vendor's) companies. The designer would merely specify the components, assemble them in a prototype "system," and turn it over to the manufacturing which would in reality be an assembly and test operation. This, of course, is largely how automobiles are built. The advent of preengineered modules, such as single-chip computers, monolithic memories, modular power supplies, complex integrated circuits for communication, interfacing, etc., has drastically altered the role of electrical engineers, transforming them into systems designers or even software engineers. Much the same is occurring in other engineering specialties, drastically affecting the content of engineering work, generally but not always for the better.

Computer-Aided Design

Computers, since their invention, have of course been used to perform engineering calculations. Today, however, we are witnessing a new phenomenon. An electrical engineer can sit before a video terminal and specify a design by its inputs and outputs. The computer will then offer up a circuit design that performs the desired function. The engineer can inspect, modify, and even "test" the design by simulation, without ever touching a soldering iron. Similarly, much of the grunt work of structural, mechanical and civil engineering can now be performed graphically on computers, shortening design time, eliminating overdesign, and improving the creative content of the design function. Finally, CAD is permitting increasing automation of the tooling function by automatically creating programs for generating integrated circuits, printed circuit cards, and machined metal parts. Many believe that we are on the threshold of explosive growth in this area. We'd better be, because it is our only hope of coping with shortened product life and customized production!

Patents

In our generally accelerated technical environments, patents are assuming a somewhat different role from that of the past. Design patents become increasingly meaningless when product lives are shorter than the time-cycle to obtain the patent. The engineering time and effort it takes to follow through and obtain a patent must be carefully weighed against the value it would have to the company, *vis a vis* keeping the design as a "trade secret."

Patents, to the extent that they are pursued at all, should have significant economic life, should focus on more fundamental techniques, processes, and innovations than perhaps was the case a few years ago. Naturally, a strong patent position makes your venture incrementally more attractive to the investment community, but short-lived design patents will not impress the financial community, and will be of little practical value to the company.

Industrial Design

Industrial design is a highly specialized field, dealing with issues of product appearance, ease of use, ease of servicing, packaging, and overall customer reaction. It is an area in which even large companies are often deficient. Small startup ventures should almost always therefore retain an industrial design consultant to look at the product and suggest ways in which to make it visually and functionally appealing. In so doing, he may also be able to show you how to reduce its costs, by combining functions, changing materials or finishes, repackaging, or using different types of vendors. These services will cost you a few thousand dollars, but the result should be well worth it. Every major city has industrial design firms. Interview a few, look at their work, and see what they can offer. Don't try to do industrial design yourself.

Care and Feeding of Engineers

Since much of your startup venture's money may be being spent on and by engineers, it behooves you to think carefully about controlling this cost and being sure the company is getting its money's worth.

Recruiting and Hiring

In this era, engineers are scarce; manpower projections indicate that they will be in short supply throughout the '80s. Therefore, to compete for the best, you must be entrepreneurial. In searching for prospects, use the list of sources in Chapter 17. In interviewing, stress the things that your little company can offer that Collossus Industries cannot: Opportunity to see design all the way through from inception to production; flexible working hours; informal, collegial environment; future opportunity for equity participation; more responsibility than at a large firm; maximum scope for initiative and creativity; and opportunity to grow with a growing firm.

In recruiting for scarce talent, be prepared to make an offer on the spot, if necessary, "subject to routine reference checks." Rest assured that your competition is similarly prepared. Be concise but complete in outlining salary, benefits, bonuses or stock plans, and be sure to mention that he must sign an invention assignment form. Give him a deadline; make sure he knows he's only one of several strong candidates being considered.

You can also be entrepreneurial in enlisting engineering talent from sources other than the large companies. For example:

1. Hire students. Some of the best talent, especially in areas such as software, is in school. Hire them part-time or on a co-op basis. Hire them as temporaries, if they want to drop out for a term to earn money.

2. Consider aliens. Many large companies cannot, or will not, hire aliens, due to defense contracts or corporate policy. However, talented aliens arrive in the U.S. daily, from technically advanced countries such as Canada, England, Russia, Taiwan, and Japan. Many are educated in the U.S. at our top schools. Where a language problem exists, you may be able to get a highly experienced engineer on a very favorable basis for all concerned.

3. Hire retired engineers. For many specialties such as mechanical engineering, tool design, production engineering, circuit design, and others, a part-time retired engineer may be the ideal worker for your firm. Especially in the mechanical, hydraulic, and electromechanical areas, his years of experience may prove priceless in a young, inexperienced design group.

Carrots and Sticks

Your primary management tools, as with each other department in your firm, are budgets and schedules. We have all heard, "You can't schedule invention," but as we have seen, very little invention is, in fact, going on in your engineering department. Their tasks are highly amenable to tracking via milestones, and their expenses are readily controllable, since they consist mainly of salaries. As always, judicious alternation of the carrot and the stick is indicated.

On-time completion of tasks, ingenious solutions to problems, and outstanding work of every type should be singled out for praise and recognition. People should receive recognition for creativity as well as task completion, however, for this establishes the climate in which engineers love to work.

The whip, when employed, must be done privately, one on one. Every effort should be made to attack the problem, not the person. If repeated experiences show that the talent or motivation is deficient, don't delay taking the necessary action to terminate. There's no room to hide your mistakes in a small company.

Supporting the Engineer

At the outset, with limited resources, your engineers may have to double in brass. However, as your resources increase, you will have some hiring latitude. At this juncture, it is important before hiring more engineers to be sure you are properly supporting the ones you already have. Do they have enough drafting technicians and clerical support? Do they have the right instruments, tools, and computation facilities? Do they have, in short, what's needed to get the job done right? If not, adding more engineers will make matters worse, not better. The new engineers won't want to be technicians, either.

Supplementing the Engineer

Most companies have engineering projects of two sorts: the mainstream product developments, and the secondary. The latter might be special options, accessories, software packages, or other improvements to the existing product line needed urgently by marketing. In such instances, rather than interrupt the larger projects, it may be optimal to contract out the special project to a consultant, on an *ad hoc* basis. This way, the work gets done quickly, you know your costs in advance, and the overall department is not disrupted. Finding the right specialist can often result in a better job than might be done in-house, as well.

Marketing versus Engineering

In small companies, a dynamic can easily be permitted to spring up that is destructive to all concerned. From marketing's viewpoint, it may look as though engineering is not being responsive to the needs of the marketplace; that the competition's engineering is always a lap ahead of yours; that the engineers are unwilling to interrupt their work to help the company by working on that "special deal."

To the engineers, the same circumstances may look like this: Marketing expects us to offer every feature that every competitor can ever think up; they don't have enough initiative to sell our standard products, so they expect us to constantly custom-engineer specials; and worst, they continually interrupt our work on the new-generation product, to add some marginal feature to the old product.

This dynamic, left unchecked, can undermine productivity and morale on all sides. To avoid it you may be able to (a) include marketing in engineering reviews, (b) include engineering in all marketing strategy/product line planning efforts, (c) provide an applications engineering function exclusively for marketing's use, or

(d) make sure that key engineers periodically make customer calls to stay in touch with the marketplace.

Evaluating your Engineering Function

The engineering function is a costly one, and must be subjected to the same investment criteria as any other, despite the fact that the "investment" in product design does not appear on the balance sheet. The engineering investment must be capitalized for planning purposes just like tooling inventories and other product costs. A project that pays out with, say, three person-years of engineering investment might never pay out if the effort eventually required five. Slippages, overruns, re-engineering, fixing units in the field, and late or incomplete production documentation are not generally problems of themselves but are rather symptoms that your engineering investment is being spent poorly. It may be that no corrective measure, short of replacing from the top will correct the problem—assuming there is still time and money enough to correct it at all.

In Conclusion

You may, from time to time, conclude that your top engineers are a bunch of prima donnas, with all that the term implies. Well, you're probably right. The opera may, in fact, be the appropriate metaphor for a high-technology startup. You may be the greatest impresario on earth, have a super orchestra, a fine stage manager, a good director, and talented extras—but without those prima donnas, your show is going nowhere. The sooner you learn to live with them, the better.

Conventional Wisdom. You can't schedule invention.

Reality. You can certainly schedule whatever it is your engineering department is doing.

References

1. Pelz, Donald C., and Andrews, Frank M.: *Scientists in Organizations,* John Wiley & Sons, N.Y., 1966.

   Explores the dilemma of organizations versus freedom, in a study of 1300 scientists doing both research and development. Came up with measures of performance, and related it to many variables. Determinants of motivation, dedication and creativity are all discussed.

2. Shames, William A.: *Venture Management,* The Free Press (Macmillan), New York, 1974.

   Contains extensive treatment of the business of inventing.

Chapter 27

LIFE AFTER DEATH: OUR BENEFICENT BANKRUPTCY LAWS

"Some days nothing *seems to go right."*

. . . Corrollary of Murphy's Law

To most of us, the term *bankruptcy* holds connotations comparable to terminal cancer, execution, or just walking off the edge. The bankrupt businessperson as social leper is a recurrent American theme. Dark though the connotations may be, however, our liberal laws provide a surprising degree of relief for the bankrupt businessman; indeed, they may be considered as just one more tool of entrepreneurial survival.

What Is Bankruptcy?

As generally construed, bankruptcy is the chronic inability to pay one's debts.[1] In the academic sense, it would be defined as having a negative net worth (technical insolvency)—however, many firms operate with negative net worth, and are never declared bankrupt by a court. In a practical sense, the bankrupt firm is usually characterized by negative working capital (current assets minus cur-

---

[1]Bankruptcy should also be differentiated from *failure*. Dun and Bradstreet define *five* failure modes: failed companies cease operation, (a) following a bankruptcy or assignment of assets, (b) following an execution, foreclosure, or attachment with loss to creditors, (c) after involvement in court actions, involving receivership, reorganization, or arrangement, and (e) voluntary compromise with creditors. Note that the company operating under Chapter XI is *not* a failure in the D&B definition.

rent liabilities)—hence the inability to meet current obligations. Indeed, for many entrepreneurs the only thing that differentiates between current conditions and bankruptcy, then, is a state of mind.

The usual causes of bankruptcy are generally a combination of undercapitalization, inept management, and overexpansion. However, there is often a major precipitating factor, such as the failure of a large account receivable, a factory fire, a major lawsuit, or the unwillingness of a lender to renew a note. It is uniquely tragic when a company that is growing, even profitably, but absorbing all its cash, is hit by one of these precipitating events. If cash management is poor, assets are illiquid (e.g., tied up in plant equipment or excessive inventory) or lending relationships in poor repair, the result can well be bankruptcy.

What the Law Says

In ancient Rome, the legal code provided that the bankrupt debtor had to surrender his *person* to the creditor for disposition, without any judicial proceeding at all. The creditor could, presumably, put you to work as a slave, or sell you off for that purpose, or possibly donate you for lion-fodder, as a wholesome example to other debtors.

By the Middle Ages, things had softened a bit, however. Kings could, among other things, grant the bankrupt debtor a delay of payment without consent of creditors. Colonial America was settled in part by debtors released from overcrowded English prisons. However, by 1978, when our present Bankruptcy Act was enacted, society had generally come to recognize that not only is it difficult to obtain further payments from a dead or imprisoned debtor; it is also very hard to obtain payment from a liquidated or caretaker-managed company. Clearly, the debtor has made great progress in the last 2,000 years or so.

The Bankruptcy Reform Act of 1978 represents the first Congressional action in 40 years to streamline and clarify the intent and operation of our bankruptcy laws. The Act covers all types of bankruptcies and liquidations. However, we will focus only on one portion: the new Chapter XI. The new Chapter XI represents a merging of the old Chapter X (involuntary) and Chapter XI (voluntary) provisions, into a single set of procedures which should be more equitable to both the creditors and entrepreneur. Chapter XI works as described below.

Voluntary

The entrepreneur (debtor) may, when confronted with the inability to pay his debts in a timely way, petition for the protection of the court (the U.S. District Court). The Court may extend protection or dismiss the petition altogether, whichever it deems to be in the creditor's interest. If the petition is accepted, the petitioner then may continue to operate his business under a set of legal ground-rules designed to protect the creditors. He then has 120 days in which to submit to the court a plan of reorganization which, if accepted, becomes his operating plan for the duration of the case. The court also has the right to appoint a trustee in cases of voluntary bankruptcy, who takes possession of all assets of the company, and oversees operations for as long as the court deems necessary. If the debtor has not submitted a plan within 120 days, or if the court has not found his plan acceptable within 180 days, the trustee may submit a plan of his own, as may the creditors. The acceptance of a plan requires at least one of the following:

1. Acceptance by creditors representing two-thirds of the total dollar claims and 51 percent of the individual claims.

2. Acceptance by any other class of interests (e.g., shareholders) representing two-thirds of the dollar interests of that class.

The court can impose a plan on any dissenting class, so long as it deems it to be "fair and equitable" to that class. Also, if there is more than one qualified plan in front of the court, the court may decide which, if any, to approve. Once the plan is accepted by the court, it becomes the new operating charter for the entrepreneur. He may have quite a lot of latitude under it. He may raise new funds by selling shares, by borrowing money, by leasing or selling assets of the firm, and by continuing operations in the most profitable manner.

Involuntary

Under the new Bankruptcy Act, the creditors still have the right to petition the court to order your reorganization. A petition may be submitted by a group of creditors whose claims total only $5,000. However, if an involuntary petition is submitted, the debtor has the right to contest it; if he is successful in having it thrown out, he is entitled to court costs, legal fees, and damages. If he is unsuccessful, he has, as before, 120 days to submit a plan. The procedures then are essentially the same as in the voluntary case.

These provisions of the new law are generally quite favorable to the entrepreneur; they give him relief from harassment by creditors, stockholders and others, as soon as the court accepts the petition. They give him an opportunity to develop a workable plan to turn the company around, rather than just assigning a receiver or liquidator. They give him a chance to raise new monies, by subordinating the claims of the old creditors; and they give him the right to fight off any attempt to place him in involuntary bankruptcy. In short, they give him far more than the benefit of the doubt, and a fair chance of recovering from his straits.

What's in a Plan of Reorganization?

The plan of reorganization for a Chapter XI reorganization is a little like your financial business plan in that it must convince some very skeptical people of your ability to make the company profitable. This includes, predictably, financial projections, market data, and product information. It also includes one other very important item, however: Your plan for treatment of creditors. These include, usually, a *reduction* in claim (called "composition of debt"), *extension* of payment date, and often a *substitution* of other securities for debt. Thus, a typical plan of reorganization could offer the following:

1. Pay off all creditors with claims under $100

2. Reduce all other claims to $100 and pay them

3. Distribute one share of common stock for each dollar of claims unpaid

Or, you could just resort to the good old ten-cents-on-the-dollar method. Or a schedule of payment in full, over a long period. Many permutations are possible.

Diving in and Digging Out

Today it looks like the end. The phone never stops ringing, and the creditors aren't just angry—they're starting to panic. You've moved heaven and earth to collect that enormous account receivable, but to no avail—it looks like your customer is going broke and taking you with him. Meanwhile, rumors of creditor's committees have reached your banker and he's getting nervous, too. The stockholders have started to call up to find out what the hell is going on. The brimstone smell of bankruptcy is in the air. What do you do?

The first thing is, don't panic. The second is, get to your attorney fast. If Chapter XI is the only logical route in his judgment, you must waste no time in filing your petition, before the creditors get organized and file theirs. Once the petition is granted, you have a breathing spell of up to 120 days to file a plan, and another 60 days while the court and the creditors are considering it. During this time you can, of course, work on the problem that sent you into U.S. District Court in the first place, but chances are you won't get it resolved. So, keep your fingers crossed, and do whatever you can to persuade holdout creditors that their best chance of recovery is your plan.

Once in Chapter XI, you've got your work cut out. You must

make the plan work, or resign yourself to the liquidation of your company. You must function on less cash than ever before. You'll be obliged to cut staff and overheads to the bone; you'll cut advertising, development, and other discretionary costs. You'll need every tactic in the book to operate under the conditions that will prevail (see Chapter 8, "Operating Without Capital"). You will have to be a veritable Norman Vincent Peale of inspiration and optimism.

There are several groups of people who will require some constant attention and inspiration during this business:

1. *Customers.* Your customers are your only hope of salvation. Their reaction to the announcement of your bankruptcy will be negative, to say the least. Personally call up or write all customers and visit key customers. Explain that the problems are only temporary, that their source of supply is secure, and that you're going to be in business to back up the products they have bought in the past.

Step up your rate of press announcements of new products, new personnel, new anything, to let the world know you're both alive and kicking.

2. *Creditors.* They are the whole reason for the exercise, and have "donated" a major portion of your new working capital. They deserve to be kept informed. Don't avoid them, be open and cooperative, and continue to try to win their confidence—not just their grudging acquiescence.

3. *Stockholders.* Even though they may have had no vote, they are still very important to you. They stand to lose more than anybody; moreover, they may be your only hope of getting additional loans or referrals, so you need them. Send them a monthly memo and let them know how the plan is being pursued.

4. *Employees and Reps.* The last thing you want at this stage is defection of key employees or reps. Keep maximum contact, be a source of inspiration, keep everybody focused on the tasks at hand, not on the past difficulties. Try sales contests, special incentives, awards for special accomplishment. If you're feeling a trifle gloomy, don't let anybody know it.

With courage and persistence, you can dig your way out of Chapter XI. Those who have say it is a uniquely educational experience in hard-nosed management. As a matter of sobering fact, however, it should be noted that fewer than one-tenth of the firms that enter Chapter XI do, in fact, make it out.

Viewed in perspective, Chapter XI is, indeed, a management tool. It permits you to raise working capital by the delightfully simple expedient of stealing it (legally) from your unsecured creditors. Then, with the court protecting you from their wrath, you're back on the old corner, selling the old goods. Business as usual, except now the stakes have been pushed up a notch: This is your last chance to make it. If you repeat the same mistakes that got you into Chapter XI, you may well expect to end up a Dun and Bradstreet statistic. But even that's a lot better than rowing a galley or nourishing a lion.

A Footnote on the Bankruptcy Reform Act of 1978

In addition to streamlining the procedures of bankruptcy, a second goal was to reduce the court backlogs by creating U.S. Trustees, to relieve the judges of many of the administrative burdens of bankruptcy proceedings. The U.S. Trustee is appointed by the U.S. Attorney General, reducing the arbitrary scope of the U.S. District Courts. This system is being tested in selected Districts; if successful, it will be adopted by the entire country, resulting, one hopes, in reduced backlogs, lower costs to the company and the government, and more speedy implementation of plans of reorganization.

Conventional Wisdom. Chapter XI: The end of the line.

Reality. Chapter XI: One more management tool.

References

1. Ma, J. C., and Henney, H. D.: "What It Takes to Come Out of Chapter XI," *Credit and Financial Management*, February, 1962.

   This is a rather interesting article written by a professor and an entrepreneur who have been through it all.

2. Altman, E. I.: *Corporate Bankruptcy in America*, D. C. Heath Co., Lexington, Mass., 1971.

   This is a rather scholarly work, the second half of which is an elaborate model for the prediction of bankruptcy from historical financial data of the firm. However, the first half gives some worthwhile background on present law and practice, for the entrepreneur.

3. Stanley, D. T., and Girth, M.: *Bankruptcy: Problems, Process, Reform*, Brookings Institution, Washington, D.C., 1971.

   This will tell you more than you want to know about bankruptcy law.

OVER AND OUT VI

Chapter 28

EXIT THIS WAY

"Getting into a deal is a cinch, compared to getting out."

. . . Anonymous

Why Get Out?

If you're a typical entrepreneur there will come a time when you will want to get out of your company. This is not necessarily just a matter of cashing out, since (a) it is possible that via a secondary issue you have enough cash, and, (b) if you liquidated your entire position you'd have to pay Uncle Sam, then reinvest it someplace else. However, there are several valid reasons why you might very well wish to get out, among which might be:

1. You have found a better opportunity which you wish to pursue, or you want to look for one.

2. You're tired/bored with the old business, even if it's successful. You'd like some new problems, some new people, maybe even a new career.

3. You feel that the major growth phase is over, or possibly you see some serious problems ahead for the company.

4. You feel that the entrepreneurial phase is over and are not sure of your ability/desire to become the skillful custodial manager needed for the next phase of growth.

For these or a number of other reasons you are statistically likely to be looking for a graceful exit somewhere between five and ten years from startup.

Life Strategy

If you're like most of us, a lot more planning goes into your business life than into your personal life. If you need some concrete evidence of this, just look at the mess your checkbook is in, and how irrational your cumulative personal investment decisions look. The months and years on the firing line of your company make it appear that the company *is* your life. It isn't. It is merely the dominant component in this phase of your life.

It would be well if, one day each year, you would sit down and update your ten-year plan. This might be very useful, even if it merely serves to identify those areas in which there is no agreement, or no possibility of predicting/influencing the outcome. Try setting some goals, just as you do for the business. Remember, a goal differs from a wish. A wish could take the form, "I want to be happy"; a goal would take the form, "By age 45 I wish to retire with a net worth of $750,000." A goal has the characteristics of *concreteness, measurability, time-relatedness,* and *attainability;* in the absence of any of these four characteristics, you don't have a working goal—you have a wish.

Your goals and schedules would include such items as the following:

1. Your wife's return to her profession as soon as the children are in school.

2. Acquisition of physical assets for personal use (e.g., a new home, country place, boat, airplane).

3. Attainment of a particular investment goal (e.g., assets of $500,000 yielding unearned income of $25,000 per year).

4. Change of jobs or career.

5. Extensive travel.

6. Return to graduate school.

7. Ability to assume support of parents.

8. Locating in a desired geographical location.

Your plan must include not only the goals, but the requisite interim steps for getting there, and the milestones which you will establish for measurement of progress toward them. You should also list the risks/obstacles to attainment, and the strategies you will employ to overcome them.

To the extent that you are able to integrate the progress of your business into your personal ten-year plan, you will be better able to make correct decisions about whether, when, and how to exit from the company. In fact, it will pull many other elements of your personal decision-making into focus, as well.

Exit Modes

There are several exit modes from the company. These include, mainly:

1. Business failure

2. Getting fired by directors

3. Selling to another firm

4. Selling your stock to private parties, including others in the company

5. Selling your stock in a public secondary offering.

Not all will be available to every entrepreneur, obviously. They differ in rate of personal exit, rate of financial exit, and range of follow-on options.

Business Failure

When the doors are closed involuntarily, it is usually the end of the road for the firm, but not necessarily for the entrepreneur. He's usually out looking for a new deal the next morning, although the failure of his last one may take some tall explaining. Some ultraentrepreneurial types have even been known to show up at their firm's liquidation auction, buy up the assets at five cents on the dollar, and behold, they are back on the old corner Monday morning.

The folding of your company, however, may provide an appropriate juncture to pause and reflect. Was it really bad luck, or are you yourself weak in certain areas that may jeopardize success in future ventures? What lessons can be gleaned from the experience? Try writing yourself an essay on the experience, complete with prescriptions for dealing with the forces that led to your last company's downfall.

Getting Fired by Directors

This is, in some respects, more undesirable than business failure, although it is possible that it leaves you with more assets, and therefore, more options as to future action. Again, some careful analysis of yourself and your company's history is in order, to establish precisely what went wrong and how to avoid a repeat performance. Be honest. Was it bad management, bad people, or bad luck?

Selling to Another Firm

This exit route, among the most common for entrepreneurs, is not necessarily an exit at all. In selling your company, it may also be necessary to sell yourself for a number of years, since without you the value of the enterprise may be much lower, and the acquiring firm knows it. This is especially true if the selling company is to be operated as a subsidiary. It is perhaps less true if you are to become a division or a department.

The new role may be bondage or a fantastic opportunity, depending upon circumstances and your state of mind. Many companies look to their subsidiary acquisitions as a major source of future top executives, as well as of growth and diversification for the parent. Others see the acquisition as a sort of portfolio investment, a part of which is the entrepreneur. He is bought with it and sold with it, as circumstances demand.

The situations of acquired executives vary widely. Some are locked in only for a given time period; others are locked in by a stock workout arrangement, which bases stock price on subsidiary performance. Some are given great latitude, for example, in acquiring other firms. Others are kept on a very short tether, indeed.

If your firm was originally financed by a large corporation, or its venture capital subsidiary, you probably have no choice as to whom to sell. In fact, the pricing formula may already exist. If this is not the case, however, selecting a corporate partner can require some serious research. If, in the case discussed in Chapter 24, you are headed for calamity, you probably haven't much leisure in which to check out the fine points. If this is not the case, however, you should review your prospective bedfellow rather carefully. Before approaching anybody, you should develop a list of criteria to aid you, your directors, and perhaps a consultant in the search for appropriate corporate partners. These criteria could for example include:

1. Size of company.

2. Present business.

3. Experience in acquisitions. Are they sophisticated, or will they make all their mistakes with you? Will you get a better price from an unsophisticated firm?

4. Familiarity with your industry and market.

5. Availability of resources needed by your company (e.g., manufacturing capacity, marketing ability, raw materials, working capital).

6. Geographical location. There are pros and cons to close proximity to one's corporate parent.

7. General progressiveness. While a progressive partner may normally be desirable, sometimes the presence of some new blood is what a company needs to revitalize it, creating a bigger opportunity for the new blood.

8. Ownership status. Is it on the NYSE, OTC, or privately held? What is the stability of its stock?

9. Character and reputation of management.

You will be able to think of several dozen more criteria. You should rank or weigh them, before putting them to use. Remember, even a bad set of criteria is better than simply selling out on the basis of willingness of the other firm to buy. Your choice should, of course, be heavily influenced by your personal ten-year plan, since you may in effect be making a long-term career choice at the same time.

Selling Your Stock to Private Parties

Such a route may be available to you on favorable terms. However, even more than the acquiring corporation, the buyers are likely to need you to run the company for some substantial period of time. To ensure this, they may be willing to offer attractive bonuses, option plans or other incentives to keep you on board.

A major exception, of course, is the case in which your partners and/or stockholders are buying you out to get rid of you. Your greatest obstacle to rational action at this point may be the involvement of your own ego in the process. If the other members of the team are inalterably opposed to your leadership, it may be best for you, too, if you bow out. You are going to have nothing but trouble from now on if you stay. A fight for the sake of winning may ensure that *everyone* loses out.

The toughest problem at this juncture is in getting a fair price for your stock. If it develops that you can't, consider leaving *with* the stock, and let them figure out how to increase its value. A partial solution of some stock and some cash may be the most equitable.

Selling Your Stock in a Public Secondary Offering

This is without a doubt the route that has made more millionaires out of entrepreneurs than any other. Subject to timing in the business cycle and other factors, the public has historically been quite willing to pay for stock in a growing company. While an acquiring corporation might be willing to pay ten times earnings, or perhaps its own price-earnings ratio, the public may pay 50 times, 100 times, or maybe infinity times earnings. There is no guarantee of this, however, and there are many more risks and hazards than in private acquisition. For example, if your initial public offering (in which you cannot sell any of your personal stock) comes out at 20, and the market promptly takes a nose dive, leaving you at 10, it may be all but impossible to get a secondary offering out. Too many people have already lost money on your stock.

Your ability to pull off a satisfactory secondary offering may also be related to the investment banker who handles your offerings. Assuming that company performance is satisfactory, your secondary offering success may depend upon who your investment banker sold the initial offering to, at what price, and how much support (i.e., buying for his own account in times of market weakness) he has given the stock. If your stock price has risen a bit and held up well, you're golden. If it's fallen a bit and stuck there, you're in for a long wait.

Selection of an investment banker deserves about the same amount of energy as selection of a corporate partner since, in the best case, he *is* a corporate partner. The worst kind takes a firm public, then disappears. The best hang on through good and bad, and try to ensure that each successful public offering sets the stage for the next.

In establishing your list of criteria for an investment banker, you may need a little help, since this is a world with which few entrepreneurs are familiar. You may wish to enlist your banker, lawyer, or accounting firm on the job. Among the possible criteria are:

1. Familiarity with initial offerings of smaller companies. The largest, most prestigious house may strike out completely in this department.

2. Success with small-company offerings. Their score is a matter of public record. Moreover, presidents of their client firms are readily identified for further checks. Look at the record. What happened to their deal?

3. General reputation in the financial community. This is a vague parameter, but one which will affect profoundly their ability to sell out your issue quickly. Ask several people, including your lawyer, attorney, and directors to rank a list of 20 firms you give them. Try the same thing on your broker, your banker, your rich uncle. A pattern may begin to emerge.

4. Present types of issues. Just because they have done your kind of offering in the past is no guarantee they would do it or do it well today. Was there a specific champion in the house who is no longer there? Where did *he* go?

5. Your intuitive reaction. Does the guy come on like a big time hustler, a torpid old aristocrat, or a reasonable fellow with whom you can discuss your business problems? Be sure it's somebody you can personally like and trust.

The selection and dealing with investment bankers is a realm where war stories abound. It may be constructive to listen to a few, and there is no better source than an entrepreneur who has just gone through it. Seek out a couple of them and see what they have to say.

Initial offerings, except in the case of *very* strong issuing companies, are seldom underwritten, that is, they are normally taken on in a best-efforts mode by the underwriter. If he is unable to sell an agreed-upon minimum (e.g., 80 percent of the issue), you both simply walk away from the agreement. Such an agreement usually involves a hefty fee for the investment banker if he's successful (say, 10 percent of the offering), plus some warrants or cheap stock for his own portfolio. This latter is very important, since it creates an incentive for him to support your stock and also to promote favorable conditions for a secondary offering so that he can cash in.

When you and an investment banker have agreed to work together, there will ensue a negotiation of the different variables of the offering: percent of ownership, pricing, timing, compensation to investment banker, and other considerations. There will be the question of expenses to be picked up by each side, of the retention of special counsel (often of the investment banker's choice) for SEC work, and many other considerations. These are all very critical areas which may have a profound effect on the company's fortunes and your personal net worth. Your attorney should, of course, be a party to this negotiation. Try to be cooperative without giving in too much. If you honestly feel that they are trying to dictate unreasonable terms, say so. There are other investment bankers; it isn't the end of the world if talks are terminated.

A note on expense is in order. In addition to the investment banker's commission, your company will be expected to pick up the bills for legal, audit, and SEC registration work incident to the offering. For an offering of, say, two million dollars, this could be as much as $50,000. This is bad enough if the offering goes well. It may be disaster for the company, however, if for some reason the offering doesn't sell. Thus, the public offering must be undertaken with an appreciation of this risk, and with a contingency plan of recovery if the worst happens. Do not let the euphoria of public issue and mushrooming paper net worth cause you to lose sight of this very real hazard.

A Final Note on Getting Out

Your ten-year plan will give you some guidance as to whether, how fast and how completely you should get out of your firm. Market conditions and the progress of the company itself will provide the constraints. However, some things must be experienced to be understood. This is particularly true of being at loose ends with a lot of money. The folklore is full of stories about entrepreneurs who cashed out, intending to retire with a bundle only to discover after six months of walking the beaches that they really only wanted to start another company. Many of these stories are probably true. The personality traits, drives, and abilities that made you an entrepreneur in the first place do not go away the day you cash out. They are part of your permanent psychological equipment. Therefore, don't be surprised if your game plan to retire at 40 must be extensively revised when you reach your goal. This will be a happy result for everyone if it happens, because it means that a decision has been reached to put back in use one of society's most valuable assets: a successful entrepreneur!

Conventional Wisdom. When you finally make your million, you retire to clip coupons in Boca Raton.

Reality. When you finally make your million, you'll have learned that starting companies is a lot more fun than retirement.

References

1. Buskirk, Richard H., and Vaughn, Percy J.: *Managing New Enterprises,* West Publishing Co., St. Paul, Minn., 1976.

    See esp. Section VIII, Terminating the Enterprise.

2. Strange, M. (ed.): *Acquisition and Merger Strategy,* Hawthorne Books Inc., N.Y., 1971.

    Book written from the viewpoint of the acquiring firm, will offer you some insights on how to be acquired on the most advantageous terms.

3. Liles, Patrick R.: *New Business Ventures and the Entrepreneur,* Irwin, Homewood, Ill., 1974.

    See section on evaluating a going company.

4. Vesper, Karl: *New Venture Strategies,* Prentice-Hall, Englewood Cliffs, N.J., 1980.

    See sec. 10, "Acquisition Dealing".

5. O'Neal, F. H.: *Expulsion or Oppression of Business Associates—Squeeze-outs in Small Enterprises,* Duke University Press, Durham, N.C., 1961.
    Reviews virtually all squeeze-out techniques in general use, and examines some of the remedies of the squeezees.

INDEX